ENGLAND *v* AUS

TEST MATCH RECORDS 1877

ENGLAND *v* AUSTRALIA

TEST MATCH RECORDS 1877–1985

Edited by David Frith

WILLOW BOOKS
Collins
8 Grafton Street London W1
1986

Willow Books
William Collins Sons & Co Ltd
London · Glasgow · Sydney · Auckland · Toronto · Johannesburg

First published 1986

BRITISH LIBRARY CATALOGUING IN PUBLICATION DATA

Frith, David, *1937–*
England v. Australia test match records 1877–1985.
1. Test matches (Cricket) – England – History
2. Test matches (Cricket) – Australia – History
I. Title
796.35′865 GV928.G7

ISBN 0 00 218198 3 (cased edition)
ISBN 0 00 218199 1 (limp edition)

Typographic design by Tim Higgins

Set in Palatino by
Rowland Phototypesetting Ltd
Bury St Edmunds, Suffolk

Printed and bound in Great Britain by
Hazell, Watson and Viney Ltd
Aylesbury, Bucks

CONTENTS

SECTION 3
The Captains 41

SECTION 4
The Players 51

SECTION 5
The Batsmen 83

SECTION 10
The Umpires 211

SECTION 11
The Grounds 215

SECTION 12
Laws and Conditions of Play 251

Illustrations by courtesy of Press Association, Associated Sports Photography, Sport & General, Sporting Pictures, Ken Kelly, Bob Thomas, and David Frith.

PREFACE

Test cricket's blue-riband series remains that between England and Australia. It has stiffer competition now than ever before: from the vibrant West Indies XIs, the streetwise players of India, Pakistan and New Zealand, and the blossoming talents of Sri Lanka. But England *versus* Australia is the oldest, the pioneer series, the saga embroidered with myriads of thrilling incidents and awesome achievements.

Ashes Test matches have inspired what is clearly an incalculable depth of coverage: books galore, miles of newspaper columnage, hundreds and hundreds of hours of air time on radio and television, and, in its day, much newsreel footage. All this has met public desire. It seemed time, therefore, for an exhaustive study of the statistics and the superlatives generated by England *v* Australia Test cricket, for it is an area that has received surprisingly scanty consideration.

Our team set about compiling the most extensive analysis of this subject yet known, the principal aim being to separate clinically the successful performances in these Tests from the mediocre, to back (or otherwise) history's handed-down verdicts of opinion with solid fact. Numerous aspects of performance are studied, with one of the more interesting techniques being the splitting of Ashes history into five eras (successively to the end of the 19th Century, to the First World War, between the Wars, 1946 to 1968, and 1970 to date) for some of the specialties under review, to show who wielded most influence. This has confirmed the status of many of the star performers, but it has also produced a few surprises, as seen by the allrounders' table, or the list of most expensive bowlers.

This volume is offered as a companion to the books containing full scorecards of the Test matches between England and Australia, and the picture histories. Figures can never be all; but nor can pictures and nor can words. And there is a secondary motive for gathering together this treasure-trove of fact: it is hoped it will prove a joy both to the cricket-lover who quests for knowledge and also his sometimes over-enthusiastic brother who, having mined his gems of information, is impelled to belabour the next person he meets.

Which counties have supplied most England players against Australia? Who have been the youngest players, and the oldest? Who scored a century upon debut, or – hitherto almost a secret – took a wicket with his first ball? Is it generally appreciated that Jack Hobbs scored a century against Australia when in his 47th year, or that Ian Botham has yet to match Joe Darling when it comes to centuries brimming with boundary hits? Who have been the slow-coaches, and who failed to score in their first visit to the crease? Would Bosanquet be your nomination for the most penetrative bowler (on figures at least)? Is anyone in doubt as to Bradman's batting supremacy? If so, let him examine some of these dissections. The wicketkeepers are not overlooked; nor are the fieldsmen – or umpires. All of this is laid out alongside the fundamental tables of career averages, partnerships, centuries, etc.

The idea of collating this mountain of information and turning it into a display of quality individual performance sprang from fellow Anglo-Australian Warren Bagust, a computer expert (but, more impressively, also a legspin bowler) whom I had last seen about 30 years before, when we were both youthful wearers of the proud red-and-white cap of Sydney's St George club. Thus the framework. The choice of collaborators came next. With accuracy being the keynote, invitations went to Steven Lynch (another legspinner), who worked for MCC for 10 years, and Jim Gibb, a schoolmaster from the North-East.

Along the way, many long-standing errors were flushed out, and, of course, an enormous amount of updating was needed. The last major work had appeared 16 years earlier. There was no need to ask Messrs Lynch and Gibb to swear upon oath: they already regarded accuracy as a sacred quality, and knew that it had to be striven for with every ounce of determination. It does not come easily.

Only a sunstruck fool would proclaim this work to be error-free in advance. But if painstaking endeavour as the midnight candle flickered entitles one to carry the bags of the true flannelled champions of Test cricket, my two compilation assistants have earned their passports. In particular I thank Steven Lynch for his additional help and sharpness in the later, gruelling stages of proofreading.

David Frith

Guildford, 1986

SECTION 1
The Matches

England captain David Gower and allrounder Ian Botham with the Ashes – The Oval 1985

1.1 *Results Series by Series*

Season	England Captains	Australian Captains	M	E	A	D	Ashes held by	Totals M	E	A	D
1876–77	Lillywhite James	Gregory DW	2	1	1	0	–	2	1	1	0
1878–79	Harris Lord	Gregory DW	1	0	1	0	–	3	1	2	0
1880	Harris Lord	Murdoch WL	1	1	0	0	–	4	2	2	0
1881–82	Shaw A	Murdoch WL	4	0	2	2	–	8	2	4	2
1882	Hornby AN	Murdoch WL	1	0	1	0	–	9	2	5	2
1882–83	Bligh Hon. IFW	Murdoch WL	4	2	2	0	*E	13	4	7	2
1884	Hornby AN (1st) Harris Lord	Murdoch WL	3	1	0	2	E	16	5	7	4
1884–85	Shrewsbury A	Murdoch WL (1st) Horan TP (2nd, 5th) Massie HH (3rd) Blackham JM (4th)	5	3	2	0	E	21	8	9	4
1886	Steel AG	Scott HJH	3	3	0	0	E	24	11	9	4
1886–87	Shrewsbury A	McDonnell PS	2	2	0	0	E	26	13	9	4
1887–88	Read WW	McDonnell PS	1	1	0	0	E	27	14	9	4
1888	Steel AG (1st) Grace WG	McDonnell PS	3	2	1	0	E	30	16	10	4
1890	Grace WG	Murdoch WL	‡2	2	0	0	E	32	18	10	4
1891–92	Grace WG	Blackham JM	3	1	2	0	A	35	19	12	4
1893	Stoddart AE (1st) Grace WG	Blackham JM	3	1	0	2	E	38	20	12	6
1894–95	Stoddart AE	Blackham JM (1st) Giffen G	5	3	2	0	E	43	23	14	6
1896	Grace WG	Trott GHS	3	2	1	0	E	46	25	15	6
1897–98	MacLaren AC (1st, 2nd, 5th) Stoddart AE (3rd, 4th)	Trott GHS	5	1	4	0	A	51	26	19	6
1899	Grace WG (1st) MacLaren AC	Darling J	5	0	1	4	A	56	26	20	10
1901–02	MacLaren AC	Darling J Trumble H (4th, 5th)	5	1	4	0	A	61	27	24	10
1902	MacLaren AC	Darling J	5	1	2	2	A	66	28	26	12
1903–04	Warner PF	Noble MA	5	3	2	0	E	71	31	28	12
1905	Jackson Hon. FS	Darling J	5	2	0	3	E	76	33	28	15
1907–08	Fane FL Jones AO (4th, 5th)	Noble MA	5	1	4	0	A	81	34	32	15

Season	England Captains	Australian Captains	M	E	A	D	Ashes held by	Totals M	E	A	D
1909	MacLaren AC	Noble MA	5	1	2	2	A	86	35	34	17
1911–12	Douglas JWHT	Hill C	5	4	1	0	E	91	39	35	17
1912	Fry CB	Gregory SE	3	1	0	2	E	94	40	35	19
1920–21	Douglas JWHT	Armstrong WW	5	0	5	0	A	99	40	40	19
1921	Douglas JWHT (1st, 2nd) Tennyson Hon. LH	Armstrong WW	5	0	3	2	A	104	40	43	21
1924–25	Gilligan AER	Collins HL	5	1	4	0	A	109	41	47	21
1926	Carr AW Chapman APF (5th)	Collins HL Bardsley W (3rd, 4th)	5	1	0	4	E	114	42	47	25
1928–29	Chapman APF White JC (5th)	Ryder J	5	4	1	0	E	119	46	48	25
1930	Chapman APF Wyatt RES (5th)	Woodfull WM	5	1	2	2	A	124	47	50	27
1932–33	Jardine DR	Woodfull WM	5	4	1	0	E	129	51	51	27
1934	Walters CF (1st) Wyatt RES	Woodfull WM	5	1	2	2	A	134	52	53	29
1936–37	Allen GOB	Bradman DG	5	2	3	0	A	139	54	56	29
1938	Hammond WR	Bradman DG	‡4	1	1	2	A	143	55	57	31
1946–47	Hammond WR Yardley NWD (5th)	Bradman DG	5	0	3	2	A	148	55	60	33
1948	Yardley NWD	Bradman DG	5	0	4	1	A	153	55	64	34
1950–51	Brown FR	Hassett AL	5	1	4	0	A	158	56	68	34
1953	Hutton L	Hassett AL	5	1	0	4	E	163	57	68	38
1954–55	Hutton L	Johnson IW Morris AR (2nd)	5	3	1	1	E	168	60	69	39
1956	May PBH	Johnson IW	5	2	1	2	E	173	62	70	41
1958–59	May PBH	Benaud R	5	0	4	1	A	178	62	74	42
1961	Cowdrey MC (1st, 2nd) May PBH	Benaud R Harvey RN (2nd)	5	1	2	2	A	183	63	76	44
1962–63	Dexter ER	Benaud R	5	1	1	3	A	188	64	77	47
1964	Dexter ER	Simpson RB	5	0	1	4	A	193	64	78	51
1965–66	Smith MJK	Booth BC (1st, 3rd) Simpson RB	5	1	1	3	A	198	65	79	54
1968	Cowdrey MC Graveney TW (4th)	Lawry WM Jarman BN (4th)	5	1	1	3	A	203	66	80	57
1970–71	Illingworth R	Lawry WM Chappell IM (7th)	‡6	2	0	4	E	209	68	80	61

Season	England Captains	Australian Captains	M	E	A	D	Ashes held by	Totals M	E	A	D
1972	Illingworth R	Chappell IM	5	2	2	1	E	214	70	82	62
1974–75	Denness MH Edrich JH (4th)	Chappell IM	6	1	4	1	A	220	71	86	63
1975	Denness MH (1st) Greig AW	Chappell IM	4	0	1	3	A	224	71	87	66
1976–77	Greig AW	Chappell GS	1	0	1	0	†–	225	71	88	66
1977	Brearley JM	Chappell GS	5	3	0	2	E	230	74	88	68
1978–79	Brearley JM	Yallop GN	6	5	1	0	E	236	79	89	68
1979–80	Brearley JM	Chappell GS	3	0	3	0	†–	239	79	92	68
1980	Botham IT	Chappell GS	1	0	0	1	†–	240	79	92	69
1981	Botham IT (1st, 2nd) Brearley JM	Hughes KJ	6	3	1	2	E	246	82	93	71
1982–83	Willis RGD	Chappell GS	5	1	2	2	A	251	83	95	73
1985	Gower DI	Border AR	6	3	1	2	E	257	86	96	75
	In England		123	37	30	56					
	In Australia		134	49	66	19					
			257	86	96	75					

*England were presented with the Ashes after the 3rd Test of the 1882–83 series, when they led 2–1. A 4th Test was played.

‡The 3rd Test at Old Trafford in 1890, the 3rd Test at Old Trafford in 1938 and the 3rd Test at Melbourne in 1970–71 were all abandoned without a ball bowled. These matches have been excluded from the above.

†The Ashes were not at stake in the Centenary Tests of 1976–77 and 1980, nor (according to the TCCB) in the 3-match series of 1979–80.

1.2 *Results Era by Era*

		M	E	%	A	%	D	%
Era 1	1876–77 to 1899	56	26	46.4	20	35.7	10	17.9
Era 2	1901–02 to 1912	38	14	36.8	15	39.5	9	23.7
Era 3	1920–21 to 1938	49	15	30.6	22	44.9	12	24.5
Era 4	1946–47 to 1968	60	11	18.3	23	38.3	26	43.3
Era 5	1970–71 to 1985	54	20	37.0	16	29.6	18	33.3

1.3 *Sequences of Results*

Most Consecutive Victories

ENGLAND	AUSTRALIA
7 Melbourne 1884–85 to Sydney 1887–88	8 Sydney 1920–21 to Headingley 1921
5 Oval 1926 to Adelaide 1928–29	6 Headingley 1948 to Adelaide 1950–51
4 Oval 1888 to Oval 1890	4 Melbourne 1897–98 to Sydney 1897–98
4 Melbourne 1911–12 to Sydney 1911–12	4 Melbourne 1901–02 to Melbourne 1901–02

Only Australia, in 1920–21, have won every match in a 5-match series.

Most Consecutive Draws

4 Trent Bridge 1926 to Old Trafford 1926
4 Trent Bridge 1953 to Headingley 1953
4 Adelaide 1962–63 to Lord's 1964
4 Old Trafford 1964 to Melbourne 1965–66

There were no drawn matches in Australia from Melbourne 1881–82 to Melbourne 1946–47, 72 consecutive Tests being played to a finish.

Most Consecutive Tests Without Defeat

ENGLAND	AUSTRALIA
11 Lord's 1968 to Old Trafford 1972	14 Brisbane 1946–47 to Adelaide 1950–51
9 Trent Bridge 1926 to Adelaide 1928–29	13 Sydney 1920–21 to Adelaide 1924–25
7 Melbourne 1884–85 to Sydney 1887–88	10 Sydney 1962–63 to Melbourne 1965–66
7 Lord's 1977 to Perth 1978–79	

1.4 *Wickets Lost*

ENGLAND	Era 1	Era 2	Era 3	Era 4	Era 5	Total
To Bowlers	880	583	729	929	885	4006
Run-Outs	31	24	26	30	19	130
Total	911	607	755	959	904	4136

AUSTRALIA	Era 1	Era 2	Era 3	Era 4	Era 5	Total
To Bowlers	914	622	729	862	854	3981
Run-Outs	46	28	34	27	30	165
Total	960	650	763	889	884	4146
Combined total	1871	1257	1518	1848	1788	8282

1.5 *Runs Scored*

ENGLAND	Era 1	Era 2	Era 3	Era 4	Era 5	Total
From the Bat	20925	16027	25877	27258	25761	115848
Extras	1064	776	1089	1207	1997	6133
Total	21989	16803	26966	28465	27758	121981
Av per wkt	24.14	27.68	35.72	29.68	30.71	29.49
AUSTRALIA	**Era 1**	**Era 2**	**Era 3**	**Era 4**	**Era 5**	**Total**
From the Bat	20409	15537	26131	27843	25332	115252
Extras	894	843	1264	1038	1504	5543
Total	21303	16380	27395	28881	26836	120795
Av per wkt	22.19	25.20	35.90	32.49	30.36	29.14
Combined total	43292	33183	54361	57346	54394	242576
Av per wkt	23.14	26.40	35.81	31.03	30.53	29.29

1.6 *Victories Losing Fewest Wickets*

ENGLAND		
5 wickets	Edgbaston 1985	won by Inns and 118
6 wickets	Sydney 1936–37	won by Inns and 22
7 wickets	Oval 1938	won by Inns and 579

AUSTRALIA

8 wickets	Sydney 1946–47	won by Inns and 33
8 wickets	Brisbane 1954–55	won by Inns and 154
9 wickets	Lord's 1930	won by 7 wkts

1.7 *Summary of Performances*

	Players	M	Inns	NO	Runs	HS	Av	100s	50s	Ct	St
England	349	257	4714	578	115848	364	28.01	179	543	2273	86
Australia	293	257	4726	580	115252	334	27.80	198	502	2246	123
Totals	642	257	9440	1158	231100	364	27.90	377	1045	4519	209

1.8 *Longest Matches* (Actual playing time)

			Days	Total time	Balls
Era 1	Sydney	1894–95	6	23 hrs 48 mins	3370
	Melbourne	1891–92	5	20 hrs 15 mins	3102
Era 2	Sydney	1903–04	6	24 hrs 12 mins	3245
	Adelaide	1901–02	6	23 hrs 10 mins	3166
Era 3	Melbourne (5th Test)	1928–29	8	33 hrs 51 mins	4244
	Melbourne (3rd Test)	1928–29	7	31 hrs 10 mins	4209
Era 4	Adelaide	1946–47	6	29 hrs 7 mins	3525
	Sydney	1962–63	5	28 hrs 30 mins	3360
Era 5	Perth	1970–71	5	29 hrs 46 mins	3049
	Adelaide	1970–71	5	29 hrs 51 mins	3027

The first Test to last 7 days was at Sydney (5th Test) in 1911–12, though there was no play on the 3rd and 6th days because of rain.

Up to the Second World War, Tests in England were limited to 3 days from 1880 to 1926, and to 4 days from 1930 to 1938, though provision was made for the final Test to be timeless in 1912, 1926, 1930, 1934 and 1938. Of the latter (all played at The Oval), only the 1934 Test lasted 6 days but there was no play on the 5th day owing to rain.

The longest Test in actual playing time in England was the Oval Test of 1975, which lasted 6 days or 32 hrs 29 mins in all (3007 balls bowled).

The longest Test in England in terms of balls bowled was at Old Trafford in 1964 (3306 balls). The match lasted 5 days or 28 hrs 40 mins.

1.9 *Shortest Completed Matches* (Actual playing time)

			Days	Total time	Balls
Era 1	Lord's	1888	2	7 hrs 20 mins	792
	Old Trafford	1888	2	6 hrs 34 mins	804
Era 2	Melbourne (5th Test)	1903–04	3	9 hrs 11 mins	1079
	Edgbaston	1909	3	9 hrs 50 mins	1120
Era 3	Trent Bridge	1921	2	10 hrs 10 mins	1241
	Lord's	1921	3	13 hrs 50 mins	1640
Era 4	Brisbane	1950–51	4	9 hrs 39 mins	1034
	Oval	1948	4	14 hrs 49 mins	1836
Era 5	Trent Bridge	1981	4	17 hrs 28 mins	1418
	Edgbaston	1975	4	16 hrs 12 mins	1451

There was only 50 minutes' play (104 balls bowled) in the drawn Trent Bridge Test of 1926.

The last Test to be finished in 3 days was at Headingley in 1972, the match lasting 16 hrs 20 mins (1662 balls).

1.10 *The Follow-on*

England have been asked to follow on 20 times.

Of these matches England have:

won 2 drawn 5 lost 13

Australia have been asked to follow on 26 times.

Of these matches Australia have:

won 0 drawn 6 lost 20

The largest deficit faced by a side following on is 702 by Australia at The Oval in 1938. The smallest deficit is 91 by Australia at Old Trafford in 1888. (At this time the follow-on was compulsory after a deficit of 80 runs or more.)

1.11 *Biggest Victories*

By an Innings

ENGLAND			AUSTRALIA		
Inns and 579	Oval	1938	Inns and 332	Brisbane	1946–47
Inns and 230	Adelaide	1891–92	Inns and 200	Melbourne	1936–37
			Inns and 154	Brisbane	1954–55
Inns and 225	Melbourne	1911–12	Inns and 149	Oval	1948
Inns and 217	Oval	1886	Inns and 147	Sydney	1894–95

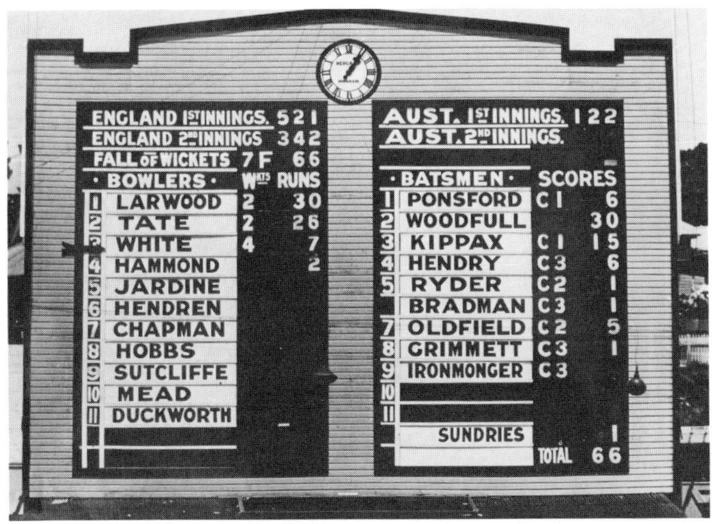

The scoreboard at the end of the 1928–29 Brisbane Test, which saw England's biggest runs victory

ENGLAND			AUSTRALIA		
Inns and 170	Old Trafford	1956	Inns and 91	Melbourne	1920–21
Inns and 137	Oval	1888	Inns and 85	Edgbaston	1975
Inns and 124	Sydney	1901–02	Inns and 55	Melbourne	1897–98
Inns and 118	Edgbaston	1985			
Inns and 106	Lord's	1886	Inns and 39	Oval	1930
Inns and 98	Melbourne	1884–85	Inns and 33	Sydney	1946–47

England have won 23 Tests by an innings, Australia 13.

By Runs

ENGLAND			AUSTRALIA		
675 runs	Brisbane	1928–29	562 runs	Oval	1934
338 runs	Adelaide	1932–33	409 runs	Lord's	1948
322 runs	Brisbane	1936–37	382 runs	Adelaide	1894–95
299 runs	Sydney	1970–71	377 runs	Sydney	1920–21
289 runs	Oval	1926	365 runs	Melbourne	1936–37

England have won by 200 runs or more on 9 occasions, Australia on 14.

By 10 Wickets

ENGLAND		AUSTRALIA	
Melbourne	1884–85	Melbourne	1878–79
Edgbaston	1909	Lord's	1899
Sydney	1932–33	Trent Bridge	1921
		Adelaide	1958–59

1.12 *Smallest Winning Margins*

By Wickets

ENGLAND				AUSTRALIA			
			Total				**Total**
1 wkt	Oval	1902	263–9	2 wkts	Sydney	1907–08	275–8
1 wkt	Melbourne	1907–08	282–9	3 wkts	Old Trafford	1896	125–7
2 wkts	Oval	1890	95–8				
3 wkts	Melbourne	1928–29	332–7				

By Runs

ENGLAND			
3 runs	Melbourne	1982–83	(Australia needed 292)
10 runs	Sydney	1894–95	(Australia needed 177)
12 runs	Adelaide	1928–29	(Australia needed 349)
13 runs	Sydney	1886–87	(Australia needed 111)
18 runs	Headingley	1981	(Australia needed 130)

AUSTRALIA			
3 runs	Old Trafford	1902	(England needed 124)
6 runs	Sydney	1884–85	(England needed 214)
7 runs	Oval	1882	(England needed 85)
11 runs	Adelaide	1924–25	(England needed 375)
28 runs	Melbourne	1950–51	(England needed 179)

On 15 occasions the winning margin has been less than 50 runs.
Of these, England have won 7 Tests, Australia 8.

SECTION 2
The Teams

ABOVE *The Australian touring team of 1948, led by Don Bradman. They returned home undefeated*
BELOW *The England XI which recaptured the Ashes by beating Australia at The Oval in 1926*

2.1 *Highest Innings Totals*

ENGLAND			AUSTRALIA		
903–7d	Oval	1938	729–6d	Lord's	1930
658–8d	Trent Bridge	1938	701	Oval	1934
636	Sydney	1928–29	695	Oval	1930
627–9d	Old Trafford	1934	659–8d	Sydney	1946–47
611	Old Trafford	1964	656–8d	Old Trafford	1964
595–5d	Edgbaston	1985	645	Brisbane	1946–47
589	Melbourne	1911–12	604	Melbourne	1936–37
577	Sydney	1903–04	601–8d	Brisbane	1954–55
576	Oval	1899	600	Melbourne	1924–25
558	Melbourne	1965–66	586	Sydney	1894–95
551	Sydney	1897–98	584	Headingley	1934
548	Melbourne	1924–25	†582	Adelaide	1920–21
†538	Oval	1975	†581	Sydney	1920–21
533	Headingley	1985	573	Adelaide	1897–98
529	Melbourne	1974–75	566	Headingley	1930
524	Sydney	1932–33	†564	Melbourne	1936–37
521	Brisbane*	1928–29	551	Oval	1884
519	Melbourne	1928–29	543–8d	Melbourne	1965–66
501	Adelaide	1911–12	539	Trent Bridge	1985
499	Adelaide	1891–92	†536	Melbourne	1946–47

*Brisbane Exhibition Ground, not Woolloongabba †Second innings

2.1a *Number of High Totals*

ENGLAND	Score	AUSTRALIA
1	900–999	0
0	800–899	0
0	700–799	2
4	600–699	7
14	500–599	17
45	400–499	46
64	Over 400	72

2.2 *Highest Totals Each Innings of Match*

First Innings of Match

ENGLAND			AUSTRALIA		
903–7d	Oval	1938	701	Oval	1934
658–8d	Trent Bridge	1938	656–8d	Old Trafford	1964
627–9d	Old Trafford	1934	645	Brisbane	1946–47
577	Sydney	1903–04	604	Melbourne	1936–37
576	Oval	1899	601–8d	Brisbane	1954–55

Second Innings of Match

ENGLAND			AUSTRALIA		
636	Sydney	1928–29	729–6d	Lord's	1930
611	Old Trafford	1964	695	Oval	1930
595–5d	Edgbaston	1985	659–8d	Sydney	1946–47
589	Melbourne	1911–12	584	Headingley	1934
558	Melbourne	1965–66	543–8d	Melbourne	1965–66

Third Innings of Match

ENGLAND			AUSTRALIA		
538	Oval	1975	582	Adelaide	1920–21
475	Melbourne	1894–95	581	Sydney	1920–21
441	Trent Bridge	1948	564	Melbourne	1936–37
437	Sydney	1894–95	536	Melbourne	1946–47
436–7d	Lord's	1975	506	Adelaide	1907–08

Fourth Innings of Match

ENGLAND			AUSTRALIA		
417	Melbourne	1976–77	404–3	Headingley	1948
411	Sydney	1924–25	402	Old Trafford	1981
370	Adelaide	1920–21	336	Adelaide	1928–29
363	Adelaide	1924–25	335	Trent Bridge	1930
332–7	Melbourne	1936–37	333	Melbourne	1894–95

2.2a *Highest Total When Following On*

ENGLAND			AUSTRALIA		
538	Oval	1975	427–6d	Trent Bridge	1938
437	Sydney	1894–95	408	Sydney	1897–98
356	Headingley	1981	349	Oval	1893
305	Old Trafford	1896	346–7d	Old Trafford	1899
304	Adelaide	1982–83	327	Oval	1880

England have followed on 20 times

Australia have followed on 26 times

2.3 *Highest Fourth-Innings Totals*

To Win

ENGLAND			AUSTRALIA		
332–7	Melbourne	1928–29	404–3	Headingley	1948
298–4	Melbourne	1894–95	315–6	Adelaide	1901–02
282–9	Melbourne	1907–08	287–5	Melbourne	1928–29
263–9	Oval	1902	276–4	Sydney	1897–98
237–3	Melbourne	1962–63	275–8	Sydney	1907–08

To Draw

ENGLAND			AUSTRALIA		
314–7	Sydney	1982–83	329–3	Lord's	1975
310–7	Melbourne	1946–47	328–3	Adelaide	1970–71
290–4	Trent Bridge	1972	238–8	Melbourne	1974–75
282–7	Lord's	1953	224–7	Headingley	1905
278–6	Brisbane	1962–63	220–3	Headingley	1975

To Lose

ENGLAND			AUSTRALIA		
417	Melbourne	1976–77	402	Old Trafford	1981
411	Sydney	1924–25	336	Adelaide	1928–29
370	Adelaide	1920–21	335	Trent Bridge	1930
363	Adelaide	1924–25	333	Melbourne	1894–95
323	Melbourne	1936–37	292	Sydney	1911–12

2.4 *Lowest Totals in Completed Innings*

ENGLAND			AUSTRALIA		
45	Sydney	1886–87	36	Edgbaston	1902
52	Oval	1948	42	Sydney	1887–88
53	Lord's	1888	44	Oval	1896
61	Melbourne	1901–02	53	Lord's	1896
61	Melbourne	1903–04	58*	Brisbane	1936–37
62	Lord's	1888	60	Lord's	1888
65*	Sydney	1894–95	63	Oval	1882
72*	Sydney	1894–95	65	Oval	1912
75	Melbourne	1894–95	66**	Brisbane†	1928–29
77	Oval	1882	68	Oval	1886
77	Sydney	1884–85	70	Old Trafford	1888
84	Oval	1896	74	Edgbaston	1909
87*	Headingley	1909	78*	Lord's	1968
87	Melbourne	1958–59	80	Oval	1888
95	Old Trafford	1884	80*	Sydney	1936–37
95	Melbourne	1976–77	81	Old Trafford	1888
99	Sydney	1901–02	82	Sydney	1887–88
100	Oval	1890	83	Sydney	1882–83
101	Oval	1882	84	Sydney	1886–87
101*	Melbourne	1903–04	84	Old Trafford	1956
101	Edgbaston	1975			

*One batsman short **Two batsmen short †Exhibition Ground

England have been dismissed for under 100 on 17 occasions
Australia have been dismissed for under 100 on 24 occasions

2.5 *Innings Closed at Low Totals*

ENGLAND			AUSTRALIA		
68–7d	Brisbane	1950–51	27–5†	Oval	1956
76–9d	Melbourne	1936–37	32–7d	Brisbane	1950–51
95–8*	Oval	1890	35–8†	Old Trafford	1953

*England won by 2 wickets †Drawn matches

2.6 *Highest Match Aggregates*

Overall

Runs–Wkts	Ground	Year	Days in Match	Won by
1753–40	Adelaide	1920–21	6	A
1723–31	Headingley	1948	5	A
1619–40	Melbourne	1924–25	7	A
1601–29	Lord's	1930	4	A
1562–37	Melbourne	1946–47	6	D
1554–35	Melbourne	1928–29	8	A
1541–35	Sydney	1903–04	6	E
1514–40	Sydney	1894–95	6	E
1502–29	Adelaide	1946–47	6	D
1497–37	Melbourne	1928–29	7	E

In England

Runs–Wkts	Ground	Year	Days in Match	Won by
1723–31	Headingley	1948	5	A
1601–29	Lord's	1930	4	A
1496–24	Trent Bridge	1938	4	D
1494–37	Oval	1934	4	A
1368–37	Lord's	1953	5	D

In Australia

Runs–Wkts	Ground	Year	Days in Match	Won by
1753–40	Adelaide	1920–21	6	A
1619–40	Melbourne	1924–25	7	A
1562–37	Melbourne	1946–47	6	D
1554–35	Melbourne	1928–29	8	A
1541–35	Sydney	1903–04	6	E

At Headingley in 1975 *the final day's play was abandoned after vandals protesting the innocence of a convicted criminal (George Davis) had dug up part of the pitch and poured oil on it. Rain from noon to approximately 4 pm would probably have ensured a draw anyway. The main sufferer was RB McCosker, who was stranded on 95 not out, just short of his maiden Test century. He scored 127 at The Oval in the next Test.*

2.7 *Lowest Match Aggregates in Completed Match*

Overall

Runs–Wkts	Ground	Year	Days in Match	Won by
291–40	Lord's	1888	2	A
323–30	Old Trafford	1888	2	E
363–40	Oval	1882	2	A
374–40	Sydney	1887–88	5**	E
389–38	Oval	1890	2	E
392–40	Oval	1896	3	E
421–28	Sydney	1894–95	3*	E
445–40	Sydney	1886–87	3	E
450–34	Brisbane	1950–51	4*	A
451–30	Edgbaston	1909	3	E

In England

Runs–Wkts	Ground	Year	Days in Match	Won by
291–40	Lord's	1888	2	A
323–30	Old Trafford	1888	2	E
363–40	Oval	1882	2	A
389–38	Oval	1890	2	E
392–40	Oval	1896	3	E

In Australia

Runs–Wkts	Ground	Year	Days in Match	Won by
374–40	Sydney	1887–88	5**	E
421–28	Sydney	1894–95	3*	E
445–40	Sydney	1886–87	3	E
450–34	Brisbane	1950–51	4*	A
539–40	Sydney	1886–87	4	E

*No play on one day **No play on two days

2.8 *Totals of Under 100 in Both Innings*

ENGLAND			AUSTRALIA		
53 and 62	Lord's	1888	42 and 82	Sydney	1887–88
65 and 72	Sydney	1894–95	81 and 70	Old Trafford	1888

2.9 *Fewest Wickets to Fall in Completed Match*

Wkts	Ground	Year	Wkts	Ground	Year
23	Oval	1938	28	Sydney	1936–37
25	Sydney	1936–37	28	Brisbane	1954–55
25	Edgbaston	1985	29	Lord's	1884
28	Sydney	1894–95	29	Lord's	1930
28	Melbourne	1920–21	29	Sydney	1950–51

2.10 *Averages Per Wicket*

ENGLAND	In England			In Australia			Total		
	Runs	Wkts	Av	Runs	Wkts	Av	Runs	Wkts	Av
Era 1	8621	348	24.77	13368	563	23.74	21989	911	24.14
Era 2	6935	252	27.52	9868	355	27.80	16803	607	27.68
Era 3	12221	319	38.31	14745	436	33.82	26966	755	35.72
Era 4	14106	454	31.07	14359	505	28.43	28465	959	29.68
Era 5	13790	427	32.30	13968	477	29.28	27758	904	30.71
Total	55673	1800	30.93	66308	2336	28.39	121981	4136	29.49

AUSTRALIA	In England			In Australia			Total		
	Runs	Wkts	Av	Runs	Wkts	Av	Runs	Wkts	Av
Era 1	8293	426	19.47	13010	534	24.36	21303	960	22.19
Era 2	5830	263	22.17	10550	387	27.26	16380	650	25.20
Era 3	12053	315	38.26	15342	448	34.25	27395	763	35.90
Era 4	13520	455	29.71	15361	434	35.39	28881	889	32.49
Era 5	13070	432	30.25	13766	452	30.46	26836	884	30.36
Total	52766	1891	27.90	68029	2255	30.17	120795	4146	29.14

In the fourth Test match at Sydney 1882–83 *the captains agreed to play each innings of the match on a separate pitch. Australia won by 4 wickets.*

2.11 *Batsmen's Matches – Highest Average Per Wicket* (By Era)

	Ground and Year	Total Runs	Total Wkts	Av
Era 1	Oval 1899	1182	25	47.28
	Oval 1884	982	22	44.64
	Sydney 1897–98	1292	31	41.68
Era 2	Lord's 1902	102	2	51.00
	Sydney 1903–04	1541	35	44.03
	Lord's 1912	592	14	42.29
Era 3	Old Trafford 1934	1307	20	65.35
	Trent Bridge 1938	1496	24	62.33
	Lord's 1926	1052	18	58.44
Era 4	Old Trafford 1964	1271	18	70.61
	Headingley 1948	1723	31	55.58
	Melbourne 1965–66	1097	20	54.85
Era 5	Trent Bridge 1985	1191	22	54.14
	Melbourne 1970–71	1215	23	52.83
	Adelaide 1970–71	1266	27	46.89

2.11a *Bowlers' Matches – Lowest Average Per Wicket* (By Era)

	Ground and Year	Total Runs	Total Wkts	Av
Era 1	Lord's 1888	291	40	7.28
	Oval 1882	363	40	9.08
	Sydney 1887–88	374	40	9.35
Era 2	Melbourne 1903–04	542	39	13.90
	Oval 1912	596	40	14.90
	Edgbaston 1909	451	30	15.03
Era 3	Trent Bridge 1921	521	30	17.37
	Melbourne 1932–33	747	40	18.18
	Headingley 1938	695	35	19.86

	Ground and Year	Total Runs	Total Wkts	Av
Era 4	Brisbane 1950–51	450	34	13.24
	Melbourne 1950–51	722	40	18.05
	Headingley 1956	608	30	20.27
Era 5	Trent Bridge 1981	621	36	17.25
	Headingley 1972	566	31	18.26
	Melbourne 1978–79	747	40	18.68

2.12 *Most Players in a Series*

	ENGLAND		AUSTRALIA	
	Players	**Series**	**Players**	**Series**
6 Tests	20	1981	19	1970–71
5 Tests	30	1921	28	1884–85
	25	1909	22	1894–95
	24	1899	20	1928–29
	21	1930		
	21	1948		
	20	1956		
	20	1964		
	20	1968		
4 Tests	18	1975	15	1881–82
3 Tests	17	1893	16	1979–80

2.13 *Fewest Players in a Series*

	ENGLAND		AUSTRALIA	
	Players	**Series**	**Players**	**Series**
6 Tests	14	1970–71	14	1974–75
	14	1978–79		

	ENGLAND		AUSTRALIA	
	Players	**Series**	**Players**	**Series**
5 Tests	11	1884–85	12	1964
	12	1894–95	13	1899
	12	1897–98	13	1902
	12	1901–02	13	1905
	13	1903–04	13	1921
	13	1982–83	13	1926
			13	1930
4 Tests	11	1881–82	12	1975
	12	1882–83		
3 Tests	12	1891–92	11	1884
	13	1886	11	1893
			12	1888

2.14 *Most Extras in an Innings*

Extras	Total	% Extras	Ground	Year	B	LB	W	NB	Wicketkeeper
ENGLAND									
52	309	16.83	Brisbane	1982–83	8	8	1	35	Marsh RW
50	903–7d	5.54	Oval	1938	22	19	1	8	Barnett BA
50	464	10.78	Oval	1985	13	11	0	26	Phillips WB
49	595–5d	8.24	Edgbaston	1985	7	20	0	22	Phillips WB
46	263	17.49	Headingley	1972	19	15	4	8	Marsh RW
AUSTRALIA									
55	345	15.94	Lord's	1981	6	11	6	32	Taylor RW
50	327	15.29	Oval	1934	37	8	1	4	Woolley FE
44	695	6.33	Oval	1930	22	18	0	4	Duckworth G
44	258	17.05	Edgbaston	1981	4	19	0	21	Taylor RW
43	627–9d	6.86	Old Trafford	1934	20	13	4	6	Ames LEG

England have conceded over 30 extras in an innings on 18 occasions
Australia have conceded over 30 extras in an innings on 24 occasions

Extras have never top-scored in an innings in these Tests

2.15 *Most Ducks in an Innings*

ENGLAND		AUSTRALIA	
5 Oval	1956	5 Oval	1888
4 Old Trafford	1884	5 Old Trafford	1888
4 Melbourne	1894–95	5 Lord's	1896
4 Sydney	1894–95	5 Trent Bridge	1953
4 Melbourne	1901–02	4 Edgbaston	1902
4 Melbourne	1903–04	4 Melbourne	1903–04
4 Oval	1912	4 Melbourne	1903–04
4 Headingley	1938	4 Melbourne	1932–33
4 Oval	1948	4 Brisbane	1936–37
4 Lord's	1977	4 Sydney	1936–37
		4 Old Trafford (1st)	1956
		4 Old Trafford (2nd)	1956
		4 Brisbane	1970–71
		4 Sydney	1970–71
		4 Headingley	1972
		4 Melbourne	1978–79
		4 Sydney	1978–79

2.16 *Most Ducks in a Match*

ENGLAND		AUSTRALIA	
7 Melbourne	1903–04	8 Old Trafford	1888
6 Sydney	1894–95	8 Old Trafford	1956
6 Melbourne	1901–02	7 Headingley	1972
6 Oval	1948	6 Sydney	1882–83
6 Adelaide	1974–75	6 Oval	1888
5 Oval	1882	6 Lord's	1896
5 Adelaide	1894–95	6 Headingley	1899
5 Sydney	1907–08	6 Melbourne	1903–04
5 Melbourne	1936–37	6 Oval	1912
5 Headingley	1938	6 Trent Bridge	1953
5 Adelaide	1950–51	6 Melbourne	1978–79
5 Oval	1956	6 Sydney	1978–79

ENGLAND		AUSTRALIA	
5 Sydney	1962–63	5 Lord's	1886
		5 Oval	1896
		5 Sydney	1901–02
		5 Sheffield	1902
		5 Sydney	1903–04
		5 Melbourne	1932–33
		5 Adelaide	1932–33
		5 Brisbane	1936–37
		5 Sydney	1936–37
		5 Old Trafford	1968
		5 Sydney	1970–71
		5 Melbourne	1974–75
		5 Trent Bridge	1977
		5 Adelaide	1978–79
		5 Old Trafford	1981

2.17 *First Wicket Down Without Scoring*

England have lost their first wicket without scoring on 35 occasions. Twice (Melbourne 1903–04 and Melbourne 1958–59) the first wicket has fallen before scoring in both innings. Twice (Lord's 1902 and Melbourne 1903–04, 1st innings) the second wicket has also fallen with the score at 0.

Australia have lost their first wicket without scoring on 38 occasions. Twice (Sydney 1932–33 and Brisbane 1950–51) the first wicket has fallen before scoring in both innings. Twice (Old Trafford 1888 and Brisbane 1950–51, 2nd innings) the second wicket has also fallen with the score at 0; at Brisbane the third wicket also fell before a run had been recorded.

England's victory at The Oval in 1968 *was made possible by the help of scores of spectators who spiked the outfield and assisted the ground staff to clear up after rain had flooded parts of the ground on the final afternoon. Unlikely resumption became a reality at 4.45 pm, with Australia 65 for 5, and DL Underwood (7 for 50) took the final wicket with 3 minutes of the match remaining.*

2.18 *Scoring Rates Per 100 Balls*

Era 1

		ENGLAND			AUSTRALIA		
Series	**Tests**	**Runs**	**Balls**	**Runs per 100 Balls**	**Runs**	**Balls**	**Runs per 100 Balls**
1876–77	2	687	1541	44.58	730	2019	36.16
1878–79	1	273	548	49.82	275	651	42.24
1880	1	477	978	48.77	476	1008	47.22
1881–82	4	1832	4486	40.84	1439	3918	36.73
1882	1	178	507	35.11	185	572	32.34
1882–83	4	1470	3582	41.04	1378	3795	36.31
1884	3	1085	2405	45.11	1107	2563	43.19
1884–85	5	1916	4323	44.32	1820	5527	32.93
1886	3	1117	3193	34.98	792	2430	32.59
1886–87	2	534	1686	31.67	450	1533	29.35
1887–88	1	250	700	35.71	124	429	28.90
1888	3	604	1395	43.30	507	1380	36.74
1890	2	505	1456	34.68	502	1761	28.51
1891–92	3	1385	3167	43.73	1281	4607	27.81
1893	3	1412	3161	44.67	1149	2211	51.97
1894–95	5	2399	5864	40.91	2822	5911	47.74
1896	3	1168	2329	50.15	1100	2447	44.95
1897–98	5	2622	6254	41.93	2691	5529	48.67
1899	5	2075	4377	47.41	2475	5488	45.10
Sub-Total	56	21989	51952	42.33	21303	53779	39.61

Era 2

Series	Tests	Runs	Balls	Runs per 100 Balls	Runs	Balls	Runs per 100 Balls
1901–02	5	2118	5292	40.02	2260	5306	42.59
1902	5	1646	3563	46.20	1395	2982	46.78
1903–04	5	2333	5669	41.15	2424	4744	51.10
1905	5	2788	6092	45.76	1862	3357	55.47
1907–08	5	2584	5654	45.70	3187	6379	49.96
1909	5	1568	3752	41.79	2101	4393	47.83
1911–12	5	2833	6008	47.15	2679	5290	50.64
1912	3	933	2302	40.53	472	1306	36.14
Sub-Total	38	16803	38332	43.84	16380	33757	48.52

Era 3

		ENGLAND			AUSTRALIA		
Series	**Tests**	**Runs**	**Balls**	**Runs per 100 Balls**	**Runs**	**Balls**	**Runs per 100 Balls**
1920–21	5	2779	5659	49.11	3368	6246	53.92
1921	5	2243	4469	50.19	1979	3502	56.51
1924–25	5	3067	7150	42.90	3630	8698	41.73
1926	5	2076	4818	43.09	1833	4577	40.05
1928–29	5	3757	9781	38.41	3069	8402	36.53
1930	5	2765	6221	44.45	2886	6378	45.25
1932–33	5	2726	7297	37.36	2490	4960	50.20
1934	5	2494	6721	37.11	3218	6276	51.27
1936–37	5	2416	6297	38.37	2785	6206	44.88
1938	4	2643	5291	49.95	2137	4212	50.74
Sub-Total	49	26966	63704	42.33	27395	59457	46.08

Era 4

Series	Tests	Runs	Balls	Runs per 100 Balls	Runs	Balls	Runs per 100 Balls
1946–47	5	2866	7598	37.72	3374	6666	50.62
1948	5	2645	6783	38.99	2981	6405	46.54
1950–51	5	1865	5032	37.06	2249	5140	43.75
1953	5	2074	5982	34.67	2289	5016	45.63
1954–55	5	2176	6075	35.82	2128	4515	47.13
1956	5	1975	5055	39.07	1611	5400	29.83
1958–59	5	2113	6358	33.23	2026	5173	39.16
1961	5	2559	6699	38.20	2400	5263	45.60
1962–63	5	2761	7025	39.30	2903	7135	40.69
1964	5	2326	5937	39.18	2091	5380	38.87
1965–66	5	2578	5792	44.51	2681	6287	42.64
1968	5	2527	6389	39.55	2148	5840	36.78
Sub-Total	60	28465	74725	38.09	28881	68220	42.34

Era 5

Series	Tests	Runs	Balls	Runs per 100 Balls	Runs	Balls	Runs per 100 Balls
1970–71	6	3580	9164	39.07	3188	8005	39.83
1972	5	2274	5667	40.13	2345	5341	43.91
1974–75	6	2883	7015	41.10	3375	7233	46.66
1975	4	2333	5127	45.50	1883	3934	47.86

		ENGLAND			AUSTRALIA		
Series	**Tests**	**Runs**	**Balls**	**Runs per 100 Balls**	**Runs**	**Balls**	**Runs per 100 Balls**
1976–77	1	512	1175	43.57	557	1124	49.56
1977	5	2300	5319	43.24	2213	4839	45.73
1978–79	6	2665	7679	34.71	2301	6620	34.76
1979–80	3	1382	3255	42.46	1525	3625	42.07
1980	1	449	872	51.49	574	1124	51.07
1981	6	3034	6367	47.65	2865	6338	45.20
1982–83	5	2946	5760	51.15	2820	5566	50.66
1985	6	3400	5604	60.67	3190	6741	47.32
Sub-Total	54	27758	63004	44.06	26836	60490	44.36
Total	257	121981	291717	41.81	120795	275703	43.81

The scoring rates shown take no account of no-balls and wides, which would in all cases slightly reduce the rates

2.19 *Biggest Difference Between Innings Totals*

ENGLAND

Difference	1st inns	2nd inns	Ground	Year
504	627–9d	123–0d	Old Trafford	1934
400	75	475	Melbourne	1894–95
347	191	438	Oval	1975
322	95	417	Melbourne	1976–77
313	494	181	Oval	1968

AUSTRALIA

Difference	1st inns	2nd inns	Ground	Year
420	586	166	Sydney	1894–95
374	701	327	Oval	1934
364	200–9d	564	Melbourne	1936–37
350	600	250	Melbourne	1924–25
343	133	476	Adelaide	1911–12

The instances by England at The Oval (1975) and Melbourne (1976–77) were in consecutive matches

2.20 *Highest Score at the Fall of Each Wicket*

	ENGLAND			AUSTRALIA		
1st	323	Melbourne	1911–12	244	Adelaide	1965–66
2nd	425	Melbourne	1911–12	472	Oval	1934
3rd	546	Oval	1938	585	Lord's	1930
4th	572	Edgbaston	1985	588	Lord's	1930
5th	592	Edgbaston	1985	643	Lord's	1930
6th	770	Oval	1938	672	Lord's	1930
7th	876	Oval	1938	670	Oval	1930
8th	626	Trent Bridge	1938	684	Oval	1930
9th	607	Old Trafford	1964	684	Oval	1930
10th	636	Sydney	1928–29	701	Oval	1934

2.21 *Lowest Score at the Fall of Each Wicket*

	ENGLAND			AUSTRALIA		
1st	0	(35 occasions)		0	(38 occasions)	
2nd	0	Lord's Melbourne	1902 1903–04	0	Old Trafford Brisbane	1888 1950–51
3rd	4	Melbourne	1903–04	0	Brisbane	1950–51
4th	5	Melbourne	1903–04	7	Old Trafford Oval Brisbane	1888 1896 1936–37
5th	13	Sydney	1886–87	7	Old Trafford	1888
6th	17	Sydney	1886–87	7	Old Trafford	1888
7th	21	Sydney	1886–87	14	Oval	1896
8th	29	Sydney	1886–87	19	Oval	1896
9th	41	Sydney	1886–87	25	Oval	1896
10th	45	Sydney	1886–87	36	Edgbaston	1902

At Sydney in the final Test of 1970–71 *England captain R Illingworth led his team from the field after a spectator tried to manhandle J A Snow. Only after the umpires threatened to award the match to Australia did England return to the field.*

2.22 *Method of Dismissal*

	Bowled (%)	Caught (%)	LBW (%)	Stumped (%)	Run Out (%)	Hit Wkt (%)	Total
Era 1	700 (37.41)	939 (50.19)	87 (4.65)	63 (3.37)	77 (4.12)	5 (0.27)	1871
Era 2	400 (31.82)	666 (52.98)	96 (7.64)	40 (3.18)	52 (4.14)	3 (0.24)	1257
Era 3	436 (28.72)	793 (52.24)	166 (10.94)	54 (3.56)	61 (4.02)	8 (0.53)	1518
Era 4	469 (25.38)	1055 (57.09)	228 (12.34)	35 (1.89)	57 (3.08)	4 (0.22)	1848
Era 5	363 (20.30)	1127 (63.03)	230 (12.86)	17 (0.95)	49 (2.74)	2 (0.11)	1788
Total	2368 (28.59)	4580 (55.30)	807 (9.74)	209 (2.52)	296 (3.57)	22 (0.27)	8282

SECTION 3
The Captains

RIGHT *Jardine and Woodfull toss during the acrimonious 'Bodyline' series of 1932–33*

LEFT *Gower and Border presided over a notably good-spirited series in 1985, won resoundingly by England*

3.1 *Captains*

ENGLAND (43)	Age when 1st Capt	No. of Tests as Capt	Tests as non-Capt	Won Toss	Batted 1st on winning Toss	Results W	D	L	% Wins
Allen GOB	34	5	8	2	2	2	0	3	40.00
Bligh Hon. IFW	23	4	0	3	3	2	0	2	50.00
Botham IT	24	3	26	0	0	0	2	1	–
Brearley JM	35	18	1	8	6	11	3	4	61.11
Brown FR	39	5	1	1	1	1	0	4	20.00
Carr AW	33	4	0	2	1	0	4	0	–
Chapman APF	25	9	7	5	5	6	2	1	66.67
Cowdrey MC	28	6	37	5	5	1	3	2	16.67
Denness MH	33	6	0	2	0	1	1	4	16.67
Dexter ER	27	10	9	6	5	1	7	2	10.00
Douglas JWHT	29	12	5	6	5	4	0	8	33.33
Edrich JH	37	1	31	0	0	0	0	1	–
Fane FL	32	3	1	1	1	1	0	2	33.33
Fry CB	40	3	15	3	3	1	2	0	33.33
Gilligan AER	29	5	0	1	1	1	0	4	20.00
Gower DI	28	6	20	4	2	3	2	1	50.00
Grace WG	40	13	9	4	4	8	2	3	61.54
Graveney TW	41	1	21	0	0	0	1	0	–
Greig AW	28	4	17	3	2	0	3	1	–
Hammond WR	34	8	25	6	6	1	4	3	12.50
Harris Lord	29	4	0	2	2	2	1	1	50.00
Hornby AN	35	2	1	1	1	0	1	1	–
Hutton L	36	10	17	2	1	4	5	1	40.00
Illingworth R	38	11	7	6	5	4	5	2	36.36
Jackson Hon. FS	34	5	15	5	5	2	3	0	40.00
Jardine DR	32	5	5	1	1	4	0	1	80.00
Jones AO	35	2	10	1	0	0	0	2	–
Lillywhite James	35	2	0	0	0	1	0	1	50.00
MacLaren AC	26	22	13	11	10	4	7	11	18.18
May PBH	26	13	8	9	8	3	4	6	23.08
Read WW	32	1	16	0	0	0	0	1	–
Shaw A	39	4	3	4	4	0	2	2	–
Shrewsbury A	28	7	16	3	3	5	0	2	71.43
Smith MJK	32	5	4	3	3	1	3	1	20.00

ENGLAND (43)	Age when 1st Capt	No. of Tests as Capt	Tests as non-Capt	Won Toss	Batted 1st on winning Toss	Results W	D	L	% Wins
Steel AG	27	4	9	2	2	3	0	1	75.00
Stoddart AE	30	8	8	2	1	3	1	4	37.50
Tennyson Hon. LH	31	3	1	2	2	0	2	1	–
Walters CF	28	1	4	0	0	0	0	1	–
Warner PF	30	5	2	2	2	3	0	2	60.00
White JC	38	1	6	1	1	0	0	1	–
Willis RGD	33	5	30	1	0	1	2	2	20.00
Wyatt RES	29	5	7	4	4	1	2	2	20.00
Yardley NWD	31	6	4	5	5	0	1	5	–

AUSTRALIA (34)	Age when 1st Capt	No. of Tests as Capt	Tests as non-Capt	Won Toss	Batted 1st on winning Toss	Results W	D	L	% Wins
Armstrong WW	41	10	32	4	4	8	2	0	80.00
Bardsley W	43	2	28	1	1	0	2	0	–
Benaud R	28	14	13	6	5	6	6	2	42.86
Blackham JM	31	8	27	4	4	3	2	3	37.50
Booth BC	32	2	13	1	1	0	1	1	–
Border AR	29	6	18	2	1	1	2	3	16.67
Bradman DG	28	19	18	6	6	11	5	3	57.89
Chappell GS	28	15	20	9	4	6	4	5	40.00
Chappell IM	27	16	14	8	5	7	5	4	43.75
Collins HL	34	8	8	5	5	4	2	2	50.00
Darling J	28	18	13	5	5	5	9	4	27.78
Giffen G	35	4	27	3	2	2	0	2	50.00
Gregory DW	31	3	0	2	2	2	0	1	66.67
Gregory SE	42	3	49	0	0	0	2	1	–
Harvey RN	32	1	36	0	0	1	0	0	100.00
Hassett AL	37	10	14	9	8	4	4	2	40.00
Hill C	34	5	36	3	3	1	0	4	20.00
Horan TP	30	2	13	1	1	0	0	2	–
Hughes KJ	27	6	16	3	1	1	2	3	16.67
Jarman BN	32	1	6	1	1	0	1	0	–
Johnson IW	35	9	13	3	2	2	3	4	22.22
Lawry WM	31	9	20	4	3	1	6	2	11.11
McDonnell PS	28	6	13	4	2	1	0	5	16.67

AUSTRALIA (34)	Age when 1st Capt	No. of Tests as Capt	Tests as non-Capt	Won Toss	Batted 1st on winning Toss	Results W	D	L	% Wins
Massie HH	30	1	8	1	1	1	0	0	100.00
Morris AR	32	1	23	1	0	0	0	1	–
Murdoch WL	25	16	2	7	7	5	4	7	31.25
Noble MA	30	15	24	11	10	8	2	5	53.33
Ryder J	39	5	12	2	2	1	0	4	20.00
Scott HJH	27	3	5	1	1	0	0	3	–
Simpson RB	28	8	11	2	2	2	6	0	25.00
Trott GHS	29	8	16	5	5	5	3	0	62.50
Trumble H	34	2	29	1	1	2	0	0	100.00
Woodfull WM	32	15	10	8	8	5	4	6	33.33
Yallop GN	26	6	7	5	3	1	0	5	16.67

The oldest England captain on debut, TW Graveney, was 41 years and 39 days at Headingley in 1968. The oldest Australian captain on debut, W Bardsley, was 43 years and 215 days at Headingley in 1926. The oldest player to captain England was WG Grace, 50 years 318 days on the opening day at Trent Bridge in 1899. The oldest player to captain Australia was W Bardsley, 43 years 229 days at Old Trafford in 1926.

The youngest England captain, the Hon. IFW Bligh, was 23 years 292 days at Melbourne in 1882–83. The youngest Australian captain, WL Murdoch, was 25 years 324 days at The Oval in 1880.

3.2 *Captain Most Often*

ENGLAND

Tests		W	L	D	Toss won
22	MacLaren AC	4	11	7	11
18	Brearley JM	11	4	3	8
13	Grace WG	8	3	2	4
13	May PBH	3	6	4	9
12	Douglas JWHT	4	8	0	6
11	Illingworth R	4	2	5	6
10	Dexter ER	1	2	7	6
10	Hutton L	4	1	5	2

AUSTRALIA

Tests		W	L	D	Toss won
19	Bradman DG	11	3	5	6
18	Darling J	5	4	9	5
16	Chappell IM	7	4	5	8
16	Murdoch WL	5	7	4	7
15	Chappell GS	6	5	4	9
15	Noble MA	8	5	2	11
15	Woodfull WM	5	6	4	8
14	Benaud R	6	2	6	6
10	Armstrong WW	8	0	2	4
10	Hassett AL	4	2	4	9

3.3 *Captains with Most Consecutive Victories*

ENGLAND			AUSTRALIA		
6	Chapman APF	1926 to 1930	8	Armstrong WW	1920–21 to 1921
4	Grace WG	1888 to 1890	4	Trott GHS	1897–98
4	Douglas JWHT	1911–12	4	Hassett AL	1950–51

WW Armstrong is the only captain to win all 5 Tests in a series, in 1920–21. JM Brearley won 5 Tests in the 6-match series of 1978–79.

3.4 *Captains with Most Matches Without Defeat*

ENGLAND			AUSTRALIA		
7	Illingworth R	1970–71 to 1972	10	Armstrong WW	1920–21 to 1921
7	Brearley JM	1977 to 1978–79	10	Bradman DG	1946–47 to 1948
			8	Simpson RB	1964 to 1965–66
			8	Chappell GS	1977 to 1982–83

3.5 *Centuries by Captains in Same Test*

England Capt		Australian Capt			
Chapman APF	121	Woodfull WM	155	Lord's	1930
Hammond WR	240	Bradman DG	102*	Lord's	1938
Hutton L	145	Hassett AL	104	Lord's	1953
Dexter ER	174	Simpson RB	311	Old Trafford	1964

3.6 *Highest Innings by Captains*

ENGLAND				AUSTRALIA			
240	Hammond WR	Lord's	1938	311	Simpson RB	Old Trafford	1964
215	Gower DI	Edgbaston	1985	270	Bradman DG	Melbourne	1936–37
188	Denness MH	Melbourne	1974–75	234	Bradman DG	Sydney	1946–47
174	Dexter ER	Old Trafford	1964	225	Simpson RB	Adelaide	1965–66
173	Stoddart AE	Melbourne	1894–95	212	Bradman DG	Adelaide	1936–37

ENGLAND				AUSTRALIA			
166	Gower DI	Trent Bridge	1985	211	Murdoch WL	Oval	1884
157	Gower DI	Oval	1985	196	Border AR	Lord's	1985
145	Hutton L	Lord's	1953	192	Chappell IM	Oval	1975
144*	Jackson Hon. FS	Headingley	1905	187	Bradman DG	Brisbane	1946–47

3.7 *Most Wickets in Innings by Captains*

ENGLAND				AUSTRALIA			
5–36	Allen GOB	Brisbane	1936–37	7–100	Noble MA	Sydney	1903–04
5–46	Douglas JWHT	Melbourne	1911–12	6–70	Benaud R	Old Trafford	1961
5–49	Brown FR	Melbourne	1950–51	6–115	Benaud R	Brisbane	1962–63
5–52	Jackson Hon. FS	Trent Bridge	1905	6–155	Giffen G	Melbourne	1894–95
5–66	Willis RGD	Brisbane	1982–83	5–26	Giffen G	Sydney	1894–95
				5–62	Trumble H	Melbourne	1901–02

3.8 *Most Wickets in Match by Captains*

ENGLAND				AUSTRALIA			
8–107	Allen GOB	Brisbane	1936–37	9–173	Benaud R	Adelaide	1958–59
				9–177	Benaud R	Sydney	1958–59
				8–40	Giffen G	Sydney	1894–95
				8–126	Trumble H	Melbourne	1901–02
				8–140	Noble MA	Sydney	1903–04

3.9 *Best Batting Average While Captain* (5 Tests or more)

ENGLAND	Tests	Inns	NO	Runs	HS	Av	100	50
Gower DI	6	9	0	732	215	81.33	3	1
Jackson Hon. FS	5	9	2	492	144*	70.29	2	2
May PBH	13	23	3	1091	113	54.55	2	8
Dexter ER	10	18	0	865	174	48.06	1	7

ENGLAND	Tests	Inns	NO	Runs	HS	Av	100	50
Hammond WR	8	14	0	571	240	40.79	1	2
Hutton L	10	18	1	663	145	39.00	1	4
Illingworth R	10	18	3	527	57	35.13	0	2
MacLaren AC	22	36	3	1156	116	35.03	2	6

AUSTRALIA	Tests	Inns	NO	Runs	HS	Av	100	50
Bradman DG	19	32	5	2432	270	90.07	10	6
Simpson RB	8	12	2	813	311	81.30	2	3
Border AR	6	11	2	597	196	66.33	2	1
Armstrong WW	10	13	2	616	158	56.00	3	1
Ryder J	5	10	1	492	112	54.67	1	4
Chappell GS	15	29	4	1225	117	49.00	4	4
Lawry WM	9	17	3	594	135	42.43	1	4
Chappell IM	16	30	1	1181	192	40.72	2	9
Hassett AL	10	19	0	731	115	38.47	2	4
Woodfull WM	15	25	2	878	155	38.17	1	7
Noble MA	15	29	3	992	133	38.15	1	7
Murdoch WL	16	29	4	877	211	35.08	2	1

3.10 *Best Bowling Average While Captain* (5 Tests or more)

ENGLAND	Tests	Balls	Mdns	Runs	Wkts	Av	5wI	10wM
Jackson Hon. FS	5	407	8	201	13	15.46	1	–
Brown FR	5	872	12	389	18	21.61	1	–
Yardley NWD	6	568	25	219	9	24.33	–	–
Willis RGD	5	999	28	486	18	27.00	1	–
Allen GOB	5	1021	12	526	17	30.94	1	–
Illingworth R	10	1584	71	546	17	32.12	–	–
Douglas JWHT	12	1733	46	885	27	32.78	1	–
Dexter ER	10	1056	13	491	14	35.07	–	–

AUSTRALIA	Tests	Balls	Mdns	Runs	Wkts	Av	5wI	10wM
Noble MA	15	2055	101	745	31	24.03	1	–
Armstrong WW	10	1379	77	416	17	24.47	–	–
Benaud R	14	5017	199	1760	63	27.94	4	–
Johnson IW	9	1602	69	546	18	30.33	–	–
Ryder J	5	413	16	180	5	36.00	–	–
Trott GHS	8	786	18	396	11	36.00	–	–

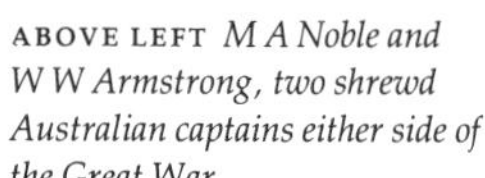

ABOVE LEFT *M A Noble and W W Armstrong, two shrewd Australian captains either side of the Great War*

ABOVE *Peter May and Richie Benaud, who fought their battles in the late 1950s and early 1960s*

LEFT *Ray Illingworth and Ian Chappell at the start of the closely-contested 1972 series*

BELOW LEFT *Kim Hughes congratulates Mike Brearley, England's captain, in 1981. Brearley's successors, Willis and Gower, stand alongside*

3.11 *Wicketkeepers as Captain*

ENGLAND	AUSTRALIA	Tests	Ct	St	Total
(No instance)	Blackham JM	8	11	4	15
	Jarman BN	1	3	0	3
	Murdoch WL	*1	1	1	2

*JM Blackham kept wicket for part of the 2nd innings of this Test

3.12 *Most Consecutive Tests as Captain*

ENGLAND		AUSTRALIA	
14 MacLaren AC	1899 to 1902	19 Bradman DG	1936–37 to 1948
14 Brearley JM	1977 to 1979–80	16 Chappell IM	1970–71 to 1975
		15 Woodfull WM	1930 to 1934
		14 Murdoch WL	1880 to 1884–85

3.13 *Captains Who Sent Opponents In*

ENGLAND

Captain	Ground	Year	Result
Stoddart AE	Sydney	1894–95	Lost by inns and 147 runs
MacLaren AC	Melbourne	1901–02	Lost by 229 runs
Jones AO	Sydney	1907–08	Lost by 49 runs
Douglas JWHT	Melbourne	1911–12	Won by inns and 225 runs
Carr AW	Headingley	1926	Drawn
Hutton L	Brisbane	1954–55	Lost by inns and 154 runs
May PBH	Adelaide	1958–59	Lost by 10 wkts
Dexter ER	Lord's	1964	Drawn
Illingworth R	Trent Bridge	1972	Drawn
Denness MH	Adelaide	1974–75	Lost by 163 runs
Denness MH	Edgbaston	1975	Lost by inns and 85 runs
Greig AW	Melbourne	1976–77	Lost by 45 runs
Brearley JM	Perth	1979–80	Lost by 138 runs
Brearley JM	Oval	1981	Drawn

ENGLAND

Captain	Ground	Year	Result
Willis RGD	Adelaide	1982–83	Lost by 8 wkts
Gower DI	Old Trafford	1985	Drawn
Gower DI	Edgbaston	1985	Won by inns and 118 runs

AUSTRALIA

Captain	Ground	Year	Result
McDonnell PS	Sydney	1886–87	Lost by 13 runs
McDonnell PS	Sydney	1887–88	Lost by 126 runs
Giffen G	Melbourne	1894–95	Lost by 94 runs
Noble MA	Lord's	1909	Won by 9 wkts
Hassett AL	Headingley	1953	Drawn
Morris AR	Sydney	1954–55	Lost by 38 runs
Johnson IW	Sydney	1954–55	Drawn
Benaud R	Melbourne	1958–59	Won by 9 wkts
Lawry WM	Perth	1970–71	Drawn
Chappell IM	Sydney	1970–71	Lost by 62 runs
Chappell IM	Perth	1974–75	Won by 9 wkts
Chappell IM	Melbourne	1974–75	Drawn
Chappell GS	Oval	1977	Drawn
Yallop GN	Perth	1978–79	Lost by 166 runs
Yallop GN	Adelaide	1978–79	Lost by 205 runs
Chappell GS	Sydney	1979–80	Won by 6 wkts
Hughes KJ	Trent Bridge	1981	Won by 4 wkts
Hughes KJ	Lord's	1981	Drawn
Chappell GS	Perth	1982–83	Drawn
Chappell GS	Brisbane	1982–83	Won by 7 wkts
Chappell GS	Melbourne	1982–83	Lost by 3 runs
Border AR	Lord's	1985	Won by 4 wkts

At The Oval in 1938 *L Hutton, who had scored 364 in England's 903–7d, tried to hasten the end of Australia's innings by kicking the ball over the boundary in order to expose a tailender to the bowling. The umpire awarded 5 runs for the stroke and the better batsman retained the strike.*

SECTION 4
The Players

ABOVE LEFT *W G Grace, England's oldest player*
ABOVE RIGHT *Bert Ironmonger, who is Australia's*
BELOW *Colin Cowdrey: most Tests for England*
RIGHT *Syd Gregory: most for Australia*

4.1 *Career Records of All Players*

†by Innings figure indicates left-hand batsman

†by Balls figure indicates left-arm bowler

ENGLAND	Born	County	Debut	M	I	NO	Runs	HS	Av	100	50	Ct	St	Balls	Mds	Runs	Wks	Av	Best	5i	10m
Abel R	30.11.1857	Surrey	1888	11	19	1	555	132*	30.83	1	2	9	–	–							
Absolom CA	07.06.1846	Kent	1878–79	1	2	–	58	52	29.00	–	1	–	–	–							
Agnew JP	04.04.1960	Leics	1985	1	1	1	2	2*	–	–	–	–	–	138	2	99	0	–	–	–	–
Allen DA	29.10.1935	Gloucs	1961	10	14	5	232	50*	25.78	–	1	2	–	2492	120	892	28	31.86	4–47	–	–
Allen GOB	31.07.1902	Middx	1930	13	21	1	479	68	23.95	–	3	15	–	2783	58	1603	43	37.28	5–36	1	–
Allott PJW	14.09.1956	Lancs	1981	5	7	2	93	52*	18.60	–	1	–	–	816	26	385	9	42.78	2–17	–	–
Ames LEG	03.12.1905	Kent	1932–33	17	27	2	675	120	27.00	1	4	33	4	–							
Amiss DL	07.04.1943	Warks	1968	11	21	1	305	90	15.25	–	2	7	–	–							
Andrew KV	15.12.1929	N'hants	1954–55	1	2	–	11	6	5.50	–	–	–	–	–							
Appleyard R	27.06.1924	Yorks	1954–55	5	6	4	45	19*	22.50	–	–	4	–	812	32	273	13	21.00	3–13	–	–
Armitage T	25.04.1848	Yorks	1876–77	2	3	–	33	21	11.00	–	–	–	–	12	0	15	0	–	–	–	–
Arnold EG	07.11.1876	Worcs	1903–04	8	12	3	144	40	16.00	–	–	6	–	1371	47	689	25	27.56	4–28	–	–
Arnold GG	03.09.1944	Surrey	1972	8	14	5	56	22	6.22	–	–	1	–	1992	51	898	30	29.93	5–86	1	–
Athey CWJ	27.09.1957	Yorks	1980	1	2	–	10	9	5.00	–	–	1	–	–							
Attewell W	12.06.1861	Notts	1884–85	10	15	6	150	43*	16.67	–	–	9	–	2850	326	626	27	23.19	4–42	–	–
Bailey TE	03.12.1923	Essex	1950–51	23	38	4	875	88	25.74	–	5	16	–	3300	105	1373	42	32.69	4–22	–	–
Bairstow DL	01.09.1951	Yorks	1980	1	1	–	6	6	6.00	–	–	2	1	–							
Barber RW	26.09.1935	Warks	1964	7	13†	1	447	185	37.25	1	–	4	–	603	4	371	6	61.83	2–56	–	–
Barlow GD	26.03.1950	Middx	1977	1	2†	–	6	5	3.00	–	–	–	–	–							
Barlow RG	28.05.1851	Lancs	1881–82	17	30	4	591	62	22.73	–	2	14	–	2456†	325	767	34	22.56	7–40	3	–
Barnes SF	19.04.1873	La(4)misc(16)	1901–02	20	30	5	210	38*	8.40	–	–	7	–	5749	262	2288	106	21.58	7–60	12	1
Barnes W	27.05.1852	Notts	1880	21	33	2	725	134	23.39	1	5	19	–	2289	271	793	51	15.55	6–28	3	–
Barnett CJ	03.07.1910	Gloucs	1936–37	9	16	–	624	129	39.00	2	2	5	–	148	6	61	0	–	–	–	–
Barrington KF	24.11.1930	Surrey	1961	23	39	6	2111	256	63.97	5	13	19	–	426	7	231	4	57.75	2–47	–	–
Bates W	19.11.1855	Yorks	1881–82	15	26	2	656	64	[illegible]	–	5	9	[illegible]	[illegible]	[illegible]	[illegible]	[illegible]	[illegible]	[illegible]	[illegible]	[illegible]

Bean G	07.03.1864	Sussex	1891–92	3	5	–	92	50	18.40	–	1	4	–	–							
Bedser AV	04.07.1918	Surrey	1946–47	21	35	9	373	79	14.35	–	1	11	–	7065	209	2859	104	27.49	7–44	7	2
Bligh Hon. IFW	13.03.1859	Kent	1882–83	4	7	1	62	19	10.33	–	–	7	–	–							
Blythe C	30.05.1879	Kent	1901–02	9	14	4	75	20	7.50	–	–	2	–	2085†	99	877	41	21.39	6–44	3	1
Bosanquet BJT	13.10.1877	Middx	1903–04	7	14	3	147	27	13.36	–	–	9	–	970	10	604	25	24.16	8–107	2	–
Botham IT	24.11.1955	Som	1977	29	49	2	1422	149*	30.26	3	6	44	–	7361	254	3556	136	26.15	6–78	8	2
Bowes WE	25.07.1908	Yorks	1932–33	6	7	3	19	10*	4.75	–	–	–	–	1459	41	741	30	24.70	6–142	3	–
Boycott G	21.10.1940	Yorks	1964	38	71	9	2945	191	47.50	7	14	12	–	224	6	107	2	53.50	2–32	–	–
Bradley WM	02.01.1875	Kent	1899	2	2	1	23	23*	23.00	–	–	–	–	625	49	233	6	38.83	5–67	1	–
Braund LC	18.10.1875	Som	1901–02	20	36	3	830	103*	25.15	2	2	37	–	3731	140	1769	46	38.46	8–81	3	–
Brearley JM	28.04.1942	Middx	1976–77	19	37	2	798	81	22.80	–	5	20	–	–							
Brearley W	11.03.1876	Lancs	1905	3	4	2	21	11*	10.50	–	–	–	–	669	23	355	17	20.88	5–110	1	–
Briggs J	03.10.1862	Lancs	1884–85	31	48	5	809	121	18.81	1	2	11	–	4941†	334	1993	97	20.55	6–45	7	3
Brockwell W	21.01.1865	Surrey	1893	7	12	–	202	49	16.83	–	–	6	–	582	31	309	5	61.80	3–33	–	–
Brown DJ	30.01.1942	Warks	1965–66	8	9	–	34	14	3.78	–	–	3	–	1728	48	810	23	35.22	5–42	2	–
Brown FR	16.12.1910	N'hants	1950–51	6	10	–	260	79	26.00	–	2	5	–	1184	23	524	22	23.82	5–49	1	–
Brown G	06.10.1887	Hants	1921	3	5†	–	250	84	50.00	–	2	2	2	–							
Brown JT	20.08.1869	Yorks	1894–95	8	16	3	470	140	36.15	1	1	7	–	35	0	22	0	–	–	–	–
Carr AW	21.05.1893	Notts	1926	4	1	–	13	13	13.00	–	–	1	–	–							
Carr DW	17.03.1872	Kent	1909	1	1	–	0	0	0.00	–	–	–	–	414	3	282	7	40.29	5–146	1	–
Cartwright TW	22.07.1935	Warks	1964	2	2	–	4	4	2.00	–	–	–	–	834	55	228	5	45.60	3–110	–	–
Chapman APF	03.09.1900	Kent	1924–25	16	25†	3	784	121	35.64	1	4	18	–	40†	1	20	0	–	–	–	–
Charlwood HRJ	19.12.1846	Sussex	1876–77	2	4	–	63	36	15.75	–	–	–	–	–							
Christopherson S	11.11.1861	Kent	1884	1	1	–	17	17	17.00	–	–	–	–	136	13	69	1	69.00	1–52	–	–
Clark EW	09.08.1902	N'hants	1934	2	3†	3	6	2*	–	–	–	–	–	608†	15	324	8	40.50	5–98	1	–
Close DB	24.02.1931	Yorks	1950–51	2	4†	–	42	33	10.50	–	–	3	–	104	2	61	1	61.00	1–20	–	–
Coldwell LJ	10.01.1933	Worcs	1962–63	4	6	4	9	6	4.50	–	–	–	–	840	19	317	7	45.29	3–48	–	–
Compton DCS	23.05.1918	Middx	1938	28	51	8	1842	184	42.84	5	9	17	–	464†	7	298	3	99.33	1–18	–	–
Cook G	09.10.1951	N'hants	1982–83	3	6	–	54	26	9.00	–	–	1	–	36†	3	23	0	–	–	–	–
Cowans NG	17.04.1961	Middx	1982–83	5	8	2	90	36	15.00	–	–	3	–	840	20	524	13	40.31	6–77	1	–
Cowdrey MC	24.12.1932	Kent	1954–55	43	75	4	2433	113	34.27	5	11	40	–	59	0	45	0	–	–	–	–
Coxon A	18.01.1916	Yorks	1948	1	2	–	19	19	9.50	–	–	–	–	378	13	172	3	57.33	2–90	–	–

ENGLAND	Born	County	Debut	M	I	NO	Runs	HS	Av	100	50	Ct	St	Balls	Mds	Runs	Wks	Av	Best	5i	10m
Cranston J	09.01.1859	Gloucs	1890	1	2†	–	31	16	15.50	–	–	1	–	–							
Cranston K	20.10.1917	Lancs	1948	1	2	–	10	10	5.00	–	–	2	–	127	1	79	1	79.00	1–28	–	–
Crapp JF	14.10.1912	Gloucs	1948	3	6†	1	88	37	17.60	–	–	6	–	–							
Crawford JN	01.12.1886	Surrey	1907–08	5	10	1	162	62	18.00	–	1	6	–	1426	36	742	30	24.73	5–48	3	–
Dean H	13.08.1884	Lancs	1912	2	2†	1	0	0*	0.00	–	–	1	–	324†	19	97	6	16.17	4–19	–	–
Denness MH	01.12.1940	Kent	1974–75	6	11	–	329	188	29.91	1	1	7	–	–							
Denton D	04.07.1874	Yorks	1905	1	2	–	12	12	6.00	–	–	–	–	–							
Dewes JG	11.10.1926	Middx	1948	3	6†	–	34	10	5.67	–	–	–	–	–							
Dexter ER	15.05.1935	Sussex	1958–59	19	35	–	1358	180	38.80	2	8	10	–	1582	29	742	23	32.26	3–16	–	–
Dilley GR	18.05.1959	Kent	1979–80	5	10†	4	230	56	38.33	–	1	2	–	906	29	418	17	24.59	4–24	–	–
Dipper AE	09.11.1885	Gloucs	1921	1	2	–	51	40	25.50	–	–	–	–	–							
D'Oliveira BL	04.10.1931	Worcs	1968	13	23	2	865	158	41.19	2	4	8	–	1644	71	515	14	36.79	2–15	–	–
Dollery HE	14.10.1914	Warks	1948	2	3	–	38	37	12.67	–	–	–	–	–							
Dolphin A	24.12.1885	Yorks	1920–21	1	2	–	1	1	0.50	–	–	1	–	–							
Douglas JWHT	03.09.1882	Essex	1911–12	17	28	2	696	75	26.77	–	5	7	–	2318	53	1227	35	35.06	5–46	1	–
Downton PR	04.04.1957	Middx	1981	7	9	1	125	54	15.63	–	1	21	1	–							
Druce NF	01.01.1875	Surrey	1897–98	5	9	–	252	64	28.00	–	1	5	–	–							
Ducat A	16.02.1886	Surrey	1921	1	2	–	5	3	2.50	–	–	1	–	–							
Duckworth G	09.05.1901	Lancs	1928–29	10	17	6	163	39*	14.82	–	–	23	3	–							
Duleepsinhji KS	13.06.1905	Sussex	1930	4	7	–	416	173	59.43	1	2	2	–	–							
Durston FJ	11.07.1893	Middx	1921	1	2	1	8	6*	8.00	–	–	–	–	202	2	136	5	27.20	4–102	–	–
Edmonds PH	08.03.1951	Middx	1975	8	10	1	80	21	8.89	–	–	9	–	1946†	81	800	21	38.10	5–28	1	–
Edrich JH	21.06.1937	Surrey	1964	32	57†	3	2644	175	48.96	7	13	16	–	–							
Edrich WJ	26.03.1916	Middx	1938	21	39	1	1184	119	31.16	2	8	19	–	1477	24	888	16	55.50	3–50	–	–
Ellison RM	21.09.1959	Kent	1985	2	1†	–	3	3	3.00	–	–	1	–	455	20	185	17	10.88	6–77	2	1
Emburey JE	20.08.1952	Middx	1978–79	15	21	5	334	57	20.88	–	1	10	–	4093	193	1388	48	28.92	5–82	1	–
Emmett GM	02.12.1912	Gloucs	1948	1	2	–	10	10	5.00	–	–	–	–	–							
Emmett T	03.09.1841	Yorks	1876–77	7	13†	1	160	48	13.33	–	–	9	–	728†	92	284	9	31.55	7–68	1	–
Evans AJ	01.05.1889	Kent	1921	1	2	–	18	14	9.00	–	–	–	–	–							

Evans TG	18.08.1920	Kent	1946–47	31	55	9	783	50	17.79	[illegible]	1	64	12								
Fagg AE	18.06.1915	Kent	1936–37	2	3	–	42	27	14.00	–	–	2	–	–							
Fane FL	27.04.1875	Essex	1907–08	4	8	–	192	50	24.00	–	1	1	–	–							
Farnes K	08.07.1911	Essex	1934	8	10	4	23	7*	3.83	–	–	1	–	2153	58	1065	38	28.03	6–96	3	1
Fender PGH	22.08.1892	Surrey	1920–21	5	9	1	198	59	24.75	–	1	3	–	806	15	522	14	37.29	5–90	2	–
Fielder A	19.07.1877	Kent	1903–04	6	12	5	78	20	11.14	–	–	4	–	1491	42	711	26	27.35	6–82	1	–
Fishlock LB	02.01.1907	Surrey	1946–47	1	2†	–	14	14	7.00	–	–	1	–	–							
Flavell JA	15.05.1929	Worcs	1961	4	6†	2	31	14	7.75	–	–	–	–	792	25	367	7	52.43	2–65	–	–
Fletcher KWR	20.05.1944	Essex	1968	15	27	1	661	146	25.42	1	3	10	–	160	1	101	1	101.00	1–48	–	–
Flowers W	07.12.1856	Notts	1884–85	8	14	–	254	56	18.14	–	1	2	–	858	92	296	14	21.14	5–46	1	–
Ford FGJ	14.12.1866	Middx	1894–95	5	9†	–	168	48	18.67	–	–	5	–	210†	6	129	1	129.00	1–47	–	–
Foster FR	31.01.1889	Warks	1911–12	8	11	1	281	71	28.10	–	3	4	–	1894†	76	742	34	21.82	6–91	3	–
Foster NA	06.05.1962	Essex	1985	1	2	–	3	3	1.50	–	–	–	–	138	1	83	1	83.00	1–83	–	–
Foster RE	16.04.1878	Worcs	1903–04	5	9	1	486	287	60.75	1	–	8	–	–							
Fowler G	20.04.1957	Lancs	1982–83	3	6†	–	207	83	34.50	–	2	1	–	–							
Freeman AP	17.05.1888	Kent	1924–25	2	4	2	80	50*	40.00	–	1	1	–	968	16	459	8	57.38	3–134	–	–
Fry CB	25.04.1872	Sx(12)Hamp(6)	1899	18	29	3	825	144	31.73	1	5	14	–	10	1	3	0	–	–	–	–
Gatting MW	06.06.1957	Middx	1980	13	23	4	960	160	50.53	2	8	9	–	48	1	29	0	–	–	–	–
Gay LH	24.03.1871	Som	1894–95	1	2	–	37	33	18.50	–	–	3	1	–							
Geary G	09.07.1893	Leics	1926	9	15	2	202	66	15.54	–	2	9	–	2628	112	963	27	35.67	5–35	2	–
Gibb PA	11.07.1913	Yorks	1946–47	1	2	–	24	13	12.00	–	–	1	–	–							
Gifford N	30.03.1940	Worcs	1964	5	8†	2	57	16*	9.50	–	–	3	–	702†	41	256	6	42.67	2–14	–	–
Gilligan AER	23.12.1894	Sussex	1924–25	5	9	2	64	31	9.14	–	–	1	–	1087	14	519	10	51.90	3–114	–	–
Goddard TWJ	01.10.1900	Gloucs	1930	1	–	–	–	–	–	–	–	–	–	193	14	49	2	24.50	2–49	–	–
Gooch GA	23.07.1953	Essex	1975	22	40	–	1105	196	27.63	1	5	17	–	518	24	197	4	49.25	2–16	–	–
Gower DI	01.04.1957	Leics	1978–79	26	48†	2	2075	215	45.11	5	7	20	–	–							
Grace EM	28.11.1841	Gloucs	1880	1	2	–	36	36	18.00	–	–	1	–	–							
Grace GF	13.12.1850	Gloucs	1880	1	2	–	0	0	0.00	–	–	2	–	–							
Grace WG	18.07.1848	Gloucs	1880	22	36	2	1098	170	32.29	2	5	39	–	666	65	236	9	26.22	2–12	–	–
Graveney TW	16.06.1927	Gs(14)Wo(8)	1953	22	38	4	1075	111	31.62	1	6	24	–	140	4	74	1	74.00	1–34	–	–
Greenwood A	20.08.1847	Yorks	1876–77	2	4	–	77	49	19.25	–	–	2	–	–							
Greig AW	06.10.1946	Sussex	1972	21	37	1	1303	110	36.19	1	10	37	–	3472	114	1663	44	37.80	4–53	–	–

ENGLAND	Born	County	Debut	M	I	NO	Runs	HS	Av	100	50	Ct	St	Balls	Mds	Runs	Wks	Av	Best	5i	10m
Gunn G	13.06.1879	Notts	1907–08	11	21	1	844	122*	42.20	2	6	13	–	–							
Gunn JR	19.07.1876	Notts	1901–02	6	10†	2	85	24	10.63	–	–	3	–	997†	54	387	18	21.50	5–76	1	–
Gunn W	04.12.1858	Notts	1886–87	11	20	2	392	102*	21.78	1	1	5	–	–							
Haig NE	12.12.1887	Middx	1921	1	2	–	3	3	1.50	–	–	–	–	138	4	88	2	44.00	2–61	–	–
Haigh S	19.03.1871	Yorks	1905	4	5	1	40	14	10.00	–	–	1	–	372	21	139	4	34.75	2–40	–	–
Hallows C	04.04.1895	Lancs	1921	1	1†	1	16	16*	–	–	–	–	–	–							
Hammond WR	19.06.1903	Gloucs	1928–29	33	58	3	2852	251	51.85	9	7	43	–	3958	136	1612	36	44.78	5–57	1	–
Hampshire JH	10.02.1941	Yorks	1970–71	4	8	–	168	55	21.00	–	1	4	–	–							
Hardinge HTW	25.02.1886	Kent	1921	1	2	–	30	25	15.00	–	–	–	–	–							
Hardstaff J (sr)	09.11.1882	Notts	1907–08	5	10	–	311	72	31.10	–	3	1	–	–							
Hardstaff J (jr)	03.07.1911	Notts	1936–37	9	16	1	559	169*	37.27	1	2	3	–	–							
Harris Lord	03.02.1851	Kent	1878–79	4	6	1	145	52	29.00	–	1	2	–	32	1	29	0	–	–	–	–
Hayes EG	06.11.1876	Surrey	1909	1	2	–	13	9	6.50	–	–	–	–	36	0	24	0	–	–	–	–
Hayward TW	29.03.1871	Surrey	1896	29	51	2	1747	137	35.65	2	12	14	–	842	38	486	12	40.50	4–22	–	–
Hearne JT	03.05.1867	Middx	1896	11	17	4	86	18	6.62	–	–	3	–	2936	209	1070	48	22.29	6–41	4	1
Hearne JW	11.02.1891	Middx	1911–12	16	24	2	554	114	25.18	1	2	8	–	2068	31	1026	16	64.13	4–84	–	–
Hemmings EE	20.02.1949	Notts	1982–83	3	6	1	157	95	31.40	–	1	2	–	1131	59	409	9	45.44	3–68	–	–
Hendren EH	05.02.1889	Middx	1920–21	28	48	4	1740	169	39.55	3	10	16	–	47	0	31	1	31.00	1–27	–	–
Hendrick M	22.10.1948	Derbs	1974–75	13	20	9	77	15	7.00	–	–	8	–	3082	107	1049	42	24.98	4–41	–	–
Higgs K	14.01.1937	Lancs	1965–66	2	3†	–	6	4	2.00	–	–	1	–	591	25	223	4	55.75	2–80	–	–
Hill A	14.11.1843	Yorks	1876–77	2	4	2	101	49	50.50	–	–	1	–	340	37	130	7	18.57	4–27	–	–
Hirst GH	07.09.1871	Yorks	1897–98	21	33	3	744	85	24.80	–	5	15	–	3445†	118	1585	49	32.35	5–48	3	–
Hitch JW	07.05.1886	Surrey	1911–12	6	9	2	103	51*	14.71	–	1	2	–	462	5	325	7	46.43	2–31	–	–
Hobbs JB	16.12.1882	Surrey	1907–08	41	71	4	3636	187	54.27	12	15	11	–	124	5	53	0	–	–	–	–
Hollies WE	05.06.1912	Warks	1948	1	2	1	0	0*	0.00	–	–	–	–	336	14	131	5	26.20	5–131	1	–
Holmes P	25.11.1886	Yorks	1921	1	2	–	38	30	19.00	–	–	–	–	–							
Hone L	30.01.1853	MCC	1878–79	1	2	–	13	7	6.50	–	–	2	–	–							
Hopwood JL	30.10.1903	Lancs	1934	2	3	1	12	8	6.00	–	–	–	–	462†	32	155	0	–	–	–	–
Hornby AN	10.02.1847	Lancs	1878–79	3	6	–	21	9	3.50	–	–	–	–	28	7	0	1	0.00	1–0	–	–

Howell H	29.11.1890	Warks	1920–21	4	8	6	15	5	7.50	–	–	–	–	798	18	490	7	70.00	4–115	–	–
Humphries J	17.05.1876	Derbs	1907–08	3	6	1	44	16	8.80	–	–	7	–	–							
Hunter J	03.08.1855	Yorks	1884–85	5	7	2	93	39*	18.60	–	–	8	3	–							
Hutchings KL	07.12.1882	Kent	1907–08	7	12	–	341	126	28.42	1	1	9	–	90	1	81	1	81.00	1–5	–	–
Hutton L	23.06.1916	Yorks	1938	27	49	6	2428	364	56.47	5	14	22	–	54	1	60	1	60.00	1–2	–	–
Ikin JT	07.03.1918	Lancs	1946–47	5	10†	–	184	60	18.40	–	1	4	–	56	0	48	0	–	–	–	–
Illingworth R	08.06.1932	Yo(7)Leic(11)	1961	18	28	3	663	57	26.52	–	2	16	–	3337	180	1094	34	32.18	6–87	1	–
Insole DJ	18.04.1926	Essex	1956	1	1	–	5	5	5.00	–	–	–	–	–							
Jackson Hon. FS	21.11.1870	Yorks	1893	20	33	4	1415	144*	48.79	5	6	10	–	1587	77	799	24	33.29	5–52	1	–
Jackson HL	05.04.1921	Derbs	1961	1	1	–	8	8	8.00	–	–	1	–	264	16	83	4	20.75	2–26	–	–
Jardine DR	23.10.1900	Surrey	1928–29	10	18	1	540	98	31.76	–	4	13	–	6	0	10	0	–	–	–	–
Jessop GL	19.05.1874	Gloucs	1899	13	18	–	433	104	24.06	1	2	7	–	730	28	346	10	34.60	4–68	–	–
Jones AO	16.08.1872	Notts	1899	12	21	–	291	34	13.86	–	–	15	–	228	14	133	3	44.33	3–73	–	–
Jones IJ	10.12.1941	Glam	1965–66	4	5	2	29	16	9.67	–	–	–	–	1032†	15	533	15	35.53	6–118	1	–
Jupp H	19.11.1841	Surrey	1876–77	2	4	–	68	63	17.00	–	1	2	–	–							
Jupp VWC	27.03.1891	Sussex	1921	2	4	–	65	28	16.25	–	–	2	–	235	4	142	5	28.40	2–45	–	–
Keeton WW	30.04.1905	Notts	1934	1	2	–	37	25	18.50	–	–	–	–	–							
Kenyon D	15.05.1924	Worcs	1953	2	4	–	29	16	7.25	–	–	1	–	–							
Kilner R	17.10.1890	Yorks	1924–25	7	7†	1	174	74	29.00	–	1	5	–	2164†	66	675	24	28.13	4–51	–	–
King JH	16.04.1871	Leics	1909	1	2†	–	64	60	32.00	–	1	–	–	162†	5	99	1	99.00	1–99	–	–
Kinneir SP	13.05.1871	Warks	1911–12	1	2†	–	52	30	26.00	–	–	–	–	–							
Knight AE	08.10.1872	Leics	1903–04	3	6	1	81	70*	16.20	–	1	1	–	–							
Knight BR	18.02.1938	Ex(3)Leic(2)	1962–63	5	7	2	52	27*	10.40	–	–	2	–	1168	29	463	15	30.87	4–84	–	–
Knight DJ	12.05.1894	Surrey	1921	2	4	–	54	38	13.50	–	–	1	–	–							
Knott APE	09.04.1946	Kent	1968	34	57	6	1682	135	32.98	2	11	97	8	–							
Laker JC	09.02.1922	Surrey	1948	15	23	4	277	63	14.58	–	1	–	–	4010	203	1444	79	18.28	10–53	5	2
Lamb AJ	20.06.1954	N'hants	1982–83	11	18	1	670	83	39.41	–	5	12	–	12	1	10	0	–	–	–	–
Larkins W	22.11.1953	N'hants	1979–80	2	4	–	86	34	21.50	–	–	1	–	–							
Larwood H	14.11.1904	Notts	1926	15	22	2	386	98	19.30	–	2	12	–	4053	120	1912	64	29.88	6–32	3	1
Leslie CFH	08.12.1861	Middx	1882–83	4	7	–	106	54	15.14	–	1	1	–	96	10	44	4	11.00	3–31	–	–
Lever JK	24.02.1949	Essex	1976–77	6	10	–	97	22	9.70	–	–	3	–	1199†	44	505	18	28.06	4–28	–	–
Lever P	17.09.1940	Lancs	1970–71	9	11	1	120	36	12.00	–	–	8	–	2117	49	928	25	37.12	6–38	1	–

ENGLAND	Born	County	Debut	M	I	NO	Runs	HS	Av	100	50	Ct	St	Balls	Mds	Runs	Wks	Av	Best	5i	10m
Leyland M	20.07.1900	Yorks	1928–29	20	34†	4	1705	187	56.83	7	3	7	–	395†	10	223	1	223.00	1–11	–	–
Lilley AFA	28.11.1866	Warks	1896	32	47	7	801	84	20.03	–	4	65	19	25	1	23	1	23.00	1–23	–	–
Lillywhite Jas	23.02.1842	Sussex	1876–77	2	3†	1	16	10	8.00	–	–	1	–	340†	37	126	8	15.75	4–70	–	–
Lloyd D	18.03.1947	Lancs	1974–75	4	8†	–	196	49	24.50	–	–	6	–	–							
Loader PJ	25.10.1929	Surrey	1958–59	2	4	2	7	6*	3.50	–	–	–	–	482	10	193	7	27.57	4–56	–	–
Lock GAR	05.07.1929	Surrey	1953	13	20	2	166	30	9.22	–	–	15	–	3442†	194	1128	31	36.39	5–45	1	–
Lockwood WH	25.03.1868	Surrey	1893	12	16	3	231	52*	17.77	–	1	4	–	1970	100	884	43	20.56	7–71	5	1
Lohmann GA	02.06.1865	Surrey	1886	15	22	2	203	62*	10.15	–	1	22	–	3301	326	1002	77	13.01	8–35	5	3
Lucas AP	20.02.1857	Sy(3)Mx(2)	1878–79	5	9	1	157	55	19.63	–	1	1	–	120	13	54	0	–	–	–	–
Luckhurst BW	05.02.1939	Kent	1970–71	11	21	2	677	131	35.63	2	3	8	–	5†	0	5	0	–	–	–	–
Lyttelton Hon. A	07.02.1857	Middx	1880	4	7	1	94	31	15.67	–	–	2	–	48	5	19	4	4.75	4–19	–	–
Macaulay GG	07.12.1897	Yorks	1926	1	1	–	76	76	76.00	–	1	–	–	192	8	123	1	123.00	1–123	–	–
McGahey CP	12.02.1871	Essex	1901–02	2	4	–	38	18	9.50	–	–	1	–	–							
MacGregor G	31.08.1869	Middx	1890	8	11	3	96	31	12.00	–	–	14	3	–							
McIntyre AJW	14.05.1918	Surrey	1950–51	1	2	–	8	7	4.00	–	–	1	–	–							
MacKinnon FA	09.04.1848	Kent	1878–79	1	2	–	5	5	2.50	–	–	–	–	–							
MacLaren AC	01.12.1871	Lancs	1894–95	35	61	4	1931	140	33.88	5	8	29	–	–							
Makepeace JWH	22.08.1881	Lancs	1920–21	4	8	–	279	117	34.88	1	2	–	–	–							
Martin F	12.10.1861	Kent	1890	1	1†	–	1	1	1.00	–	–	–	–	287†	21	102	12	8.50	6–50	2	1
Mason JR	26.03.1874	Kent	1897–98	5	10	–	129	32	12.90	–	–	3	–	324	13	149	2	74.50	1–8	–	–
May PBH	31.12.1929	Surrey	1953	21	37	3	1566	113	46.06	3	10	10	–	–							
Mead CP	09.03.1887	Hants	1911–12	7	10†	2	415	182*	51.88	1	1	3	–	–							
Mead W	25.03.1868	Essex	1899	1	2	–	7	7	3.50	–	–	1	–	265	24	91	1	91.00	1–91	–	–
Midwinter WE	19.06.1851	Gloucs	1881–82	4	7	–	95	36	13.57	–	–	5	–	776	79	272	10	27.20	4–81	–	–
Milburn C	23.10.1941	N'hants	1968	2	3	–	109	83	36.33	–	1	2	–	–							
Miller G	08.09.1952	Derbs	1977	14	24	1	479	64	20.83	–	2	5	–	2713	113	856	39	21.95	5–44	1	–
Milton CA	10.03.1928	Gloucs	1958–59	2	4	–	38	17	9.50	–	–	1	–	–							
Mitchell TB	04.09.1902	Derbs	1932–33	3	4	1	14	9	4.67	–	–	1	–	468	12	285	4	71.25	2–49	–	–
Mold AW	27.05.1863	Lancs	1893	3	3	1	0	0*	0.00	–	–	1	–	491	32	234	7	33.43	3–44	–	–

Morley F	16.12.1850	Notts	1880	4	6†	2	6	2*	1.50	–	–	4	–	972†	124	296	16	18.50	5–56	1	[illegible]
Mortimore JB	14.05.1933	Gloucs	1958–59	2	3	1	67	44*	33.50	–	–	–	–	382	14	163	1	163.00	1–41	–	–
Moss AE	14.11.1930	Middx	1956	1	–	–	–	–	–	–	–	–	–	24	3	1	0	–	–	–	–
Murray JT	01.04.1935	Middx	1961	6	10	1	163	40	18.11	–	–	18	1	–							
Newham W	12.12.1860	Sussex	1887–88	1	2	–	26	17	13.00	–	–	–	–	–							
Nichols MS	06.10.1900	Essex	1930	1	1†	1	7	7*	–	–	–	–	–	126	5	33	2	16.50	2–33	–	–
Oakman ASM	20.04.1930	Sussex	1956	2	2	–	14	10	7.00	–	–	7	–	48	3	21	0	–	–	–	–
O'Brien TC	05.11.1861	Middx	1884	2	4	–	24	20	6.00	–	–	1	–	–							
Old CM	22.12.1948	Yorks	1974–75	12	20†	4	277	43	17.31	–	–	6	–	2789	90	1232	40	30.80	4–104	–	–
Palairet LCH	27.05.1870	Som	1902	2	4	–	49	20	12.25	–	–	2	–	–							
Parfitt PH	08.12.1936	Middx	1962–63	9	15†	1	302	80	21.57	–	2	12	–	12	0	10	0	–	–	–	–
Parker CWL	14.10.1882	Gloucs	1921	1	1	1	3	3*	–	–	–	–	–	168†	16	32	2	16.00	2–32	–	–
Parker PWG	15.01.1956	Sussex	1981	1	2	–	13	13	6.50	–	–	–	–	–							
Parkhouse WGA	12.10.1925	Glam	1950–51	2	4	–	77	28	19.25	–	–	1	–	–							
Parkin CH	18.02.1886	Lancs	1920–21	9	15	2	152	36	11.69	–	–	3	–	1999	50	1090	32	34.06	5–38	2	–
Parks JM	21.10.1931	Sussex	1964	10	13	–	497	89	38.23	–	5	17	4	–							
Pataudi Nawab of	16.03.1910	Worcs	1932–33	3	5	–	144	102	28.80	1	–	–	–	–							
Paynter E	05.11.1901	Lancs	1932–33	7	11†	4	591	216*	84.43	1	3	3	–	–							
Peate E	02.03.1856	Yorks	1881–82	9	14†	8	70	13	11.67	–	–	2	–	2096†	250	682	31	22.00	6–85	2	–
Peebles IAR	20.01.1908	Middx	1930	2	3	2	9	6	9.00	–	–	–	–	756	17	354	9	39.33	6–204	1	–
Peel R	12.02.1857	Yorks	1884–85	20	33†	4	427	83	14.72	–	3	17	–	5216†	444	1715	102	16.81	7–31	6	2
Penn F	07.03.1851	Kent	1880	1	2	1	50	27*	50.00	–	–	–	–	12	1	2	0	–	–	–	–
Philipson H	08.06.1866	Middx	1891–92	5	8	1	63	30	9.00	–	–	8	3	–							
Pilling R	05.07.1855	Lancs	1881–82	8	13	1	91	23	7.58	–	–	10	4	–							
Pocock PI	24.09.1946	Surrey	1968	1	2	–	16	10	8.00	–	–	2	–	348	15	156	6	26.00	6–79	1	–
Pollard R	19.06.1912	Lancs	1948	2	2	1	3	3	3.00	–	–	1	–	612	29	218	5	43.60	3–53	–	–
Price JSE	22.07.1937	Middx	1964	3	4†	2	24	19	12.00	–	–	2	–	595	11	365	7	52.14	3–183	–	–
Price WFF	25.04.1902	Middx	1938	1	2	–	6	6	3.00	–	–	2	–	–							
Prideaux RM	31.07.1939	N'hants	1968	1	2	–	66	64	33.00	–	1	–	–	–							
Pringle DR	18.09.1958	Essex	1982–83	3	6	2	108	47*	27.00	–	–	–	–	443	12	214	4	53.50	2–97	–	–
Pullar G	01.08.1935	Lancs	1961	9	18†	1	457	63	26.88	–	4	–	–	–							
Quaife WG	17.03.1872	Warks	1899	7	13	1	228	68	19.00	–	1	4	–	15	1	6	0	–	–	–	–

ENGLAND	Born	County	Debut	M	I	NO	Runs	HS	Av	100	50	Ct	St	Balls	Mds	Runs	Wks	Av	Best	5i	10m
Randall DW	24.02.1951	Notts	1976–77	18	34	4	1161	174	38.70	3	6	12	–	–							
Ranjitsinhji KS	10.09.1872	Sussex	1896	15	26	4	989	175	44.95	2	6	13	–	97	6	39	1	39.00	1–23	–	–
Read JM	09.02.1859	Surrey	1882	15	26	2	447	57	18.63	–	2	8	–	–							
Read WW	23.11.1855	Surrey	1882–83	17	26	1	680	117	27.20	1	5	16	–	60	2	63	0	–	–	–	–
Relf AE	26.06.1874	Sussex	1903–04	3	5	2	64	31	21.33	–	–	5	–	448	24	173	7	24.71	5–85	1	–
Rhodes W	29.10.1877	Yorks	1899	41	69	14	1706	179	31.02	1	9	36	–	5796†	234	2616	109	24.00	8–68	6	1
Richardson PE	04.07.1931	Worcs	1956	9	16†	–	526	104	32.88	1	3	1	–	–							
Richardson T	11.08.1870	Surrey	1893	14	24	8	177	25*	11.06	–	–	5	–	4497	191	2220	88	25.23	8–94	11	4
Richmond TL	23.06.1890	Notts	1921	1	2	–	6	4	3.00	–	–	–	–	114	3	86	2	43.00	2–69	–	–
Robins RWV	03.06.1906	Middx	1930	6	10	2	183	61	22.88	–	2	2	–	960	10	558	14	39.86	4–51	–	–
Robinson RT	21.11.1958	Notts	1985	6	9	1	490	175	61.25	2	1	5	–	–							
Roope GRJ	12.07.1946	Surrey	1975	3	4	–	149	77	37.25	–	1	1	–	–							
Root CF	16.04.1890	Worcs	1926	3	–	–	–	–	–	–	–	1	–	642	47	194	8	24.25	4–84	–	–
Royle VPFA	29.01.1854	Lancs	1878–79	1	2	–	21	18	10.50	–	–	2	–	16	1	6	0	–	–	–	–
Rumsey FE	04.12.1935	Som	1964	1	1	1	3	3*	–	–	–	–	–	215†	4	99	2	49.50	2–99	–	–
Russell CAG	07.10.1887	Essex	1920–21	6	11	2	474	135*	52.67	3	1	3	–	–							
Russell WE	03.07.1936	Middx	1965–66	1	1	1	0	0*	–	–	–	–	–	–							
Sandham A	06.07.1890	Surrey	1921	3	5	–	49	21	9.80	–	–	–	–	–							
Schultz SS	29.08.1857	Lancs	1878–79	1	2	1	20	20	20.00	–	–	–	–	35	3	26	1	26.00	1–16	–	–
Scotton WH	15.01.1856	Notts	1881–82	15	25†	2	510	90	22.17	–	3	4	–	20†	1	20	0	–	–	–	–
Selby J	01.07.1849	Notts	1876–77	6	12	1	256	70	23.27	–	2	1	–	–							
Sharp J	15.02.1878	Lancs	1909	3	6	2	188	105	47.00	1	1	1	–	183	3	111	3	37.00	3–67	–	–
Sharpe JW	09.12.1866	Surrey	1890	3	6	4	44	26	22.00	–	–	2	–	975	61	305	11	27.73	6–84	1	–
Sharpe PJ	27.12.1936	Yorks	1964	2	3	1	71	35*	35.50	–	–	–	–	–							
Shaw A	29.08.1842	Notts	1876–77	7	12	1	111	40	10.09	–	–	4	–	1099	155	285	12	23.75	5–38	1	–
Sheppard Rev. DS	06.03.1929	Sussex	1950–51	9	16	–	580	113	36.25	2	3	2	–	–							
Sherwin M	26.02.1851	Notts	1886–87	3	6	4	30	21*	15.00	–	–	5	2	–							
Shrewsbury A	11.04.1856	Notts	1881–82	23	40	4	1277	164	35.47	3	4	29	–	12	2	2	0	–	–	–	–
Shuter J	09.02.1855	Surrey	1888	1	1	–	28	28	28.00	–	–	–	–	–							

Shuttleworth K	13.11.1944	Lancs	1970–71	2	2	–	9	7	4.50	–	–	1	–	605	13	242	7	34.57	5–47	1	–
Sidebottom A	01.04.1954	Yorks	1985	1	1	–	2	2	2.00	–	–	–	–	112	3	65	1	65.00	1–65	–	–
Simpson RT	27.02.1920	Notts	1950–51	9	17	2	434	156*	28.93	1	1	5	–	–							
Sims JM	13.05.1903	Middx	1936–37	2	2	–	3	3	1.50	–	–	5	–	408	2	244	3	81.33	2–109	–	–
Sinfield RA	24.12.1900	Gloucs	1938	1	1	–	6	6	6.00	–	–	–	–	378	16	123	2	61.50	1–51	–	–
Smith AC	25.10.1936	Warks	1962–63	4	5	1	47	21	11.75	–	–	13	–	–							
Smith EJ	06.02.1886	Warks	1911–12	7	9	1	69	22	8.63	–	–	12	1	–							
Smith MJK	30.06.1933	Warks	1961	9	15	2	248	41	19.08	–	–	8	–	16	0	8	0	–	–	–	–
Smith TPB	30.10.1908	Essex	1946–47	2	4	–	32	24	8.00	–	–	1	–	376	1	218	2	109.00	2–172	–	–
Snow JA	13.10.1941	Sussex	1968	20	29	3	392	48	15.08	–	–	7	–	5073	168	2126	83	25.61	7–40	4	–
Southerton J	16.11.1827	Surrey	1876–77	2	3	1	7	6	3.50	–	–	2	–	263	30	107	7	15.29	4–46	–	–
Spooner RH	21.10.1880	Lancs	1905	7	11	–	233	79	21.18	–	3	2	–	–							
Statham JB	16.06.1930	Lancs	1953	22	32†	13	236	36*	12.42	–	–	11	–	5405	131	2138	69	30.99	7–57	3	–
Steel AG	24.09.1858	Lancs	1880	13	20	3	600	148	35.29	2	–	5	–	1364	108	605	29	20.86	3–27	–	–
Steele DS	29.09.1941	N'hants	1975	3	6	–	365	92	60.83	–	4	4	–	70†	5	21	2	10.50	1–1	–	–
Stevens GTS	07.01.1901	Middx	1926	2	3	–	63	24	21.00	–	–	3	–	384	7	184	5	36.80	3–86	–	–
Stoddart AE	11.03.1863	Middx	1887–88	16	30	2	996	173	35.57	2	3	6	–	162	7	94	2	47.00	1–10	–	–
Storer W	25.01.1867	Derbs	1897–98	6	11	–	215	51	19.55	–	1	11	–	168	5	108	2	54.00	1–24	–	–
Strudwick H	28.01.1880	Surrey	1911–12	17	26	9	149	24	8.76	–	–	37	5	–							
Studd CT	02.12.1860	Middx	1882	5	9	1	160	48	20.00	–	–	5	–	384	60	98	3	32.67	2–35	–	–
Studd GB	20.10.1859	Middx	1882–83	4	7	–	31	9	4.43	–	–	8	–	–							
Subba Row R	29.01.1932	N'hants	1961	5	10†	–	468	137	46.80	2	1	2	–	–							
Sugg FH	11.01.1862	Lancs	1888	2	2	–	55	31	27.50	–	–	–	–	–							
Sutcliffe H	24.11.1894	Yorks	1924–25	27	46	5	2741	194	66.85	8	16	15	–	–							
Swetman R	25.10.1933	Surrey	1958–59	2	4	–	56	41	14.00	–	–	3	–	–							
Tate FW	24.07.1867	Sussex	1902	1	2	1	9	5*	9.00	–	–	2	–	96	4	51	2	25.50	2–7	–	–
Tate MW	30.05.1895	Sussex	1924–25	20	30	1	578	54	19.93	–	2	7	–	7686	330	2540	83	30.60	6–99	6	1
Tattersall R	17.08.1922	Lancs	1950–51	3	4†	–	18	10	4.50	–	–	3	–	717	17	338	7	48.29	3–22	–	–
Tavaré CJ	27.10.1954	Kent	1981	7	14	–	397	89	28.36	–	4	3	–	–							
Taylor K	21.08.1935	Yorks	1964	1	2	–	24	15	12.00	–	–	–	–	–							
Taylor LB	25.10.1953	Leics	1985	2	1	1	1	1*	–	–	–	1	–	381	11	178	4	44.50	2–34	–	–
Taylor RW	17.07.1941	Derbs	1978–79	17	32	5	468	97	17.33	–	1	54	3	–							

ENGLAND	Born	County	Debut	M	I	NO	Runs	HS	Av	100	50	Ct	St	Balls	Mds	Runs	Wks	Av	Best	5i	10m
Tennyson Hon. LH	07.11.1889	Hants	1921	4	5	1	229	74*	57.25	–	3	2	–	–							
Thompson GJ	27.10.1877	N'hants	1909	1	1	–	6	6	6.00	–	–	2	–	24	0	19	0	–	–	–	–
Titmus FJ	24.11.1932	Middx	1962–63	19	30	5	716	61	28.64	–	6	9	–	5765	228	1794	47	38.17	7–79	2	–
Townsend CL	07.11.1876	Gloucs	1899	2	3†	–	51	38	17.00	–	–	–	–	140	5	75	3	25.00	3–50	–	–
Trueman FS	06.02.1931	Yorks	1953	19	29	1	338	38	12.07	–	–	21	–	4361	83	1999	79	25.30	6–30	5	1
Tyldesley GE	05.02.1889	Lancs	1921	5	7	1	257	81	42.83	–	2	2	–	–							
Tyldesley JT	22.11.1873	Lancs	1899	26	46	1	1389	138	30.87	3	8	12	–	–							
Tyldesley RK	11.03.1897	Lancs	1924–25	3	5	–	17	6	3.40	–	–	–	–	830	26	370	7	52.86	3–77	–	–
Tylecote EFS	23.06.1849	Kent	1882–83	6	9	1	152	66	19.00	–	1	5	5	–							
Tyson FH	06.06.1930	N'hants	1954–55	8	12	1	117	37*	10.64	–	–	3	–	1724	21	810	32	25.31	7–27	2	1
Ulyett G	21.10.1851	Yorks	1876–77	23	36	–	901	149	25.03	1	7	16	–	2527	286	992	48	20.67	7–36	1	–
Underwood DL	08.06.1945	Kent	1968	29	43	14	371	45*	12.79	–	–	14	–	8000†	408	2770	105	26.38	7–50	4	2
Verity H	18.05.1905	Yorks	1932–33	18	27	8	344	60*	18.11	–	1	14	–	4930†	257	1656	59	28.07	8–43	3	1
Vernon GF	20.06.1856	Middx	1882–83	1	2	1	14	11*	14.00	–	–	–	–	–							
Vine J	15.05.1875	Sussex	1911–12	2	3	2	46	36	46.00	–	–	–	–	–							
Voce W	08.08.1909	Notts	1932–33	11	17	6	67	18	6.09	–	–	8	–	2450†	56	1128	41	27.51	6–41	1	1
Waddington A	04.02.1893	Yorks	1920–21	2	4	–	16	7	4.00	–	–	1	–	276†	7	119	1	119.00	1–35	–	–
Wainwright E	08.04.1865	Yorks	1893	5	9	–	132	49	14.67	–	–	2	–	127	6	73	0	–	–	–	–
Walters CF	28.08.1905	Worcs	1934	5	9	1	401	82	50.13	–	4	5	–	–							
Ward A	21.11.1865	Lancs	1893	7	13	–	487	117	37.46	1	3	1	–	–							
Wardle JH	08.01.1923	Yorks	1953	8	12†	3	166	38	18.44	–	–	1	–	1661†	81	632	24	26.33	5–79	1	–
Warner PF	02.10.1873	Middx	1903–04	7	13	1	287	79	23.92	–	2	2	–	–							
Warr JJ	16.07.1927	Middx	1950–51	2	4	–	4	4	1.00	–	–	–	–	584	6	281	1	281.00	1–76	–	–
Warren AR	02.04.1875	Derbs	1905	1	1	–	7	7	7.00	–	–	1	–	236	9	113	6	18.83	5–57	1	–
Washbrook C	06.12.1914	Lancs	1946–47	17	31	1	996	143	33.20	2	5	8	–	–							
Watkins AJ	21.04.1922	Glam	1948	1	2†	–	2	2	1.00	–	–	–	–	24†	1	19	0	–	–	–	–
Watson W	07.03.1920	Yo(5)Leic(2)	1953	7	13†	–	272	109	20.92	1	–	1	–	–							
Webbe AJ	16.01.1855	Middx	1878–79	1	2	–	4	4	2.00	–	–	2	–	–							
Wellard AW	08.04.1902	Som	1938	1	2	–	42	38	21.00	–	–	–	–	192	3	126	3	42.00	2–96	–	–

White JC	19.02.1891	Som	1921	7	12	6	110	29	18.33	–	–	1	–	2974†	148	1033	31	33.32	6–126	3	1
Whysall WW	31.10.1887	Notts	1924–25	4	7	–	209	76	29.86	–	2	7	–	16	0	9	0	–	–	–	–
Willey P	06.12.1949	Nort(8)Lei(1)	1979–80	9	17	1	258	82	16.13	–	1	2	–	216	5	98	1	98.00	1–31	–	–
Willis RGD	30.05.1949	Sy(4)Warw(31)	1970–71	35	58	21	383	26	10.35	–	–	16	–	7294	198	3346	128	26.14	8–43	7	–
Wilson ER	25.03.1879	Yorks	1920–21	1	2	–	10	5	5.00	–	–	–	–	123	5	36	3	12.00	2–28	–	–
Wood A	25.08.1898	Yorks	1938	1	1	–	53	53	53.00	–	1	3	–	–							
Wood B	26.12.1942	Lancs	1972	4	8	–	262	90	32.75	–	2	–	–	36	2	16	0	–	–	–	–
Wood H	14.12.1854	Surrey	1888	1	1	–	8	8	8.00	–	–	1	1	–							
Wood R	07.03.1860	Lancs	1886–87	1	2†	–	6	6	3.00	–	–	–	–	–							
Woolley FE	27.05.1887	Kent	1909	32	51†	1	1664	133*	33.28	2	11	36	–	3590†	129	1555	43	36.16	5–20	2	1
Woolmer RA	14.05.1948	Kent	1975	10	18	1	663	149	39.00	3	1	5	–	300	14	103	3	34.33	1–8	–	–
Worthington TS	21.08.1905	Derbs	1936–37	3	6	–	74	44	12.33	–	–	3	–	80	0	78	0	–	–	–	–
Wright DVP	21.08.1914	Kent	1938	14	22	7	126	22	8.40	–	–	4	–	3709	61	2039	48	42.48	7–105	2	–
Wyatt RES	02.05.1901	Warks	1930	12	21	2	633	78	33.32	–	5	6	–	120	1	98	1	98.00	1–58	–	–
Wynyard EG	01.04.1861	Hants	1896	1	2	–	13	10	6.50	–	–	–	–	–							
Yardley NWD	19.03.1915	Yorks	1946–47	10	19	2	402	61	23.65	–	2	4	–	1416	37	576	19	30.32	3–67	–	–
Young HI	05.02.1876	Essex	1899	2	2	–	43	43	21.50	–	–	1	–	556†	38	262	12	21.83	4–30	–	–
Young JA	14.10.1912	Middx	1948	3	5	2	17	9	5.67	–	–	2	–	936†	64	292	5	58.40	2–118	–	–
Young RA	16.09.1885	Sussex	1907–08	2	4	–	27	13	6.75	–	–	6	–	–							

AUSTRALIA	Born	State	Debut	M	I	NO	Runs	HS	Av	100	50	Ct	St	Balls	Mds	Runs	Wks	Av	Best	5i	10m
a'Beckett EL	11.08.1907	Vic	1928–29	3	5	–	133	41	26.60	–	–	4	–	936	41	282	3	94.00	1–41	–	–
Alderman TM	12.06.1956	WA	1981	7	9	5	22	12*	5.50	–	–	8	–	2208	91	977	43	22.72	6–135	4	–
Alexander G	22.04.1851	Vic	1880	2	4	–	52	33	13.00	–	–	2	–	168	13	93	2	46.50	2–69	–	–
Alexander HH	09.06.1905	Vic	1932–33	1	2	1	17	17*	17.00	–	–	–	–	276	3	154	1	154.00	1–129	–	–
Allan FE	02.12.1849	Vic	1878–79	1	1†	–	5	5	5.00	–	–	–	–	180†	15	80	4	20.00	2–30	–	–
Allan PJ	31.12.1935	Qld	1965–66	1	–	–	–	–	–	–	–	–	–	192	6	83	2	41.50	2–58	–	–
Allen RC	02.07.1858	NSW	1886–87	1	2	–	44	30	22.00	–	–	2	–	–							
Andrews TJE	26.08.1890	NSW	1921	13	19	–	541	94	28.47	–	4	9	–	156	5	116	1	116.00	1–23	–	–

AUSTRALIA	Born	State	Debut	M	I	NO	Runs	HS	Av	100	50	Ct	St	Balls	Mds	Runs	Wks	Av	Best	5i	10m
Archer KA	18.01.1928	Qld	1950–51	3	5	–	152	48	30.40	–	–	–	–	–							
Archer RG	25.10.1933	Qld	1953	12	20	1	294	49	15.47	–	–	11	–	2445	126	761	35	21.74	5–53	1	–
Armstrong WW	22.05.1879	Vic	1901–02	42	71	9	2172	158	35.03	4	6	37	–	6782	364	2288	74	30.92	6–35	3	–
Badcock CL	10.04.1914	SA	1936–37	7	12	1	160	118	14.55	1	–	3	–	–							
Bannerman AC	21.03.1854	NSW	1878–79	28	50	2	1108	94	23.08	–	8	21	–	292	17	163	4	40.75	3–111	–	–
Bannerman C	23.07.1851	NSW	1876–77	3	6	2	239	165*	59.75	1	–	–	–	–							
Bardsley W	07.12.1882	NSW	1909	30	49†	4	1487	193*	33.04	3	8	6	–	–							
Barnes SG	05.06.1916	NSW	1938	9	14	2	846	234	70.50	2	4	6	–	314	5	118	1	118.00	1–84	–	–
Barnett BA	23.03.1908	Vic	1938	4	8†	1	195	57	27.86	–	1	3	2	–							
Barrett JE	15.10.1866	Vic	1890	2	4†	1	80	67*	26.67	–	1	1	–	–							
Benaud R	06.10.1930	NSW	1953	27	41	2	767	97	19.67	–	4	32	–	7284	289	2641	83	31.82	6–70	4	–
Bennett MJ	06.10.1956	NSW	1985	1	2	–	23	12	11.50	–	–	1	–	192†	8	111	1	111.00	1–111	–	–
Blackham JM	11.05.1854	Vic	1876–77	35	62	11	800	74	15.69	–	4	37	24	–							
Blackie DD	05.04.1882	Vic	1928–29	3	6†	3	24	11*	8.00	–	–	2	–	1260	51	444	14	31.71	6–94	1	–
Bonnor GJ	25.02.1855	Vic(12)NSW(5)	1880	17	30	–	512	128	17.07	1	2	16	–	164	16	84	2	42.00	1–5	–	–
Boon DC	29.12.1960	Tas	1985	4	7	–	124	61	17.71	–	1	4	–	–							
Booth BC	19.10.1933	NSW	1961	15	26	5	824	112	39.24	2	4	8	–	2	0	4	0	–	–	–	–
Border AR	27.07.1955	NSW(7)Qld(17)	1978–79	24	45†	12	1869	196	56.64	5	10	35	–	536†	21	181	1	181.00	1–31	–	–
Boyle HF	10.12.1847	Vic	1878–79	12	16	4	153	36*	12.75	–	–	10	–	1743	175	641	32	20.03	6–42	1	–
Bradman DG	27.08.1908	NSW(18)SA(19)	1928–29	37	63	7	5028	334	89.79	19	12	20	–	92	2	51	1	51.00	1–23	–	–
Bright RJ	13.07.1954	Vic	1977	10	16	1	198	33	13.20	–	–	7	–	2009†	135	667	18	37.06	5–68	1	–
Bromley EH	02.09.1912	Vic	1932–33	2	4†	–	38	26	9.50	–	–	2	–	60†	4	19	0	–	–	–	–
Brown WA	31.07.1912	NSW(5)Qld(8)	1934	13	24	1	980	206*	42.61	3	3	9	–	–							
Bruce W	22.05.1864	Vic	1884–85	14	26†	2	702	80	29.25	–	5	12	–	988†	72	440	12	36.67	3–88	–	–
Burge PJP	17.05.1932	Qld	1954–55	22	37	6	1179	181	38.03	4	2	10	–	–							
Burke JW	12.06.1930	NSW	1950–51	14	28	5	676	101*	29.39	1	3	8	–	288	15	83	2	41.50	2–26	–	–
Burn EJK	17.09.1862	Tas	1890	2	4	–	41	19	10.25	–	–	–	–	–							
Burton FJ	1866	NSW	1886–87	2	4	2	4	2*	2.00	–	–	1	1	–							
Callaway ST	06.02.1868	NSW	1891–92	3	6	1	87	41	17.40	–	–	–	–	471	33	142	6	23.67	5–37	1	

Carlson PH	08.08.1951	Qld	1978–79	2	4	–	23	21	5.75	–	–	2	–	368	10	99	2	49.50	2–41	–	–
Carter H	15.03.1878	NSW	1907–08	21	35	4	776	72	25.03	–	4	35	17	–							
Chappell GS	07.08.1948	SA(10)Qld(25)	1970–71	35	65	8	2619	144	45.95	9	12	61	–	1867	70	679	13	52.23	2–36	–	–
Chappell IM	26.09.1943	SA	1965–66	30	56	4	2138	192	41.12	4	16	31	–	1022	36	429	6	71.50	1–10	–	–
Chappell TM	12.10.1952	NSW	1981	3	6	1	79	27	15.80	–	–	2	–	–							
Charlton PC	09.04.1867	NSW	1890	2	4	–	29	11	7.25	–	–	–	–	45	1	24	3	8.00	3–18	–	–
Chipperfield AG	17.11.1905	NSW	1934	9	15	3	356	99	29.67	–	2	13	–	870	27	409	5	81.80	3–91	–	–
Colley DJ	15.03.1947	NSW	1972	3	4	–	84	54	21.00	–	1	1	–	729	20	312	6	52.00	3–83	–	–
Collins HL	21.01.1889	NSW	1920–21	16	26	–	1012	162	38.92	3	5	11	–	522†	16	236	3	78.67	2–47	–	–
Coningham A	14.07.1863	Qld	1894–95	1	2†	–	13	10	6.50	–	–	–	–	186†	9	76	2	38.00	2–17	–	–
Connolly AN	29.06.1939	Vic	1965–66	7	12	6	19	14	3.17	–	–	4	–	2123	83	800	25	32.00	5–72	1	–
Cooper BB	15.03.1844	Vic	1876–77	1	2	–	18	15	9.00	–	–	2	–	–							
Cooper WH	11.09.1849	Vic	1881–82	2	3	1	13	7	6.50	–	–	1	–	446	31	226	9	25.11	6–120	1	–
Corling GE	13.07.1941	NSW	1964	5	4	1	5	3	1.67	–	–	–	–	1159	50	447	12	37.25	4–60	–	–
Cosier GJ	25.04.1953	SA(1)Qld(2)	1976–77	3	6	–	66	47	11.00	–	–	4	–	96	3	35	0	–	–	–	–
Cottam JT	05.09.1867	NSW	1886–87	1	2	–	4	3	2.00	–	–	1	–	–							
Cotter A	03.12.1884	NSW	1903–04	16	29	1	377	45	13.46	–	–	5	–	3464	63	1916	67	28.60	7–148	6	–
Coulthard G	01.08.1856	Vic	1881–82	1	1	1	6	6*	–	–	–	–	–	–							
Cowper RM	05.10.1940	Vic	1964	9	15†	1	686	307	49.00	1	3	11	–	794	41	317	10	31.70	4–48	–	–
Craig ID	12.06.1935	NSW	1956	2	4	–	55	38	13.75	–	–	–	–	–							
Crawford WPA	03.08.1933	NSW	1956	1	2	1	0	0*	0.00	–	–	–	–	29	2	4	0	–	–	–	–
Darling J	21.11.1870	SA	1894–95	31	55†	2	1632	178	30.79	3	8	23	–	–							
Darling LS	14.08.1909	Vic	1932–33	7	12†	–	245	85	20.42	–	1	6	–	162	7	65	0	–	–	–	–
Darling WM	01.05.1957	SA	1978–79	4	8	–	221	91	27.63	–	1	4	–	–							
Davidson AK	14.06.1929	NSW	1953	25	36†	5	750	77*	24.19	–	3	27	–	5993†	221	1996	84	23.76	6–64	5	–
Davis IC	25.06.1953	NSW	1976–77	4	8	–	180	68	22.50	–	1	2	–	–							
de Courcy JH	18.04.1927	NSW	1953	3	6	1	81	41	16.20	–	–	3	–	–							
Dell AR	10.08.1947	Qld	1970–71	1	2	2	6	3*	–	–	–	–	–	343†	11	97	5	19.40	3–65	–	–
Donnan H	12.11.1864	NSW	1891–92	5	10	1	75	15	8.33	–	–	1	–	54	2	22	0	–	–	–	–
Dooland B	01.11.1923	SA	1946–47	2	3	–	49	29	16.33	–	–	2	–	784	9	351	8	43.88	4–69	–	–
Duff RA	17.08.1878	NSW	1901–02	19	34	1	1079	146	32.70	2	5	13	–	180	8	85	4	21.25	2–43	–	–

AUSTRALIA	Born	State	Debut	M	I	NO	Runs	HS	Av	100	50	Ct	St	Balls	Mds	Runs	Wks	Av	Best	5i	10m
Duncan JRF	25.03.1944	Qld	1970–71	1	1	–	3	3	3.00	–	–	–	–	112	4	30	0	–	–	–	–
Dymock G	21.07.1946	Qld	1974–75	7	12†	2	76	20*	7.60	–	–	–	–	2008†	65	659	25	26.36	6–34	1	–
Dyson J	11.06.1954	NSW	1981	10	20	2	489	102	27.17	1	2	6	–	–							
Eady CJ	29.10.1870	Tas	1896	2	4	1	20	10*	6.67	–	–	2	–	223	14	112	7	16.00	3–30	–	–
Eastwood KH	23.11.1935	Vic	1970–71	1	2†	–	5	5	2.50	–	–	–	–	40†	0	21	1	21.00	1–21	–	–
Ebeling HI	01.01.1905	Vic	1934	1	2	–	43	41	21.50	–	–	–	–	186	9	89	3	29.67	3–74	–	–
Edwards JD	12.06.1862	Vic	1888	3	6	1	48	26	9.60	–	–	1	–	–							
Edwards R	01.12.1942	WA	1972	13	22	3	805	170*	42.37	2	5	1	–	12	0	20	0	–	–	–	–
Edwards WJ	23.12.1949	WA	1974–75	3	6†	–	68	30	11.33	–	–	–	–	–							
Emery SH	16.10.1885	NSW	1912	2	–	–	–	–	–	–	–	1	–	114	2	68	2	34.00	2–46	–	–
Evans E	06.03.1849	NSW	1881–82	6	10	2	82	33	10.25	–	–	5	–	1237	166	332	7	47.43	3–64	–	–
Fairfax AG	16.06.1906	NSW	1928–29	5	6	2	215	65	53.75	–	2	10	–	1010	38	439	14	31.36	4–101	–	–
Favell LE	06.10.1929	SA	1954–55	6	10	1	203	54	22.56	–	1	3	–	–							
Ferris JJ	21.05.1867	NSW	1886–87	8	16†	4	98	20*	8.17	–	–	4	–	2030†	224	684	48	14.25	5–26	4	–
Fingleton JHW	28.04.1908	NSW	1932–33	12	21	–	671	136	31.95	2	2	7	–	–							
Fleetwood-Smith LO'B	30.03.1910	Vic	1936–37	7	9	4	48	16*	9.60	–	–	–	–	2359†	54	1190	33	36.06	6–110	2	1
Francis BC	18.02.1948	NSW	1972	3	5	–	52	27	10.40	–	–	1	–	–							
Freeman EW	13.07.1944	SA	1968	2	3	–	37	21	12.33	–	–	1	–	407	17	186	6	31.00	4–78	–	–
Freer FW	04.12.1915	Vic	1946–47	1	1	1	28	28*	–	–	–	–	–	160	3	74	3	24.67	2–49	–	–
Garrett TW	26.07.1858	NSW	1876–77	19	33	6	339	51*	12.56	–	1	7	–	2708	297	970	36	26.94	6–78	2	–
Gaunt RA	26.02.1934	Vic	1961	1	1†	–	3	3	3.00	–	–	1	–	276	10	86	3	28.67	3–53	–	–
Gehrs DRA	29.11.1880	SA	1903–04	2	4	–	19	11	4.75	–	–	4	–	–							
Giffen G	27.03.1859	SA	1881–82	31	53	–	1238	161	23.36	1	6	24	–	6391	434	2791	103	27.10	7–117	7	1
Giffen WF	10.09.1863	SA	1886–87	3	6	–	11	3	1.83	–	–	1	–	–							
Gilbert DR	19.12.1960	NSW	1985	1	2	1	1	1	1.00	–	–	–	–	126	2	96	1	96.00	1–96	–	–
Gilmour GJ	26.06.1951	NSW	1975	2	3†	–	26	16	8.67	–	–	–	–	380†	18	190	9	21.11	6–85	1	–
Gleeson JW	14.03.1938	NSW	1968	13	19	2	131	30	7.71	–	–	6	–	3391	150	1179	29	40.66	4–83	–	–

Gregory DW	15.04.1845	NSW	1876–77	3	5	2	60	43	20.00	[illegible]	[illegible]	[illegible]	[illegible]	20	1	9	0				
Gregory EJ	29.05.1839	NSW	1876–77	1	2	–	11	11	5.50	–	–	1	–	–							
Gregory JM	14.08.1895	NSW	1920–21	21	30†	3	941	100	34.85	1	6	30	–	4888	109	2364	70	33.77	7–69	3	–
Gregory RG	28.02.1916	Vic	1936–37	2	3	–	153	80	51.00	–	2	1	–	24	0	14	0	–	–	–	–
Gregory SE	14.04.1870	NSW	1890	52	92	7	2193	201	25.80	4	8	24	–	30	0	33	0	–	–	–	–
Grimmett CV	25.12.1891	SA	1924–25	22	34	6	366	50	13.07	–	1	7	–	9164	427	3439	106	32.44	6–37	11	2
Groube TU	02.09.1857	Vic	1880	1	2	–	11	11	5.50	–	–	–	–	–							
Grout ATW	30.03.1927	Qld	1958–59	22	26	4	301	74	13.68	–	1	69	7	–							
Guest CEJ	07.10.1937	Vic	1962–63	1	1	–	11	11	11.00	–	–	–	–	144	0	59	0	–	–	–	–
Hamence RA	25.11.1915	SA	1946–47	1	2	1	31	30*	31.00	–	–	–	–	–							
Harry J	01.08.1857	Vic	1894–95	1	2	–	8	6	4.00	–	–	1	–	–							
Hartigan RJ	12.12.1879	Qld	1907–08	2	4	–	170	116	42.50	1	–	1	–	12	0	7	0	–	–	–	–
Hartkopf AEV	28.12.1889	Vic	1924–25	1	2	–	80	80	40.00	–	1	–	–	240	2	134	1	134.00	1–120	–	–
Harvey MR	29.04.1918	Vic	1946–47	1	2	–	43	31	21.50	–	–	–	–	–							
Harvey RN	08.10.1928	V(22)NSW(15)	1948	37	68†	5	2416	167	38.35	6	12	25	–	56	4	15	0	–	–	–	–
Hassett AL	28.08.1913	Vic	1938	24	42	1	1572	137	38.34	4	6	16	–	90	2	60	0	–	–	–	–
Hawke NJN	27.06.1939	SA	1962–63	12	13	5	115	37	14.38	–	–	6	–	3176	128	1119	37	30.24	7–105	4	–
Hazlitt GR	04.09.1888	Vic(2)NSW(4)	1907–08	6	9	3	87	34*	14.50	–	–	4	–	1107	50	443	16	27.69	7–25	1	–
Hendry HSTL	24.05.1895	NSW(4)Vic(5)	1921	9	15	2	284	112	21.85	1	–	5	–	1430	65	504	14	36.00	3–36	–	–
Higgs JD	11.07.1950	Vic	1978–79	6	11	4	48	16	6.86	–	–	–	–	1580	47	471	19	24.79	5–148	1	–
Hilditch AMJ	20.05.1956	NSW(1)SA(6)	1978–79	7	13	–	428	119	32.92	1	1	5	–	–							
Hill C	18.03.1877	SA	1896	41	76†	1	2660	188	35.47	4	16	30	–	–							
Hill JC	25.06.1923	Vic	1953	2	4	2	12	8*	6.00	–	–	1	–	396	18	158	7	22.57	3–35	–	–
Hodges JH	31.07.1856	Vic	1876–77	2	4†	1	10	8	3.33	–	–	–	–	136†	9	84	6	14.00	2–7	–	–
Hogg RM	05.03.1951	SA	1978–79	11	20	4	121	36	7.56	–	–	1	–	2629	94	952	56	17.00	6–74	5	2
Hole GB	06.01.1931	SA	1950–51	9	17	–	439	66	25.82	–	4	11	–	150	8	46	1	46.00	1–10	–	–
Holland RG	19.10.1946	NSW	1985	4	5	1	15	10	3.75	–	–	1	–	1032	41	465	6	77.50	5–68	1	–
Hookes DW	03.05.1955	SA	1976–77	11	19†	1	700	85	38.89	–	7	4	–	48†	2	20	0	–	–	–	–
Hopkins AJY	04.05.1874	NSW	1901–02	17	28	2	434	43	16.69	–	–	9	–	1183	47	581	21	27.67	4–81	–	–
Horan TP	08.03.1854	Vic	1876–77	15	27	2	471	124	18.84	1	1	6	–	373	45	143	11	13.00	6–40	1	–
Hordern HV	10.02.1883	NSW	1911–12	5	10	2	173	49*	21.63	–	–	5	–	1665	42	780	32	24.38	7–90	4	2
Hornibrook PM	27.07.1899	Qld	1928–29	6	7†	1	60	26	10.00	–	–	7	–	1579†	63	664	17	39.06	7–92	1	–

AUSTRALIA	Born	State	Debut	M	I	NO	Runs	HS	Av	100	50	Ct	St	Balls	Mds	Runs	Wks	Av	Best	5i	10m
Howell WP	29.12.1869	NSW	1897–98	16	24†	6	147	35	8.17	–	–	10	–	3508	229	1233	35	35.23	4–43	–	–
Hughes KJ	26.01.1954	WA	1977	22	40	1	1499	137	38.44	3	6	12	–	–							
Hurst AG	15.07.1950	Vic	1978–79	6	12	2	44	17*	4.40	–	–	1	–	1634	44	577	25	23.08	5–28	1	–
Inverarity RJ	31.01.1944	WA	1968	5	9	1	160	56	20.00	–	1	2	–	372†	26	93	4	23.25	3–26	–	–
Iredale FA	19.06.1867	NSW	1894–95	14	23	1	807	140	36.68	2	4	16	–	12	1	3	0	–	–	–	–
Ironmonger H	07.04.1882	Vic	1928–29	6	12†	3	18	8	2.00	–	–	2	–	2446†	155	711	21	33.86	4–26	–	–
Iverson JB	27.07.1915	Vic	1950–51	5	7	3	3	1*	0.75	–	–	2	–	1108	29	320	21	15.24	6–27	1	–
Jackson AA	05.09.1909	NSW	1928–29	4	6	–	350	164	58.33	1	1	1	–	–							
Jarman BN	17.02.1936	SA	1962–63	7	11	3	111	41	13.88	–	–	18	–	–							
Jarvis AH	19.10.1860	SA	1884–85	11	21	3	303	82	16.83	–	1	9	9	–							
Jenner TJ	08.09.1944	SA	1970–71	4	7	1	136	74	22.67	–	1	5	–	862	25	312	9	34.67	3–42	–	–
Jennings CB	05.06.1884	Qld	1912	3	4	1	44	21	14.67	–	–	4	–	–							
Johnson IW	08.12.1918	Vic	1946–47	22	35	6	485	77	16.72	–	2	14	–	4592	187	1590	42	37.86	6–42	1	–
Johnston WA	26.02.1922	Vic	1948	17	25†	12	138	29	10.62	–	–	4	–	5263†	224	1818	75	24.24	5–35	3	–
Jones E	30.09.1869	SA	1894–95	18	25	1	126	20	5.25	–	–	19	–	3580	152	1757	60	29.28	7–88	3	1
Jones SP	01.08.1861	NSW	1881–82	12	24	4	432	87	21.60	–	1	12	–	262	26	112	6	18.67	4–47	–	–
Kelleway C	25.04.1886	NSW	1911–12	18	30	2	874	147	31.21	1	4	12	–	3340	112	1155	37	31.22	4–27	–	–
Kelly JJ	10.05.1867	NSW	1896	33	52	17	613	46*	17.51	–	–	39	16	–							
Kelly TJD	03.05.1844	Vic	1876–77	2	3	–	64	35	21.33	–	–	1	–	–							
Kendall T	24.08.1851	Vic	1876–77	2	4†	1	39	17*	13.00	–	–	2	–	563†	56	215	14	15.36	7–55	1	–
Kent MF	23.11.1953	Qld	1981	3	6	–	171	54	28.50	–	2	6	–	–							
Kippax AF	25.05.1897	NSW	1924–25	13	23	1	753	100	34.23	1	5	6	–	72	5	19	0	–	–	–	–
Kline LF	29.09.1934	Vic	1958–59	2	2†	2	5	4*	–	–	–	2	–	200†	6	77	0	–	–	–	–
Laird BM	21.11.1950	WA	1979–80	3	6	–	162	74	27.00	–	1	1	–	–							
Langley GRA	19.09.1919	SA	1953	9	13	2	97	18	8.82	–	–	35	2	–							
Laughlin TJ	30.01.1951	Vic	1978–79	1	2†	–	7	5	3.50	–	–	2	–	200	6	60	0	–	–	–	–
Laver F	07.12.1869	Vic	1899	15	23	6	196	45	11.53	–	–	8	–	2361	121	964	37	26.05	8–31	2	–
Lawry WM	11.02.1937	Vic	1961	29	51†	5	2233	166	48.54	7	13	16	–	8†	1	0	0	–	–	–	–
Lawson GF	07.12.1957	NSW	1981	14	22	3	255	53	13.42	–	2	3	–	3497	119	1802	68	26.50	7–81	6	1

Lee PK	[illegible]	SA	1932–33	1	2	[illegible]	57	42	28.50	–	–	–	[illegible]	316	14	163	4	40.75	4–111	–	–
Lillee DK	18.07.1949	WA	1970–71	29	39	13	469	73*	18.04	–	1	6	–	8516	361	3507	167	21.00	7–89	11	4
Lindwall RR	03.10.1921	NSW(19)Q(10)	1946–47	29	43	7	795	100	22.08	1	4	17	–	6728	216	2559	114	22.45	7–63	6	–
Love HSB	10.08.1895	NSW	1932–33	1	2	–	8	5	4.00	–	–	3	–	–							
Loxton SJE	29.03.1921	Vic	1948	6	8	–	219	93	27.38	–	1	7	–	450	12	174	3	58.00	3–55	–	–
Lyons JJ	21.05.1863	SA	1886–87	14	27	–	731	134	27.07	1	3	3	–	316	17	149	6	24.83	5–30	1	–
McAlister PA	11.07.1869	Vic	1903–04	8	16	1	252	41	16.80	–	–	10	–	–							
Macartney CG	27.06.1886	NSW	1907–08	26	42	4	1640	170	43.16	5	7	11	–	2579†	122	908	33	27.52	7–58	1	1
McCabe SJ	16.07.1910	NSW	1930	24	43	3	1931	232	48.28	4	10	21	–	2585	84	1076	21	51.24	4–41	–	–
McCool CL	09.12.1915	Qld	1946–47	5	7	2	272	104*	54.40	1	1	3	–	1456	27	491	18	27.28	5–44	2	–
McCormick EL	16.05.1906	Vic	1936–37	7	9†	2	35	17*	5.00	–	–	7	–	1356	26	661	21	31.48	4–101	–	–
McCosker RB	11.12.1946	NSW	1974–75	15	27	2	977	127	39.08	2	6	8	–	–							
McDermott CJ	14.04.1965	Qld	1985	6	9	1	103	35	12.88	–	–	2	–	1406	21	901	30	30.03	8–141	2	–
McDonald CC	17.11.1928	Vic	1954–55	15	28	1	1043	170	38.63	2	5	3	–	–							
McDonald EA	06.01.1891	Vic	1920–21	8	9	4	101	36	20.20	–	–	2	–	1991	42	1060	33	32.12	5–32	2	–
McDonnell PS	13.11.1858	Vic(13)NSW(6)	1880	19	34	1	950	147	28.79	3	2	6	–	52	1	53	0	–	–	–	–
McIlwraith J	07.09.1857	Vic	1886	1	2	–	9	7	4.50	–	–	1	–	–							
Mackay KD	24.10.1925	Qld	1956	16	23†	1	497	86*	22.59	–	4	7	–	2828	126	875	24	36.46	5–121	1	–
McKenzie GD	24.06.1941	WA	1961	25	35	8	252	34	9.33	–	–	11	–	7486	233	3009	96	31.34	7–153	6	–
McKibbin TR	10.12.1870	NSW	1894–95	5	8†	2	88	28*	14.67	–	–	4	–	1032	41	496	17	29.18	3–35	–	–
McLaren JW	24.12.1887	Qld	1911–12	1	2	2	0	0*	–	–	–	–	–	144	3	70	1	70.00	1–23	–	–
Maclean JA	27.04.1946	Qld	1978–79	4	8	1	79	33*	11.29	–	–	18	–	–							
McLeod CE	24.10.1869	Vic	1894–95	17	29	5	573	112	23.88	1	4	9	–	3374	171	1325	33	40.15	5–65	2	–
McLeod RW	19.01.1868	Vic	1891–92	6	11†	–	146	31	13.27	–	–	3	–	1089	67	384	12	32.00	5–55	1	–
McShane PG	1857	Vic	1884–85	3	6†	1	26	12*	5.20	–	–	2	–	108†	9	48	1	48.00	1–39	–	–
Maddocks LV	24.05.1926	Vic	1954–55	5	9	–	156	69	17.33	–	1	12	1	–							
Mailey AA	03.01.1886	NSW	1920–21	18	25	8	201	46*	11.82	–	–	12	–	5201	90	2935	86	34.13	9–121	6	2
Mallett AA	13.07.1945	SA	1968	16	20	6	224	43*	16.00	–	–	15	–	3995	174	1581	50	31.62	5–114	1	–
Malone MF	09.10.1950	WA	1977	1	1	–	46	46	46.00	–	–	–	–	342	24	77	6	12.83	5–63	1	–
Marr AP	28.03.1862	NSW	1884–85	1	2	–	5	5	2.50	–	–	–	–	48	6	14	0	–	–	–	–
Marsh RW	04.11.1947	WA	1970–71	42	68†	8	1633	110*	27.22	1	9	141	7	–							
Massie HH	11.04.1854	NSW	1881–82	9	16	–	249	55	15.56	–	1	5	–	–							

AUSTRALIA	Born	State	Debut	M	I	NO	Runs	HS	Av	100	50	Ct	St	Balls	Mds	Runs	Wks	Av	Best	5i	10m
Massie RAL	14.04.1947	WA	1972	4	5†	–	22	18	4.40	–	–	–	–	1195	58	409	23	17.78	8–53	2	1
Matthews GRJ	15.12.1959	NSW	1985	1	2†	–	21	17	10.50	–	–	–	–	54	2	21	0	–	–	–	–
Matthews TJ	03.04.1884	Vic	1911–12	5	7	–	74	53	10.57	–	1	4	–	680	28	277	3	92.33	2–23	–	–
Mayne ER	02.07.1882	SA	1912	1	–	–	–	–	–	–	–	–	–	–							
Meckiff I	06.01.1935	Vic	1958–59	4	4	–	9	5	2.25	–	–	1	–	898†	24	292	17	17.18	6–38	1	–
Midwinter WE	19.06.1851	Vic	1876–77	8	14	1	174	37	13.38	–	–	5	–	949	104	333	14	23.79	5–78	1	–
Miller KR	28.11.1919	Vic(5)NSW(24)	1946–47	29	49	4	1511	145*	33.58	3	6	20	–	5717	225	1949	87	22.40	7–60	3	1
Minnett RB	13.06.1888	NSW	1911–12	6	12	–	309	90	25.75	–	3	–	–	415	15	213	9	23.67	4–34	–	–
Misson FM	19.11.1938	NSW	1961	2	1	1	25	25*	–	–	–	1	–	456	18	243	7	34.71	2–48	–	–
Moroney J	24.07.1917	NSW	1950–51	1	2	–	0	0	0.00	–	–	–	–	–							
Morris AR	19.01.1922	NSW	1946–47	24	43†	2	2080	206	50.73	8	8	9	–	71†	1	39	1	39.00	1–5	–	–
Morris S	22.06.1855	Vic	1884–85	1	2	1	14	10*	14.00	–	–	–	–	136	14	73	2	36.50	2–73	–	–
Moses H	13.02.1858	NSW	1886–87	6	10†	–	198	33	19.80	–	–	1	–	–							
Moule WH	31.01.1858	Vic	1880	1	2	–	40	34	20.00	–	–	1	–	51	4	23	3	7.67	3–23	–	–
Murdoch WL	18.10.1854	NSW	1876–77	18	33	5	896	211	32.00	2	1	13	1	–							
Musgrove H	27.11.1860	Vic	1884–85	1	2	–	13	9	6.50	–	–	–	–	–							
Nagel LE	06.03.1905	Vic	1932–33	1	2	1	21	21*	21.00	–	–	–	–	262	9	110	2	55.00	2–110	–	–
Nash LJ	02.05.1910	Vic	1936–37	1	1	–	17	17	17.00	–	–	3	–	197	2	104	5	20.80	4–70	–	–
Noble MA	28.01.1873	NSW	1897–98	39	68	6	1905	133	30.73	1	15	26	–	6895	353	2860	115	24.87	7–17	9	2
Nothling OE	01.08.1900	Qld	1928–29	1	2	–	52	44	26.00	–	–	–	–	276	15	72	0	–	–	–	–
O'Brien LPJ	02.07.1907	Vic	1932–33	3	6†	–	104	61	17.33	–	1	2	–	–							
O'Connor JDA	09.09.1875	SA	1907–08	4	8†	1	86	20	12.29	–	–	3	–	692	24	340	13	26.15	5–40	1	–
O'Donnell SP	26.01.1963	Vic	1985	5	8	1	184	48	26.29	–	–	3	–	874	31	487	6	81.17	3–37	–	–
O'Keeffe KJ	25.11.1949	NSW	1970–71	6	11	4	181	48*	25.86	–	–	4	–	1675	67	677	12	56.42	3–48	–	–
Oldfield WAS	09.09.1894	NSW	1920–21	38	62	14	1116	65*	23.25	–	3	59	31	–							
O'Neill NC	19.02.1937	NSW	1958–59	19	30	3	1072	117	39.70	2	7	10	–	364	10	176	2	88.00	1–7	–	–
O'Reilly WJ	20.12.1905	NSW	1932–33	19	32†	6	277	42	10.65	–	–	4	–	7864	439	2587	102	25.36	7–54	8	3
Oxenham RK	28.07.1891	Qld	1928–29	3	5	–	88	39	17.60	–	–	1	–	1208	72	349	7	49.86	4–67	–	–
Palmer GE	22.02.1860	Vic	1880	17	25	4	296	48	14.10	–	–	13	–	4417	452	1678	78	21.51	7–65	6	2

Park RL	30.07.1892	Vic	1920–21	1	1	–	0	0	0.00	–	–	–	–	6	0	9	0	–	–	–	–
Pascoe LS	13.02.1950	NSW	1977	6	7	4	34	20	11.33	–	–	1	–	1599	58	736	29	25.38	5–59	1	–
Pellew CE	21.09.1893	SA	1920–21	9	13	1	478	116	39.83	2	1	4	–	78	3	34	0	–	–	–	–
Phillips WB	01.03.1958	SA	1985	6	11†	1	350	91	35.00	–	2	11	–	–							
Philpott PI	21.11.1934	NSW	1965–66	3	4	1	22	10	7.33	–	–	2	–	801	9	371	8	46.38	5–90	1	–
Ponsford WH	19.10.1900	Vic	1924–25	20	35	2	1558	266	47.21	5	5	17	–	–							
Pope RJ	18.02.1864	NSW	1884–85	1	2	–	3	3	1.50	–	–	–	–	–							
Rackemann CG	03.06.1960	Qld	1982–83	1	1	–	4	4	4.00	–	–	1	–	200	11	96	2	48.00	2–61	–	–
Ransford VS	20.03.1885	Vic	1907–08	15	29†	6	893	143*	38.83	1	3	9	–	19†	1	19	0	–	–	–	–
Redpath IR	11.05.1941	Vic	1964	23	43	4	1512	171	38.77	2	10	29	–	–							
Reedman JC	09.10.1865	SA	1894–95	1	2	–	21	17	10.50	–	–	1	–	57	2	24	1	24.00	1–12	–	–
Richardson AJ	24.07.1888	SA	1924–25	9	13	–	403	100	31.00	1	2	1	–	1812	91	521	12	43.42	2–20	–	–
Richardson VY	07.09.1894	SA	1924–25	14	25	–	622	138	24.88	1	1	15	–	–							
Rigg KE	21.05.1906	Vic	1936–37	3	5	–	118	47	23.60	–	–	2	–	–							
Ring DT	14.10.1918	Vic	1948	2	3	–	34	18	11.33	–	–	–	–	426	20	171	3	57.00	2–84	–	–
Ritchie GM	23.01.1960	Qld	1985	6	11	1	422	146	42.20	1	2	3	–	6	0	10	0	–	–	–	–
Robertson WR	06.10.1861	Vic	1884–85	1	2	–	2	2	1.00	–	–	–	–	44	3	24	0	–	–	–	–
Robinson RD	08.06.1946	Vic	1977	3	6	–	100	34	16.67	–	–	4	–	–							
Robinson RH	26.03.1914	NSW	1936–37	1	2	–	5	3	2.50	–	–	1	–	–							
Rorke GF	27.06.1938	NSW	1958–59	2	2†	2	2	2*	–	–	–	–	–	565	17	165	8	20.63	3–23	–	–
Ryder J	08.08.1889	Vic	1920–21	17	28	4	1060	201*	44.17	2	6	15	–	1531	52	630	13	48.46	2–20	–	–
Saggers RA	15.05.1917	NSW	1948	1	1	–	5	5	5.00	–	–	3	–	–							
Saunders JV	03.02.1876	Vic	1901–02	12	20†	5	34	11*	2.27	–	–	5	–	3268†	108	1620	64	25.31	5–28	5	–
Scott HJH	26.12.1858	Vic	1884	8	14	1	359	102	27.62	1	1	8	–	28	1	26	0	–	–	–	–
Serjeant CS	01.11.1951	WA	1977	3	5	–	106	81	21.20	–	1	1	–	–							
Sheahan AP	30.09.1946	Vic	1968	9	16	3	341	88	26.23	–	1	5	–	–							
Shepherd BK	23.04.1937	WA	1962–63	2	3†	1	94	71*	47.00	–	1	1	–	–							
Sievers MW	13.04.1912	Vic	1936–37	3	6	1	67	25*	13.40	–	–	4	–	602	25	161	9	17.89	5–21	1	–
Simpson RB	03.02.1936	WA(6)NSW(13)	1958–59	19	31	3	1405	311	50.18	2	9	30	–	1828	79	838	16	52.38	5–57	1	–
Sincock DJ	01.02.1942	SA	1965–66	1	2	–	56	29	28.00	–	–	–	–	160†	1	98	0	–	–	–	–
Slater KN	12.03.1935	WA	1958–59	1	1	1	1	1*	–	–	–	–	–	256	9	101	2	50.50	2–40	–	–
Slight J	20.10.1855	Vic	1880	1	2	–	11	11	5.50	–	–	–	–	–							

AUSTRALIA	Born	State	Debut	M	I	NO	Runs	HS	Av	100	50	Ct	St	Balls	Mds	Runs	Wks	Av	Best	5i	10m
Smith DBM	14.09.1884	Vic	1912	2	3	1	30	24*	15.00	–	–	–	–	–							
Spofforth FR	09.09.1853	NSW(14)Vic(4)	1876–77	18	29	6	217	50	9.43	–	1	11	–	4185	416	1731	94	18.41	7–44	7	4
Stackpole KR	10.07.1940	Vic	1965–66	13	24	1	1164	207	50.61	3	7	15	–	1099	32	412	4	103.00	2–33	–	–
Taber HB	29.04.1940	NSW	1968	1	1	–	16	16	16.00	–	–	2	–	–							
Tallon D	17.02.1916	Qld	1946–47	15	20	2	340	92	18.89	–	2	38	4	–							
Taylor JM	10.10.1895	NSW	1920–21	18	25	–	957	108	38.28	1	8	9	–	48	1	26	1	26.00	1–25	–	–
Thomas G	21.03.1938	NSW	1965–66	3	4	–	147	52	36.75	–	2	1	–	–							
Thompson N	21.04.1838	NSW	1876–77	2	4	–	67	41	16.75	–	–	3	–	112	16	31	1	31.00	1–14	–	–
Thomson AL	02.12.1945	Vic	1970–71	4	5	4	22	12*	22.00	–	–	–	–	1519	33	654	12	54.50	3–79	–	–
Thomson JR	16.08.1950	Qld	1974–75	21	29	9	295	49	14.75	–	–	9	–	4957	166	2418	100	24.18	6–46	5	–
Toohey PM	20.04.1954	NSW	1978–79	6	12	1	171	81*	15.55	–	1	6	–	–							
Toshack ERH	15.12.1914	NSW	1946–47	9	9	5	65	20*	16.25	–	–	3	–	2467†	120	801	28	28.61	6–82	2	–
Travers JPF	10.01.1871	SA	1901–02	1	2†	–	10	9	5.00	–	–	1	–	48†	2	14	1	14.00	1–14	–	–
Tribe GE	04.10.1920	Vic	1946–47	3	3†	1	35	25*	17.50	–	–	–	–	760†	9	330	2	165.00	2–48	–	–
Trott AE	06.02.1873	Vic	1894–95	3	5	3	205	85*	102.50	–	2	4	–	474	17	192	9	21.33	8–43	1	–
Trott GHS	05.08.1866	Vic	1888	24	42	–	921	143	21.93	1	4	21	–	1890	48	1019	29	35.14	4–71	–	–
Trumble H	12.05.1867	Vic	1890	31	55	13	838	70	19.95	–	4	45	–	7895	448	2945	141	20.89	8–65	9	3
Trumble JW	16.09.1863	Vic	1884–85	7	13	1	243	59	20.25	–	1	3	–	600	59	222	10	22.20	3–29	–	–
Trumper VT	02.11.1877	NSW	1899	40	74	5	2263	185*	32.80	6	9	25	–	348	18	142	2	71.00	2–35	–	–
Turner A	23.07.1950	NSW	1975	3	5†	–	77	37	15.40	–	–	2	–	–							
Turner CTB	16.11.1862	NSW	1886–87	17	32	4	323	29	11.54	–	–	8	–	5179	457	1670	101	16.53	7–43	11	2
Veivers TR	06.04.1937	Qld	1964	9	10†	2	242	67*	30.25	–	3	5	–	1904	83	694	15	46.27	3–39	–	–
Waite MG	07.01.1911	SA	1938	2	3	–	11	8	3.67	–	–	1	–	552	23	190	1	190.00	1–150	–	–
Walker MHN	12.09.1948	Vic	1974–75	16	22	5	407	78*	23.94	–	1	7	–	4912	200	1858	56	33.18	8–143	2	–
Wall TW	13.05.1904	SA	1928–29	14	19	4	83	20	5.53	–	–	6	–	3881	115	1663	43	38.67	5–66	2	–
Walters FH	09.02.1860	Vic	1884–85	1	2	–	12	7	6.00	–	–	2	–	–							
Walters KD	21.12.1945	NSW	1965–66	36	62	6	1981	155	35.38	4	13	23	–	1839	44	730	26	28.08	4–34	–	–
Ward FA	23.02.1909	SA	1936–37	4	8	2	36	18	6.00	–	–	1	–	1268	30	574	11	52.18	6–102	1	–

Watson WJ	31.01.1931	NSW	1954–55	1	2	–	21	18	10.50	–	–	[illegible]	[illegible]	[illegible]							
Wellham DM	13.03.1959	NSW	1981	2	4	–	145	103	36.25	1	–	1	–	–							
Wessels KC	14.09.1957	Qld	1982–83	10	19†	–	754	162	39.68	1	4	11	–	36	2	18	0	–	–	–	–
Whitney MR	24.02.1959	NSW	1981	2	4	–	4	4	1.00	–	–	–	–	468†	16	246	5	49.20	2–50	–	–
Whitty WJ	15.08.1886	SA	1909	6	8	4	35	14	8.75	–	–	2	–	1302†	74	498	15	33.20	4–43	–	–
Wiener JM	01.05.1955	Vic	1979–80	2	4	–	104	58	26.00	–	1	4	–	48	3	22	0	–	–	–	–
Wood GM	06.11.1956	WA	1978–79	19	37†	1	1063	172	29.53	3	3	13	–	–							
Woodfull WM	22.08.1897	Vic	1926	25	41	3	1675	155	44.08	6	8	5	–	–							
Woods SMJ	14.04.1867	–*	1888	3	6	–	32	18	5.33	–	–	1	–	217	18	121	5	24.20	2–35	–	–
Worrall J	12.05.1863	Vic	1884–85	11	22	3	478	76	25.16	–	5	13	–	255	29	127	1	127.00	1–97	–	–
Wright KJ	27.12.1953	WA	1978–79	2	4	–	37	29	9.25	–	–	7	1	–							
Yallop GN	07.10.1952	Vic	1978–79	13	25†	–	709	121	28.36	3	1	10	–	48†	2	17	0	–	–	–	–
Yardley B	07.09.1947	WA	1978–79	9	15	1	289	61*	20.64	–	2	10	–	2660	103	1182	29	40.76	5–107	1	–

*Woods, born in NSW, did not represent the State, but was chosen to play for the 1888 Australians while playing for Cambridge University.

4.2 *Counties and States Supplying Test Cricketers*

ENGLAND

County	No. Supplied
Derbyshire	9
Essex	17
Glamorgan	3
Gloucestershire	19
Hampshire	5
Kent	32
Lancashire	40
Leicestershire	10
Middlesex	43
Northamptonshire	13
Nottinghamshire	25
Somerset	7
Surrey	39
Sussex	21
Warwickshire	16
Worcestershire	12
Yorkshire	45
Others*	1

AUSTRALIA

State	No. Supplied
New South Wales	106
Queensland	32
South Australia	42
Tasmania	3
Victoria	105
Western Australia	19
Others†	1

*L Hone, an Irish player, was playing for MCC at the time of his selection for the 1878–79 tour.
†SMJ Woods, born in NSW, did not represent the State, but was chosen to play for the 1888 Australians while playing for Cambridge University.

8 England players have played for more than one county during their Test career.

15 Australian players have played for more than one State during their Test career.

4.3 *Most Appearances*

ENGLAND

Tests	Player	Period
43	Cowdrey MC	1954–75
41	Hobbs JB	1907–30
41	Rhodes W	1899–1926
38	Boycott G	1964–81
35	MacLaren AC	1894–1909
35	Willis RGD	1970–83
34	Knott APE	1968–81

AUSTRALIA

Tests	Player	Period
52	Gregory SE	1890–1912
42	Armstrong WW	1901–21
42	Marsh RW	1970–83
41	Hill C	1896–1912
40	Trumper VT	1899–1912
39	Noble MA	1897–1909
38	Oldfield WAS	1920–37

ENGLAND			AUSTRALIA		
Tests	**Player**	**Period**	**Tests**	**Player**	**Period**
33	Hammond WR	1928–47	37	Bradman DG	1928–48
32	Edrich JH	1964–75	37	Harvey RN	1948–63
32	Lilley AFA	1896–1909	36	Walters KD	1965–77
32	Woolley FE	1909–34	35	Blackham JM	1876–95
31	Briggs J	1884–99	35	Chappell GS	1970–83
31	Evans TG	1946–59	33	Kelly JJ	1896–1905

JM Blackham played in 15 different series for Australia. The record for England is 11 by J Briggs and W Rhodes.

The most consecutive appearances for each country are:

England
33 by WR Hammond from 1928–29 to 1946–47
32 by APE Knott from 1968 to 1977
29 by FE Woolley from 1909 to 1926.

Australia
40 by VT Trumper from 1899 to 1911–12
39 by MA Noble from 1897–98 to 1909
37 by RN Harvey from 1948 to 1962–63.

4.4 *Youngest Players at Debut*

ENGLAND

Age in Years and Days			
19 – 301	Close DB	Melbourne	1950–51
20 – 18	Compton DCS	Trent Bridge	1938
20 – 210	Dilley GR	Perth	1979–80
20 – 307	Hearne JW	Sydney	1911–12
20 – 324	MacGregor G	Lord's	1890

AUSTRALIA

Age in Years and Days			
18 – 232	Garrett TW	Melbourne	1876–77
19 – 85	Cotter A	Sydney	1903–04
19 – 96	Hill C	Lord's	1896
19 – 100	Hazlitt GR	Sydney	1907–08
19 – 149	Jackson AA	Adelaide	1928–29
19 – 173	Cottam JT	Sydney	1886–87
19 – 252	Ferris JJ	Sydney	1886–87
19 – 257	Archer RG	Old Trafford	1953

AUSTRALIA

Age in Years and Days			
19 – 288	Harvey RN	Headingley	1948
19 – 332	McCabe SJ	Trent Bridge	1930
19 – 354	Walters KD	Brisbane	1965–66
19 – 363	McKenzie GD	Lord's	1961
20 – 48	Hole GB	Melbourne	1950–51
20 – 60	McDermott CJ	Headingley	1985
20 – 95	Bradman DG	Brisbane*	1928–29
20 – 98	Gregory SE	Lord's	1890
20 – 161	Bromley EH	Brisbane	1932–33
20 – 197	Palmer GE	Oval	1880
20 – 200	Jones SP	Sydney	1881–82
20 – 217	Rorke GF	Adelaide	1958–59
20 – 224	Bruce W	Melbourne	1884–85
20 – 227	Hodges JH	Melbourne	1876–77
20 – 235	Burke JW	Adelaide	1950–51
20 – 318	Pope RJ	Melbourne	1884–85
20 – 336	Gregory RG	Adelaide	1936–37

*Exhibition Ground

4.5 *Oldest Players at Debut*

ENGLAND

Age in Years and Days			
49 – 119	Southerton J	Melbourne	1876–77
41 – 337	Wilson ER	Sydney	1920–21
40 – 216	Kinneir SP	Sydney	1911–12
40 – 92	Jackson HL	Headingley	1961
40 – 57	Fishlock LB	Sydney	1946–47
39 – 360	Wood A	Oval	1938
39 – 350	Brown FR	Brisbane	1950–51
39 – 131	Makepeace JWH	Melbourne	1920–21
38 – 282	Grace EM	Oval	1880
38 – 282	Parker CWL	Old Trafford	1921
38 – 59	King JH	Lord's	1909
38 – 43	Smith TPB	Sydney	1946–47
37 – 164	Sinfield RA	Trent Bridge	1938
37 – 145	Carr DW	Oval	1909

ENGLAND

Age in Years and Days			
37 – 137	Taylor RW	Brisbane	1978–79
37 – 77	Whysall WW	Adelaide	1924–25

AUSTRALIA

Age in Years and Days			
46 – 253	Blackie DD	Sydney	1928–29
46 – 237	Ironmonger H	Brisbane*	1928–29
38 – 328	Thompson N	Melbourne	1876–77
38 – 251	Holland RG	Lord's	1985
37 – 290	Gregory EJ	Melbourne	1876–77
37 – 184	Love HSB	Brisbane	1932–33
37 – 154	Oxenham RK	Melbourne	1928–29
36 – 141	Richardson AJ	Sydney	1924–25
35 – 127	Iverson JB	Brisbane	1950–51
35 – 81	Eastwood KH	Sydney	1970–71
35 – 4	Hartkopf AEV	Melbourne	1924–25

*Exhibition Ground

4.6 *Oldest Players*

ENGLAND

Age in Years and Days			
50 – 320	Grace WG	Trent Bridge	1899
49 – 139	Southerton J	Melbourne	1876–77
48 – 293	Rhodes W	Oval	1926
47 – 249	Hobbs JB	Oval	1930
47 – 87	Woolley FE	Oval	1934
46 – 202	Strudwick H	Oval	1926
45 – 199	Hendren EH	Headingley	1934
44 – 238	Abel R	Old Trafford	1902

AUSTRALIA

Age in Years and Days			
50 – 327	Ironmonger H	Sydney	1932–33
46 – 309	Blackie DD	Adelaide	1928–29

AUSTRALIA

Age in Years and Days			
43 – 254	Bardsley W	Oval	1926
43 – 133	Carter H	Old Trafford	1921
42 – 240	Grimmett CV	Oval	1934
42 – 224	Kelleway C	Brisbane	1928–29
42 – 175	Oldfield WAS	Melbourne	1936–37
42 – 130	Gregory SE	Oval	1912
42 – 86	Armstrong WW	Oval	1921

4.7 *Played in Only One Test*

72 players appeared for England only once.
54 players appeared for Australia only once.

The following did not score a run or take a wicket:

ENGLAND			AUSTRALIA		
Grace GF	Oval	1880	Mayne ER	Old Trafford	1912
Moss AE	Trent Bridge	1956	Park RL	Melbourne	1920–21
Russell WE	Brisbane	1965–66	Moroney J	Brisbane	1950–51
			Crawford WPA	Lord's	1956

CF Root played in 3 Tests for England without batting once.

4.8 *'One-Series Men'*

There are several players who appeared in only one series, performed outstandingly and then disappeared:

Batting

ENGLAND		M	I	NO	Runs	HS	Av
Foster RE	1903–04	5	9	1	486	287	60.75
Brown G	1921	3	5	0	250	84	50.00
Tennyson Hon. LH	1921	4	5	1	229	74*	57.25
Duleepsinhji KS	1930	4	7	0	416	173	59.43
Walters CF	1934	5	9	1	401	82	50.13
Subba Row R	1961	5	10	0	468	137	46.80
Steele DS	1975	3	6	0	365	92	60.83

AUSTRALIA		M	I	NO	Runs	HS	Av
Trott AE	1894–95	3	5	3	205	85*	102.50
McCool CL	1946–47	5	7	2	272	104*	54.40

Bowling

ENGLAND		Runs	Wkts	Av
Crawford JN	1907–08	742	30	24.73

AUSTRALIA		Runs	Wkts	Av
Hordern HV	1911–12	780	32	24.38
Iverson JB	1950–51	320	21	15.24
Massie RAL	1972	409	23	17.78
Hurst AG	1978–79	577	25	23.08

4.9 *Longest Gaps Between Selection*

ENGLAND		AUSTRALIA	
From/To	**Tests**	**From/To**	**Tests**
1950–51 to 1961	26 Close DB	1970–71 to 1976–77	15 O'Keeffe KJ
1978–79 to 1985	21 Edmonds PH	1975 to 1979–80	14 Mallett AA
1964 to 1972	18 Gifford N	1975 to 1979–80	13 Chappell IM
1964 to 1972	18 Parfitt PH		
1964 to 1972	17 Price JSE		
1965–66 to 1974–75	17 Titmus FJ		

4.10 *Related Players*

Fathers and Sons

ENGLAND	Tests		AUSTRALIA	Tests	
Hardstaff J	5	1907–08	Gregory EJ	1	1876–77
Hardstaff J jr	9	1936–48	Gregory SE	52	1890–1912
Tate FW	1	1902			
Tate MW	20	1924–30			

Grandfather and Grandsons

AUSTRALIA	Tests	
Richardson VY	14	1924–33
Chappell GS	35	1970–83
Chappell IM	30	1965–80
Chappell TM	3	1981

Great-Grandfather and Great-Grandson

AUSTRALIA	Tests	
Cooper WH	2	1881–85
Sheahan AP	9	1968–72

Brothers in Same Test Team

ENGLAND	Tests	
Grace EM Grace GF Grace WG	1	1880
Studd CT Studd GB	4	1882–83

AUSTRALIA	Tests	
Gregory EJ Gregory DW	1	1876–77
Bannerman C Bannerman AC	1	1878–79
Giffen G Giffen WF	2	1891–92
Trott GHS Trott AE	3	1894–95
Chappell IM Chappell GS	22	1970–80

Brothers Never in Same Test Team

ENGLAND	Tests	
Gunn JR	6	1901–05
Gunn G	11	1907–12
Tyldesley JT	26	1899–1909
Tyldesley GE	5	1921–29

AUSTRALIA	Tests	
Archer KA	3	1950–51
Archer RG	12	1953–56
Harvey MR	1	1946–47
Harvey RN	37	1948–63
McLeod RW	6	1891–93
McLeod CE	17	1894–1905
Trumble JW	7	1884–86
Trumble H	31	1890–1904
Chappell IM & GS		(see above)
Chappell TM		1981

At Lord's in 1975 *play was interrupted for the first time by a 'streaker' (a naked spectator intruding on the field of play).*

4.11 *Longest Time on Field*

ENGLAND

Hours	Mins			
27	52	*Sutcliffe H	Melbourne	1924–25
26	39	Hammond WR	Adelaide	1928–29
25	53	Boycott G	Trent Bridge	1977
24	28	Barrington KF	Old Trafford	1964
23	12	Hutton L	Adelaide	1950–51

*Sutcliffe was on the field for all but 86 minutes of the match

AUSTRALIA

Hours	Mins			
27	59	*Simpson RB	Old Trafford	1964
24	30	Stackpole KR	Adelaide	1970–71
23	46	Wood GM	Trent Bridge	1985
22	50	Cowper RM	Melbourne	1965–66
22	22	Border AR	Lord's	1985

*Simpson was on the field for all but 16 minutes of the match

G Boycott (Eng) was on the field for the whole match at Headingley in 1977, a total time of 18 hours 41 minutes.

4.12 *Replacements or Additions to Touring Parties*

ENGLAND

Wood R	1886–87	Willis RGD	1970–71
Gunn G	1907–08	Cowdrey MC	1974–75
*Statham JB	1950–51	*Bairstow DL	1978–79
Tattersall R	1950–51	*Emburey JE	1979–80
Dexter ER	1958–59	*Stevenson GB	1979–80
Mortimore JB	1958–59	*Jesty TE	1982–83
Knight BR	1965–66	*Indicates did not play in a Test on the tour	

AUSTRALIA

Woods SMJ	1888	Whitney MR	1981

4.13 *Tallest and Shortest Players*

Tallest (Approximate heights)

ENGLAND		AUSTRALIA	
6ft 7½ins	Greig AW	6ft 6ins	Bonnor GJ
6ft 7ins	Oakman ASM	6ft 6ins	Nagel LE
6ft 6ins	Willis RGD	6ft 5ins	Dell AR
6ft 4½ins	Farnes K	6ft 4½ins	Hendry HSTL
6ft 4½ins	Pringle DR	6ft 4ins	Trumble H
6ft 4ins	Durston FJ	6ft 4ins	Eady CJ
6ft 4ins	Bowes WE	6ft 4ins	Rorke GF
6ft 4ins	Rumsey FE	6ft 4ins	Walker MHN
6ft 4ins	Agnew JP	6ft 4ins	Lawson GF
		6ft 4ins	Rackemann CG
		6ft 4ins	McDermott CJ

Shortest

The height of the shortest players is usually a matter of conjecture. The following are believed to have been under 5ft 6ins tall:

ENGLAND	AUSTRALIA
Abel R, Briggs J, Freeman AP, Jupp H, Quaife WG, Strudwick H	Bannerman AC, Gregory SE

Heaviest

Figures for the heaviest are also somewhat conjectural.
WW Armstrong (Aus) weighed around 22 stone at the end of his career in 1921, while C Milburn (18 stone) was probably the heaviest England player.

SECTION 5
The Batsmen

D G (later Sir Donald) Bradman, the supreme batsman

5.1 *Highest Averages – Whole Series* (300 runs or more)

ENGLAND	M	I	NO	Runs	HS	Av	100	50
Paynter E	7	11	4	591	216*	84.43	1	3
Sutcliffe H	27	46	5	2741	194	66.85	8	16
Barrington KF	23	39	6	2111	256	63.97	5	13
Robinson RT	6	9	1	490	175	61.25	2	1
Steele DS	3	6	0	365	92	60.83	0	4
Foster RE	5	9	1	486	287	60.75	1	0
Duleepsinhji KS	4	7	0	416	173	59.43	1	2
Leyland M	20	34	4	1705	187	56.83	7	3
Hutton L	27	49	6	2428	364	56.47	5	14
Hobbs JB	41	71	4	3636	187	54.27	12	15
Russell CAG	6	11	2	474	135	52.67	3	1
Mead CP	7	10	2	415	182*	51.88	1	1
Hammond WR	33	58	3	2852	251	51.85	9	7
Gatting MW	13	23	4	960	160	50.53	2	8
Walters CF	5	9	1	401	82	50.13	0	4
Edrich JH	32	57	3	2644	175	48.96	7	13
Jackson Hon.FS	20	33	4	1415	144*	48.79	5	6
Boycott G	38	71	9	2945	191	47.50	7	14
Subba Row R	5	10	0	468	137	46.80	2	1
May PBH	21	37	3	1566	113	46.06	3	10
Gower DI	26	48	2	2075	215	45.11	5	7

AUSTRALIA	M	I	NO	Runs	HS	Av	100	50
Bradman DG	37	63	7	5028	334	89.79	19	12
Barnes SG	9	14	2	846	234	70.50	2	4
Jackson AA	4	6	0	350	164	58.33	1	1
Border AR	24	45	12	1869	196	56.64	5	10
Morris AR	24	43	2	2080	206	50.73	8	8
Stackpole KR	13	24	1	1164	207	50.61	3	7
Simpson RB	19	31	3	1405	311	50.18	2	9
Cowper RM	9	15	1	686	307	49.00	1	3
Lawry WM	29	51	5	2233	166	48.54	7	13
McCabe SJ	24	43	3	1931	232	48.28	4	10
Ponsford WH	20	35	2	1558	266	47.21	5	5
Chappell GS	35	65	8	2619	144	45.95	9	12
Ryder J	17	28	4	1060	201*	44.17	2	6
Woodfull WM	25	41	3	1675	155	44.08	6	8
Macartney CG	26	42	4	1640	170	43.16	5	7

ENGLAND	M	I	NO	Runs	HS	Av	100	50
Brown WA	13	24	1	980	206*	42.61	3	3
Edwards R	13	22	3	805	170*	42.37	2	5
Ritchie GM	6	11	1	422	146	42.20	1	2
Chappell IM	30	56	4	2138	192	41.12	4	16

5.2 *Highest Averages in Each Era* (Min: 6 innings and 300 runs)

A dot before a player's name indicates an incomplete career record.

Era 1 1876–99

ENGLAND	M	I	NO	Runs	HS	Av	100	50
•Ranjitsinhji KS	12	22	4	970	175	53.89	2	6
•Hayward TW	12	20	2	787	137	43.72	2	3
•Jackson Hon. FS	10	16	1	612	118	40.80	2	2
Ward A	7	13	0	487	117	37.46	1	3
Brown JT	8	16	3	470	140	36.15	1	1
Stoddart AE	16	30	2	996	173	35.57	2	3
Shrewsbury A	23	40	4	1277	164	35.47	3	4
Steel AG	13	20	3	600	148	35.29	2	0
•MacLaren AC	16	30	3	933	124	34.56	3	3
•Abel R	9	15	1	482	132*	34.43	1	2
Grace WG	22	36	2	1098	170	32.29	2	5

AUSTRALIA	M	I	NO	Runs	HS	Av	100	50
•McLeod CE	7	12	4	477	112	59.63	1	4
•Noble MA	9	14	3	473	89	43.00	0	4
•Hill C	11	19	0	783	188	41.21	2	5
Iredale FA	14	23	1	807	140	36.68	2	4
•Darling J	18	33	1	1139	178	35.59	3	4
Murdoch WL	18	33	5	896	211	32.00	2	1
Graham H	6	10	0	301	107	30.10	2	0
Bruce W	14	26	2	702	80	29.25	0	5
McDonnell PS	19	34	1	950	147	28.79	3	2
Gregory SE	24	42	3	1096	201	28.10	3	4
Scott HJH	8	14	1	359	102	27.62	1	1
Lyons JJ	14	27	0	731	134	27.07	1	3

The highest aggregate for Australia in Era 1 was 1238 by G Giffen (av 23.36).

Era 2 1901–1912

ENGLAND	M	I	NO	Runs	HS	Av	100	50
Foster RE	5	9	1	486	287	60.75	1	0
•Jackson Hon.FS	10	17	3	803	144*	57.36	3	4
•Hobbs JB	15	27	3	1320	187	55.00	4	6
Gunn G	11	21	1	844	122*	42.20	2	6
•Rhodes W	31	51	13	1379	179	36.29	1	8
•Woolley FE	9	12	1	396	133*	36.00	1	2
•Fry CB	13	21	3	638	144	35.44	1	3
•MacLaren AC	19	31	1	998	140	33.27	2	5
•Tyldesley JT	24	42	1	1339	138	32.66	3	8
Hardstaff J sr	5	10	0	311	72	31.10	0	3

AUSTRALIA	M	I	NO	Runs	HS	Av	100	50
Ransford VS	15	29	6	893	143*	38.83	1	3
•Hill C	30	57	1	1877	160	33.52	2	11
Duff RA	19	34	1	1079	146	32.70	2	5
•Trumper VT	35	65	4	1983	185*	32.51	5	8
•Armstrong WW	32	58	7	1556	133*	30.51	1	5
•Noble MA	30	54	3	1432	133	28.07	1	11
•Bardsley W	12	21	0	576	136	27.42	2	1
•Macartney CG	14	24	1	607	99	26.39	0	5
Minnett RB	6	12	0	309	90	25.75	0	3
•Carter H	15	28	4	599	72	24.95	0	4

Era 3 1920–38

ENGLAND	M	I	NO	Runs	HS	Av	100	50
Paynter E	7	11	4	591	216*	84.43	1	3
Sutcliffe H	27	46	5	2741	194	66.85	8	16
Duleepsinhji KS	4	7	0	416	173	59.43	1	2
•Hammond WR	29	50	3	2684	251	57.11	9	7
Leyland M	20	34	4	1705	187	56.83	7	3
•Hobbs JB	26	44	1	2316	154	53.86	8	9
Russell CAG	6	11	2	474	135*	52.67	3	1
Walters CF	5	9	1	401	82	50.13	0	4
•Barnett CJ	8	14	0	610	129	43.57	2	2
•Hardstaff J jr	7	12	1	440	169*	40.00	1	1

AUSTRALIA	M	I	NO	Runs	HS	Av	100	50
•Bradman DG	27	46	4	3840	334	91.43	15	8
•Macartney CG	12	18	3	1033	170	68.87	5	2
Jackson AA	4	6	0	350	164	58.33	1	1
•Armstrong WW	10	13	2	616	158	56.00	3	1
McCabe SJ	24	43	3	1931	232	48.28	4	10
Ponsford WH	20	35	2	1558	266	47.21	5	5
•Brown WA	11	21	1	907	206*	45.35	3	3
Ryder J	17	28	4	1060	201*	44.17	2	6
Woodfull WM	25	41	3	1675	155	44.08	6	8
Pellew CE	9	13	1	478	116	39.83	2	1

Era 4 1946–68

ENGLAND	M	I	NO	Runs	HS	Av	100	50
Barrington KF	23	39	6	2111	256	63.97	5	13
•Edrich JH	13	21	0	1090	164	51.90	4	5
•Hutton L	24	45	6	1955	156*	50.13	3	14
Subba Row R	5	10	0	468	137	46.80	2	1
May PBH	21	37	3	1566	113	46.06	3	10
•Compton DCS	24	45	7	1628	184	42.84	4	8
•Boycott G	12	20	2	753	113	41.83	1	4
Dexter ER	19	35	0	1358	180	38.80	2	8
Parks JM	10	13	0	497	89	38.23	0	5
•Cowdrey MC	35	62	4	2186	113	37.69	5	11
Barber RW	7	13	1	447	185	37.25	1	0

AUSTRALIA	M	I	NO	Runs	HS	Av	100	50
•Bradman DG	10	17	3	1188	234	84.86	4	4
•Barnes SG	8	12	2	772	234	77.20	2	4
Morris AR	24	43	2	2080	206	50.73	8	8
•Lawry WM	24	41	3	1909	166	50.24	7	10
•Walters KD	10	16	1	753	155	50.20	2	4
Simpson RB	19	31	3	1405	311	50.18	2	9
Cowper RM	9	15	1	686	307	49.00	1	3
•Hassett AL	20	34	1	1373	137	41.61	4	5
O'Neill NC	19	30	3	1072	117	39.70	2	7
Booth BC	15	26	5	824	112	39.24	2	4

Era 5 1970–85

ENGLAND	M	I	NO	Runs	HS	Av	100	50
Robinson RT	6	9	1	490	175	61.25	2	1
Steele DS	3	6	0	365	92	60.83	0	4
Gatting MW	13	23	4	960	160	50.53	2	8
•Boycott G	26	51	7	2192	191	49.82	6	10
•Edrich JH	19	36	3	1554	175	47.09	3	8
Gower DI	26	48	2	2075	215	45.11	5	7
Lamb AJ	11	18	1	670	83	39.41	0	5
Woolmer RA	10	18	1	663	149	39.00	3	1
Randall DW	18	34	4	1161	174	38.70	3	6
Greig AW	21	37	1	1303	110	36.19	1	10

AUSTRALIA	M	I	NO	Runs	HS	Av	100	50
Border AR	24	45	12	1869	196	56.64	5	10
•Stackpole KR	11	22	1	1112	207	52.95	3	7
•Redpath IR	12	24	3	969	171	46.14	2	6
Chappell GS	35	65	8	2619	144	45.95	9	12
Edwards R	13	22	3	805	170*	42.37	2	5
Ritchie GM	6	11	1	422	146	42.20	1	2
•Chappell IM	23	44	2	1754	192	41.76	4	12
•Lawry WM	5	10	2	324	84	40.50	0	3
Wessels KC	10	19	0	754	162	39.68	1	4
McCosker RB	15	27	2	977	127	39.08	2	6

5.3 *Highest Individual Scores in Each Era*

Era 1 1876–99

ENGLAND

Score	6s	5s	4s	Mins			
175	–	–	24	223	Ranjitsinhji KS	Sydney	1897–98
173	–	3	14	320	Stoddart AE	Melbourne	1894–95
170	–	–	22	270	Grace WG	Oval	1886
164	–	–	16	411	Shrewsbury A	Lord's	1886
154*	–	–	23	185	Ranjitsinhji KS	Old Trafford	1896

ENGLAND

Score	6s	5s	4s	Mins			
152	–	–	12	235	Grace WG	Oval	1880
149	–	–	13	240	Ulyett G	Melbourne	1881–82
148	–	–	13	230	Steel AG	Lord's	1884
140	–	–	16	145	Brown JT	Melbourne	1894–95
137	–	–	20	270	Hayward TW	Old Trafford	1899

AUSTRALIA

Score	6s	5s	4s	Mins			
211	–	–	24	485	Murdoch WL	Oval	1884
201	–	–	28	243	Gregory SE	Sydney	1894–95
188	–	1	21	294	Hill C	Melbourne	1897–98
178	1	2	26	285	Darling J	Adelaide	1897–98
165*	–	–	18	285	Bannerman C	Melbourne	1876–77
161	–	1	22	255	Giffen G	Sydney	1894–95
160	–	–	30	175	Darling J	Sydney	1897–98
153*	–	1	18	315	Murdoch WL	Oval	1880
147	–	1	16	250	McDonnell PS	Sydney	1881–82
143	–	–	24	210	Trott GHS	Lord's	1896

Era 2 1901–12

ENGLAND

Score	6s	5s	4s	Mins			
287	–	–	37	419	Foster RE	Sydney	1903–04
187	–	–	16	334	Hobbs JB	Adelaide	1911–12
179	–	–	14	417	Rhodes W	Melbourne	1911–12
178	–	–	22	268	Hobbs JB	Melbourne	1911–12
144*	–	–	18	268	Jackson Hon. FS	Headingley	1905
144	–	–	23	213	Fry CB	Oval	1905
140	–	–	22	220	MacLaren AC	Trent Bridge	1905
138	–	1	20	262	Tyldesley JT	Edgbaston	1902
133*	–	–	12	215	Woolley FE	Sydney	1911–12
128	–	–	16	255	Jackson Hon. FS	Old Trafford	1902

AUSTRALIA

Score	6s	5s	4s	Mins			
185*	–	–	26	230	Trumper VT	Sydney	1903–04
166	–	–	18	241	Trumper VT	Sydney	1907–08
160	–	–	18	319	Hill C	Adelaide	1907–08
146	–	–	20	197	Duff RA	Oval	1905
143*	–	–	21	245	Ransford VS	Lord's	1909
136	1	–	12	225	Bardsley W	Oval	1909
133*	2	–	14	289	Armstrong WW	Melbourne	1907–08
133	–	–	16	287	Noble MA	Sydney	1903–04
130	–	–	10	225	Bardsley W	Oval	1909
119	–	–	16	145	Hill C	Sheffield	1902

Era 3 1920–38

ENGLAND

Score	6s	5s	4s	Mins			
364	–	–	35	797	Hutton L	Oval	1938
251	–	–	30	461	Hammond WR	Sydney	1928–29
240	–	–	32	367	Hammond WR	Lord's	1938
231*	–	–	27	458	Hammond WR	Sydney	1936–37
216*	1	1	26	319	Paynter E	Trent Bridge	1938
200	–	–	17	398	Hammond WR	Melbourne	1928–29
194	–	–	13	436	Sutcliffe H	Sydney	1932–33
187	–	–	17	381	Leyland M	Oval	1938
182*	–	–	21	309	Mead CP	Oval	1921
177	–	–	17	440	Hammond WR	Adelaide	1928–29

AUSTRALIA

Score	6s	5s	4s	Mins			
334†	–	–	46	383	Bradman DG	Headingley	1930
304	2	–	43	430	Bradman DG	Headingley	1934
270	–	–	22	458	Bradman DG	Melbourne	1936–37
266	–	1	27	460	Ponsford WH	Oval	1934
254	–	–	25	339	Bradman DG	Lord's	1930
244	1	–	32	316	Bradman DG	Oval	1934
232	–	–	16	438	Bradman DG	Oval	1930

AUSTRALIA

Score	6s	5s	4s	Mins			
232	1	–	34	235	McCabe SJ	Trent Bridge	1938
212	–	–	14	437	Bradman DG	Adelaide	1936–37
206*	–	1	22	369	Brown WA	Lord's	1938
201*	1	1	12	395	Ryder J	Adelaide	1924–25

†DG Bradman's 334 came off 436 balls

Era 4 1946–68

ENGLAND

Score	6s	5s	4s	Mins			
256	–	–	26	683	Barrington KF	Old Trafford	1964
185†	–	–	19	296	Barber RW	Sydney	1965–66
184	–	–	19	410	Compton DCS	Trent Bridge	1948
180	–	–	31	344	Dexter ER	Edgbaston	1961
174	–	–	22	481	Dexter ER	Old Trafford	1964
164	–	–	20	462	Edrich JH	Oval	1968
158	–	–	21	315	D'Oliveira BL	Oval	1968
156*	–	–	11	370	Hutton L	Adelaide	1950–51
156*	–	–	12	338	Simpson RT	Melbourne	1950–51
147	–	–	15	286	Compton DCS	Adelaide	1946–47

†RW Barber's 185 came off 255 balls

AUSTRALIA

Score	6s	5s	4s	Mins			
311	1	–	23	762	Simpson RB	Old Trafford	1964
307	–	–	20	727	Cowper RM	Melbourne	1965–66
234	–	–	17	642	Barnes SG	Sydney	1946–47
234†	–	–	24	393	Bradman DG	Sydney	1946–47
225	1	–	18	545	Simpson RB	Adelaide	1965–66
206	–	–	23	462	Morris AR	Adelaide	1950–51
196	–	–	16	400	Morris AR	Oval	1948
187	–	–	19	316	Bradman DG	Brisbane	1946–47
182	–	–	33	290	Morris AR	Headingley	1948
181	–	–	22	411	Burge PJP	Oval	1961

†DG Bradman's 234 came off 398 balls

Era 5 1970–85

ENGLAND

Score	6s	5s	4s	Mins	Balls			
215	1	–	25	449	314	Gower DI	Edgbaston	1985
196	–	–	27	425	310	Gooch GA	Oval	1985
191	–	1	23	629	471	Boycott G	Headingley	1977
188	–	–	17	492	448	Denness MH	Melbourne	1974–75
175	–	–	21	538	420	Edrich JH	Lord's	1975
175	–	–	27	412	271	Robinson RT	Headingley	1985
174	–	–	21	448	353	Randall DW	Melbourne	1976–77
166	–	–	17	379	283	Gower DI	Trent Bridge	1985
160	–	–	21	356	266	Gatting MW	Old Trafford	1985
157	–	–	20	337	215	Gower DI	Oval	1985

AUSTRALIA

Score	6s	5s	4s	Mins	Balls			
207	1	–	25	454	356	Stackpole KR	Brisbane	1970–71
196	–	–	22	450	318	Border AR	Lord's	1985
192	–	1	17	438	367	Chappell IM	Oval	1975
172	–	–	21	600	449	Wood GM	Trent Bridge	1985
171	–	1	14	484	372	Redpath IR	Perth	1970–71
170*	–	1	13	343	290	Edwards R	Trent Bridge	1972
162	–	–	17	464	343	Wessels KC	Brisbane	1982–83
146*	–	–	13	346	334	Border AR	Old Trafford	1985
146	–	–	16	357	308	Ritchie GM	Trent Bridge	1985
144	–	–	16	252	209	Chappell GS	Sydney	1974–75

5.4 *Highest Run Aggregates* (1000 runs or more)

ENGLAND	M	I	NO	Runs	HS	Av	100
Hobbs JB	41	71	4	3636	187	54.27	12
Boycott G	38	71	9	2945	191	47.50	7
Hammond WR	33	58	3	2852	251	51.85	9
Sutcliffe H	27	46	5	2741	194	66.85	8
Edrich JH	32	57	3	2644	175	48.96	7

ENGLAND	M	I	NO	Runs	HS	Av	100
Cowdrey MC	43	75	4	2433	113	34.27	5
Hutton L	27	49	6	2428	364	56.47	5
Barrington KF	23	39	6	2111	256	63.97	5
Gower DI	26	48	2	2075	215	45.11	5
MacLaren AC	35	61	4	1931	140	33.88	5
Compton DCS	28	51	8	1842	184	42.83	5
Hayward TW	29	51	2	1747	137	35.65	2
Hendren EH	28	48	4	1740	169	39.55	3
Rhodes W	41	69	14	1706	179	31.02	1
Leyland M	20	34	4	1705	187	56.83	7
Knott APE	34	57	6	1682	135	32.98	2
Woolley FE	32	51	1	1664	133*	33.28	2
May PBH	21	37	3	1566	113	46.06	3
Botham IT	29	49	2	1422	149*	30.26	3
Jackson Hon. FS	20	33	4	1415	144*	48.79	5
Tyldesley JT	26	46	1	1389	138	30.87	3
Dexter ER	19	35	0	1358	180	38.80	2
Greig AW	21	37	1	1303	110	36.19	1
Shrewsbury A	23	40	4	1277	164	35.47	3
Edrich WJ	21	39	1	1184	119	31.16	2
Randall DW	18	34	4	1161	174	38.70	3
Gooch GA	22	40	0	1105	196	27.63	1
Grace WG	22	36	2	1098	170	32.29	2
Graveney TW	22	38	4	1075	111	31.62	1

AUSTRALIA	M	I	NO	Runs	HS	Av	100
Bradman DG	37	63	7	5028	334	89.79	19
Hill C	41	76	1	2660	188	35.47	4
Chappell GS	35	65	8	2619	144	45.95	9
Harvey RN	37	68	5	2416	167	38.35	6
Trumper VT	40	74	5	2263	185*	32.80	6
Lawry WM	29	51	5	2233	166	48.54	7
Gregory SE	52	92	7	2193	201	25.80	4
Armstrong WW	42	71	9	2172	158	35.03	4
Chappell IM	30	56	4	2138	192	41.12	4
Morris AR	24	43	2	2080	206	50.73	8
Walters KD	36	62	6	1981	155	35.38	4
McCabe SJ	24	43	3	1931	232	48.28	4
Noble MA	39	68	6	1905	133	30.73	1

AUSTRALIA	M	I	NO	Runs	HS	Av	100
Border AR	24	45	12	1869	196	56.64	5
Woodfull WM	25	41	3	1675	155	44.08	6
Macartney CG	26	42	4	1640	170	43.16	5
Marsh RW	42	68	8	1633	110*	27.22	1
Darling J	31	55	2	1632	178	30.79	3
Hassett AL	24	42	1	1572	137	38.34	4
Ponsford WH	20	35	2	1558	266	47.21	5
Redpath IR	23	43	4	1512	171	38.77	2
Miller KR	29	49	4	1511	145*	33.58	3
Hughes KJ	22	40	1	1499	137	38.44	3
Bardsley W	30	49	4	1487	193*	33.04	3
Simpson RB	19	31	3	1405	311	50.18	2
Giffen G	31	53	0	1238	161	23.36	1
Burge PJP	22	37	6	1179	181	38.03	4
Stackpole KR	13	24	1	1164	207	50.61	3
Oldfield WAS	38	62	14	1116	65*	23.25	0
Bannerman AC	28	50	2	1108	94	23.08	0
Duff RA	19	34	1	1079	146	32.70	2
O'Neill NC	19	30	3	1072	117	39.70	2
Wood GM	19	37	1	1063	172	29.53	3
Ryder J	17	28	4	1060	201*	44.17	2
McDonald CC	15	28	1	1043	170	38.63	2
Collins HL	16	26	0	1012	162	38.92	3

5.5 *Centuries for England (179)*

Hobbs JB (12)

126*	Melbourne	1911–12
187	Adelaide	1911–12
178	Melbourne	1911–12
107	Lord's	1912
122	Melbourne	1920–21
123	Adelaide	1920–21
115	Sydney	1924–25
154	Melbourne	1924–25
119	Adelaide	1924–25
119	Lord's	1926
100	Oval	1926
142	Melbourne	1928–29

Hammond WR (9)

251	Sydney	1928–29
200	Melbourne	1928–29
119* 177	Adelaide	1928–29
113	Headingley	1930
112	Sydney	1932–33
101	Sydney	1932–33
231*	Sydney	1936–37
240	Lord's	1938

Sutcliffe H (8)

115	Sydney	1924–25
176 127	Melbourne	1924–25
143	Melbourne	1924–25
161	Oval	1926
135	Melbourne	1928–29
161	Oval	1930
194	Sydney	1932–33

Boycott G (7)

113	Oval	1964
142*	Sydney	1970–71
119*	Adelaide	1970–71
107	Trent Bridge	1977
191	Headingley	1977
128*	Lord's	1980
137	Oval	1981

Edrich JH (7)

120	Lord's	1964
109	Melbourne	1965–66
103	Sydney	1965–66
164	Oval	1968
115*	Perth	1970–71
130	Adelaide	1970–71
175	Lord's	1975

Leyland M (7)

137	Melbourne	1928–29
109	Lord's	1934
153	Old Trafford	1934
110	Oval	1934
126	Brisbane	1936–37
111*	Melbourne	1936–37
187	Oval	1938

Barrington KF (5)

132*	Adelaide	1962–63
101	Sydney	1962–63
256	Old Trafford	1964
102	Adelaide	1965–66
115	Melbourne	1965–66

Compton DCS (5)

102	Trent Bridge	1938
147 103*	Adelaide	1946–47
184	Trent Bridge	1948
145*	Old Trafford	1948

Cowdrey MC (5)

102	Melbourne	1954–55
100*	Sydney	1958–59
113	Melbourne	1962–63
104	Melbourne	1965–66
104	Edgbaston	1968

Gower DI (5)

102	Perth	1978–79
114	Adelaide	1982–83
166	Trent Bridge	1985
215	Edgbaston	1985
157	Oval	1985

Hutton L (5)

100	Trent Bridge	1938
364	Oval	1938
122*	Sydney	1946–47
156*	Adelaide	1950–51
145	Lord's	1953

Jackson Hon. FS (5)

103	Oval	1893
118	Oval	1899
128	Old Trafford	1902
144*	Headingley	1905
113	Old Trafford	1905

MacLaren AC (5)

120	Melbourne	1894–95
109	Sydney	1897–98
124	Adelaide	1897–98
116	Sydney	1901–02
140	Trent Bridge	1905

Botham IT (3)

119*	Melbourne	1979–80
149*	Headingley	1981
118	Old Trafford	1981

Hendren EH (3)

127*	Lord's	1926
169	Brisbane†	1928–29
132	Old Trafford	1934

May PBH (3)

104	Sydney	1954–55
101	Headingley	1956
113	Melbourne	1958–59

Randall DW (3)

174	Melbourne	1976–77
150	Sydney	1978–79
115	Perth	1982–83

Russell CAG (3)

135*	Adelaide	1920–21
101	Old Trafford	1921
102*	Oval	1921

Shrewsbury A (3)

105*	Melbourne	1884–85
164	Lord's	1886
106	Lord's	1893

Tyldesley JT (3)

138	Edgbaston	1902
100	Headingley	1905
112*	Oval	1905

Woolmer RA (3)

149	Oval	1975
120	Lord's	1977
137	Old Trafford	1977

Barnett CJ (2)

129	Adelaide	1936–37
126	Trent Bridge	1938

†Exhibition Ground

Braund LC (2)

103*	Adelaide	1901–02
102	Sydney	1903–04

Dexter ER (2)

180	Edgbaston	1961
174	Old Trafford	1964

D'Oliveira BL (2)

158	Oval	1968
117	Melbourne	1970–71

Edrich WJ (2)

119	Sydney	1946–47
111	Headingley	1948

Gatting MW (2)

160	Old Trafford	1985
100*	Edgbaston	1985

Grace WG (2)

152	Oval	1880
170	Oval	1886

Gunn G (2)

119	Sydney	1907–08
122*	Sydney	1907–08

Hayward TW (2)

130	Old Trafford	1899
137	Oval	1899

Knott APE (2)

106*	Adelaide	1974–75
135	Trent Bridge	1977

Luckhurst BW (2)

131	Perth	1970–71
109	Melbourne	1970–71

Ranjitsinhji KS (2)

154*	Old Trafford	1896
175	Sydney	1897–98

Robinson RT (2)

175 Headingley 1985
148 Edgbaston 1985

Sheppard Rev. DS (2)

113 Old Trafford 1956
113 Melbourne 1962–63

Steel AG (2)

135* Sydney 1882–83
148 Lord's 1884

Stoddart AE (2)

134 Adelaide 1891–92
173 Melbourne 1894–95

Subba Row R (2)

112 Edgbaston 1961
137 Oval 1961

Washbrook C (2)

112 Melbourne 1946–47
143 Headingley 1948

Woolley FE (2)

133* Sydney 1911–12
123 Sydney 1924–25

Abel R (1)

132* Sydney 1891–92

Ames LEG (1)

120 Lord's 1934

Barber RW (1)

185 Sydney 1965–66

Barnes W (1)

134 Adelaide 1884–85

Briggs J (1)

121 Melbourne 1884–85

Brown JT (1)

140 Melbourne 1894–95

Chapman APF (1)

121 Lord's 1930

Denness MH (1)

188 Melbourne 1974–75

Duleepsinhji KS (1)

173 Lord's 1930

Fletcher KWR (1)

146 Melbourne 1974–75

Foster RE (1)

287 Sydney 1903–04

Fry CB (1)

144 Oval 1905

Gooch GA (1)

196 Oval 1985

Graveney TW (1)

111 Sydney 1954–55

Greig AW (1)

110 Brisbane 1974–75

Gunn W (1)

102* Old Trafford 1893

Hardstaff J jr (1)

169* Oval 1938

Hearne JW (1)

114 Melbourne 1911–12

Hutchings KL (1)

126 Melbourne 1907–08

Jessop GL (1)

104 Oval 1902

Makepeace JWH (1)

117 Melbourne 1920–21

Mead CP (1)

182* Oval 1921

Pataudi Nawab of (1)

102	Sydney	1932–33

Paynter E (1)

216*	Trent Bridge	1938

Read WW (1)

117	Oval	1884

Rhodes W (1)

179	Melbourne	1911–12

Richardson PE (1)

104	Old Trafford	1956

Sharp J (1)

105	Oval	1909

Simpson RT (1)

156*	Melbourne	1950–51

Ulyett G (1)

149	Melbourne	1881–82

Ward A (1)

117	Sydney	1894–95

Watson W (1)

109	Lord's	1953

5.6 *Centuries for Australia (198)*

Bradman DG (19)

112	Melbourne	1928–29
123	Melbourne	1928–29
131	Trent Bridge	1930
254	Lord's	1930
334	Headingley	1930
232	Oval	1930
103*	Melbourne	1932–33
304	Headingley	1934
244	Oval	1934
270	Melbourne	1936–37
212	Adelaide	1936–37
169	Melbourne	1936–37
144*	Trent Bridge	1938
102*	Lord's	1938
103	Headingley	1938
187	Brisbane	1946–47
234	Sydney	1946–47
138	Trent Bridge	1948
173*	Headingley	1948

Chappell GS (9)

108	Perth	1970–71
131	Lord's	1972
113	Oval	1972
144	Sydney	1974–75
102	Melbourne	1974–75
112	Old Trafford	1977
114	Melbourne	1979–80
117	Perth	1982–83
115	Adelaide	1982–83

Morris AR (8)

155	Melbourne	1946–47
122 124*	Adelaide	1946–47
105	Lord's	1948
182	Headingley	1948
196	Oval	1948
206	Adelaide	1950–51
153	Brisbane	1954–55

Lawry WM (7)

130	Lord's	1961
102	Old Trafford	1961
106	Old Trafford	1964
166	Brisbane	1965–66
119	Adelaide	1965–66
108	Melbourne	1965–66
135	Oval	1968

Harvey RN (6)

112	Headingley	1948
122	Old Trafford	1953
162	Brisbane	1954–55

ABOVE *Victor Trumper, Australian stylist: first to hit a century before lunch*
BELOW *Woodfull and Ponsford, Australia's rock-like opening pair in the between-wars period*

ABOVE *Hobbs and Sutcliffe, England's legendary, prolific openers of the 1920s*
BELOW *Geoff Boycott, a Yorkshireman with almost unique powers of concentration*

(**Harvey RN** *cont*)

167	Melbourne	1958–59
114	Edgbaston	1961
154	Adelaide	1962–63

Trumper VT (6)

135*	Lord's	1899
104	Old Trafford	1902
185*	Sydney	1903–04
113	Adelaide	1903–04
166	Sydney	1907–08
113	Sydney	1911–12

Woodfull WM (6)

141	Headingley	1926
117	Old Trafford	1926
111	Sydney	1928–29
107	Melbourne	1928–29
102	Melbourne	1928–29
155	Lord's	1930

Border AR (5)

115	Perth	1979–80
123*	Old Trafford	1981
106*	Oval	1981
196	Lord's	1985
146*	Old Trafford	1985

Macartney CG (5)

170	Sydney	1920–21
115	Headingley	1921
133*	Lord's	1926
151	Headingley	1926
109	Old Trafford	1926

Ponsford WH (5)

110	Sydney	1924–25
128	Melbourne	1924–25
110	Oval	1930
181	Headingley	1934
266	Oval	1934

Armstrong WW (4)

133*	Melbourne	1907–08
158	Sydney	1920–21
121	Adelaide	1920–21
123*	Melbourne	1920–21

Burge PJP (4)

181	Oval	1961
103	Sydney	1962–63
160	Headingley	1964
120	Melbourne	1965–66

Chappell IM (4)

111	Melbourne	1970–71
104	Adelaide	1970–71
118	Oval	1972
192	Oval	1975

Gregory SE (4)

201	Sydney	1894–95
103	Lord's	1896
117	Oval	1899
112	Adelaide	1903–04

Hassett AL (4)

128	Brisbane	1946–47
137	Trent Bridge	1948
115	Trent Bridge	1953
104	Lord's	1953

Hill C (4)

188	Melbourne	1897–98
135	Lord's	1899
119	Sheffield	1902
160	Adelaide	1907–08

McCabe SJ (4)

187*	Sydney	1932–33
137	Old Trafford	1934
112	Melbourne	1936–37
232	Trent Bridge	1938

Walters KD (4)

155 Brisbane 1965–66
115 Melbourne 1965–66
112 Brisbane 1970–71
103 Perth 1974–75

Bardsley W (3)

136 / 130 Oval 1909
193* Lord's 1926

Brown WA (3)

105 Lord's 1934
133 Trent Bridge 1938
206* Lord's 1938

Collins HL (3)

104 Sydney 1920–21
162 Adelaide 1920–21
114 Sydney 1924–25

Darling J (3)

101 Sydney 1897–98
178 Adelaide 1897–98
160 Sydney 1897–98

Hughes KJ (3)

129 Brisbane 1978–79
117 Lord's 1980
137 Sydney 1982–83

McDonnell PS (3)

147 Sydney 1881–82
103 Oval 1884
124 Adelaide 1884–85

Miller KR (3)

141* Adelaide 1946–47
145* Sydney 1950–51
109 Lord's 1953

Stackpole KR (3)

207 Brisbane 1970–71
136 Adelaide 1970–71
114 Trent Bridge 1972

Wood GM (3)

100 Melbourne 1978–79
112 Lord's 1980
172 Trent Bridge 1985

Yallop GN (3)

102 Brisbane 1978–79
121 Sydney 1978–79
114 Old Trafford 1981

Barnes SG (2)

234 Sydney 1946–47
141 Lord's 1948

Booth BC (2)

112 Brisbane 1962–63
103 Melbourne 1962–63

Duff RA (2)

104 Melbourne 1901–02
146 Oval 1905

Edwards R (2)

170* Trent Bridge 1972
115 Perth 1974–75

Fingleton JHW (2)

100 Brisbane 1936–37
136 Melbourne 1936–37

Graham H (2)

107 Lord's 1893
105 Sydney 1894–95

Iredale FA (2)

140 Adelaide 1894–95
108 Old Trafford 1896

McCosker RB (2)

127 Oval 1975
107 Trent Bridge 1977

McDonald CC (2)

170 Adelaide 1958–59
133 Melbourne 1958–59

Murdoch WL (2)

153*	Oval	1880
211	Oval	1884

O'Neill NC (2)

117	Oval	1961
100	Adelaide	1962–63

Pellew CE (2)

116	Melbourne	1920–21
104	Adelaide	1920–21

Redpath IR (2)

171	Perth	1970–71
105	Sydney	1974–75

Ryder J (2)

201*	Adelaide	1924–25
112	Melbourne	1928–29

Simpson RB (2)

311	Old Trafford	1964
225	Adelaide	1965–66

Badcock CL (1)

118	Melbourne	1936–37

Bannerman C (1)

165*	Melbourne	1876–77

Bonnor GJ (1)

128	Sydney	1884–85

Burke JW (1)

101*	Adelaide	1950–51

Cowper RM (1)

307	Melbourne	1965–66

Dyson J (1)

102	Headingley	1981

Giffen G (1)

161	Sydney	1894–95

Gregory JM (1)

100	Melbourne	1920–21

Hartigan RJ (1)

116	Adelaide	1907–08

Hendry HSTL (1)

112	Sydney	1928–29

Hilditch AMJ (1)

119	Headingley	1985

Horan TP (1)

124	Melbourne	1881–82

Jackson AA (1)

164	Adelaide	1928–29

Kelleway C (1)

147	Adelaide	1920–21

Kippax AF (1)

100	Melbourne	1928–29

Lindwall RR (1)

100	Melbourne	1946–47

Lyons JJ (1)

134	Sydney	1891–92

McCool CL (1)

104*	Melbourne	1946–47

McLeod CE (1)

112	Melbourne	1897–98

Marsh RW (1)

110*	Melbourne	1976–77

Noble MA (1)

133	Sydney	1903–04

Ransford VS (1)

143*	Lord's	1909

Richardson AJ (1)

100	Headingley	1926

Richardson VY (1)

138	Melbourne	1924–25

Ritchie GM (1)

146 Trent Bridge 1985

Scott HJH (1)

102 Oval 1884

Taylor JM (1)

108 Sydney 1924–25

Trott GHS (1)

143 Lord's 1896

Wellham DM (1)

103 Oval 1981

Wessels KC (1)

162 Brisbane 1982–83

5.7 *Highest Percentage of Centuries*

(Among batsmen scoring 5 or more centuries)

ENGLAND	Inns	100s	%age	AUSTRALIA	Inns	100s	%age
Leyland M	34	7	20.59	Bradman DG	63	19	30.16
Hobbs JB	71	12	16.90	Morris AR	43	8	18.60
Sutcliffe H	46	8	17.39	Woodfull WM	41	6	14.63
Hammond WR	58	9	15.52	Ponsford WH	35	5	14.29
Jackson Hon. FS	33	5	15.15	Chappell GS	65	9	13.85
Barrington KF	39	5	12.82	Lawry WM	51	7	13.73
Edrich JH	57	7	12.28	Macartney CG	42	5	11.90
Gower DI	48	5	10.42	Border AR	45	5	11.11
Hutton L	49	5	10.20	Harvey RN	68	6	8.82
Boycott G	71	7	9.86	Trumper VT	74	6	8.11
Compton DCS	51	5	9.80				
MacLaren AC	61	5	8.20				
Cowdrey MC	75	5	6.67				

5.8 *Century in First Test*

ENGLAND (15)			
Grace WG	152	Oval	1880
Ranjitsinhji KS	†154*	Old Trafford	1896
Foster RE	287	Sydney	1903–04
Gunn G	119	Sydney	1907–08
Sutcliffe H	†115	Sydney	1924–25
Leyland M	137	Melbourne	1928–29
Duleepsinhji KS	173	Lord's	1930
Pataudi Nawab of	102	Sydney	1932–33

ENGLAND (15)			
Hutton L	100	Trent Bridge	1938
Compton DCS	102	Trent Bridge	1938
Watson W	†109	Lord's	1953
Subba Row R	†112	Edgbaston	1961
Edrich JH	120	Lord's	1964
Randall DW	†174	Melbourne	1976–77
Robinson RT	175	Headingley	1985

AUSTRALIA (14)			
Bannerman C	165*	Melbourne	1876–77
Graham H	107	Lord's	1893
Duff RA	†104	Melbourne	1901–02
Hartigan RJ	†116	Adelaide	1907–08
Collins HL	†104	Sydney	1920–21
Ponsford WH	110	Sydney	1924–25
Jackson AA	164	Adelaide	1928–29
Harvey RN	112	Headingley	1948
Burke JW	†101*	Adelaide	1950–51
Walters KD	155	Brisbane	1965–66
Chappell GS	108	Perth	1970–71
Yallop GN	†102	Brisbane	1978–79
Wellham DM	†103	Oval	1981
Wessels KC	162	Brisbane	1982–83

H Sutcliffe scored 3 centuries in his first 2 Tests (115, 176 and 127) in 1924–25.
WH Ponsford (110 and 128 in 1924–25) and KD Walters (155 and 115 in 1965–66) scored centuries in their first 2 Tests.
H Graham is the only batsman to have scored a century in his first Test innings in each country.

†Denotes second innings

5.9 *Near Misses – 90 or More in First Test*

ENGLAND				**AUSTRALIA**			
Jackson Hon. FS	91	Lord's	1893	Minnett RB	90	Sydney	1911–12
Wood B	†90	Oval	1972	Richardson AJ	†98	Sydney	1924–25
				Chipperfield AG	99	Trent Bridge	1934
				McCool CL	95	Brisbane	1946–47
				Phillips WB	†91	Headingley	1985

†Denotes second innings

5.10 *Most Runs in First Test*

ENGLAND

306 (287 & 19)	Foster RE	Sydney	1903–04
221 (173 & 48)	Duleepsinhji KS	Lord's	1930
216 (62 & 154*)	Ranjitsinhji KS	Old Trafford	1896
196 (175 & 21)	Robinson RT	Headingley	1985
193 (119 & 74)	Gunn G	Sydney	1907–08
190 (137 & 53*)	Leyland M	Melbourne	1928–29
178 (4 & 174)	Randall DW	Melbourne	1976–77
174 (59 & 115)	Sutcliffe H	Sydney	1924–25
171 (59 & 112)	Subba Row R	Edgbaston	1961
161 (152 & 9*)	Grace WG	Oval	1880

AUSTRALIA

208 (162 & 46)	Wessels KC	Brisbane	1982–83
200 (164 & 36)	Jackson AA	Adelaide	1928–29
174 (70 & 104)	Collins HL	Sydney	1920–21
169 (165* & 4)	Bannerman C	Melbourne	1876–77
164 (48 & 116)	Hartigan RJ	Adelaide	1907–08
155 (155)	Walters KD	Brisbane	1965–66
137 (110 & 27)	Ponsford WH	Sydney	1924–25
136 (32 & 104)	Duff RA	Melbourne	1901–02

5.11 *Century in Last Test*

ENGLAND

105	Sharp J	Oval	1909
102*	Russell CAG	Oval	1921
187	Leyland M	Oval	1938
137	Subba Row R	Oval	1961
†137	Boycott G	Oval	1981
†196	Gooch GA	Oval	1985
†157	Gower DI	Oval	1985

AUSTRALIA

146	Duff RA	Oval	1905
266	Ponsford WH	Oval	1934
†137	Hughes KJ	Sydney	1982–83

†Still playing first-class cricket in 1986

5.12 *Two Centuries in a Match*

ENGLAND

6s	5s	4s	Mins				
–	–	18	431	176	Sutcliffe H	Melbourne	1924–25
–	–	12	379	127			
–	–	9	263	119*	Hammond WR	Adelaide	1928–29
–	–	17	440	177			
–	–	15	286	147	Compton DCS	Adelaide	1946–47
–	–	10	284	103*			

AUSTRALIA

6s	5s	4s	Mins				
1	–	12	225	136	Bardsley W	Oval	1909
–	–	10	225	130			
2	–	12	270	122	Morris AR	Adelaide	1946–47
–	–	11	195	124*			

The following batsmen achieved 'near misses':

ENGLAND

106	&	81	Shrewsbury A	Lord's	1893
95	&	93	Woolley FE	Lord's	1921
101	&	94	Barrington KF	Sydney	1962–63
107	&	80*	Boycott G	Trent Bridge	1977

AUSTRALIA

124	&	83	McDonnell PS	Adelaide	1884–85
98	&	97	Hill C	Adelaide	1901–02
201*	&	88	Ryder J	Adelaide	1924–25
87	&	136	Stackpole KR	Adelaide	1970–71
84	&	144	Chappell GS	Sydney	1974–75
117	&	84	Hughes KJ	Lord's	1980
106*	&	84	Border AR	Oval	1981
119	&	80	Hilditch AMJ	Headingley	1985

5.13 *Summary of Centuries*

	Tests	For Eng	For Aus	Total
In England	123	85	85	170
In Australia	134	94	113	207
Totals	257	179	198	377

For England 72 players out of a total of 349 have scored a century.

For Australia 73 players out of a total of 293 have scored a century.

	Single	Double	Triple	Most 200s
England	170	8	1	Hammond WR (4)
Australia	178	16	4	Bradman DG (8)

5.14 *Three Centuries in Successive Innings*

ENGLAND			AUSTRALIA		
115, 176 and 127	Sutcliffe H	1924–25	133*, 151, 109	Macartney CG	1926
			155, 122 and 124*	Morris AR	1946–47

5.15 *Most Centuries in Successive Matches*

Six	Bradman DG*	270, 212, 169	1936–37
		144*, 102*, 103	1938
Four	Bradman DG	123	1928–29
		131, 254, 334	1930

*Bradman did not bat in the final Test of 1938. In his next 2 Tests, in 1946–47, he scored 187 and 234, giving him 8 centuries in successive Tests in which he batted.

WR Hammond scored 4 centuries in 3 successive matches in 1928–29, his scores being 251, 200 and 32, 119* and 177. Only Hammond and Bradman (304 and 244) have scored double-centuries in successive innings.

5.16 *Youngest Players to Score a Century*

ENGLAND

Age in Years and Days

20 – 19	Compton DCS	102	Trent Bridge	1938
20 – 324	Hearne JW	114	Melbourne	1911–12
21 – 227	Gower DI	102	Perth	1978–79
21 – 352	Hutton L	100	Trent Bridge	1938
22 – 7	Cowdrey MC	102	Melbourne	1954–55

AUSTRALIA

Age in Years and Days

19 – 152	Jackson AA	164	Adelaide	1928–29
19 – 290	Harvey RN	112	Headingley	1948
19 – 357	Walters KD	155	Brisbane	1965–66
20 – 129	Bradman DG	112	Melbourne	1928–29
20 – 240	Burke JW	101*	Adelaide	1950–51
20 – 317	Hill C	188	Melbourne	1897–98

The youngest player to score a double-century is DG Bradman (Aus), who was 21 years 307 days when he scored 254 at Lord's in 1930.

The youngest player to score a double-century for England is L Hutton, who was 22 years 60 days when he scored 364 at The Oval in 1938.

Walters and Bradman both scored 2 centuries before the age of 21.

5.17 *Oldest Players to Score a Century*

ENGLAND

Age in Years and Days

46 – 83	Hobbs JB	142	Melbourne	1928–29
45 – 181	Hendren EH	132	Old Trafford	1934
40 – 312	Boycott G	137	Oval	1981
39 – 113	D'Oliveira BL	117	Melbourne	1970–71
38 – 173	Makepeace JWH	117	Melbourne	1920–21

Hobbs scored 6 centuries (1924–25 to 1928–29) after reaching the age of 40.

AUSTRALIA

Age in Years and Days

43 – 201	Bardsley W	193*	Lord's	1926
41 – 268	Armstrong WW	123*	Melbourne	1920–21
40 – 29	Macartney CG	109	Old Trafford	1926
39 – 334	Bradman DG	173*	Headingley	1948
39 – 301	Hassett AL	104	Lord's	1953

Both Armstrong (in 1920–21) and Macartney (in 1926) scored 3 centuries in one series after reaching the age of 40.

The oldest player to score a double-century is Bradman (Aus), who was 38 years 112 days when he scored 234 at Sydney in 1946–47.

The oldest player to score a double-century for England is E Paynter, who was 36 years 218 days when he scored 216* at Trent Bridge in 1938.

5.18 *Most Individual 100s in an Innings*

ENGLAND				AUSTRALIA			
4	658–8 dec	Trent Bridge	1938	3	551	Oval	1884
3	524	Sydney	1932–33	3	582	Adelaide	1920–21
3	903–7 dec	The Oval	1938	3	494	Headingley	1926
3	595–5 dec	Edgbaston	1985	3	604	Melbourne	1936–37

5.19 *Most Individual 100s in a Match*

7	England (4)	v	Australia (3)	Trent Bridge	1938
6	Australia (4)	v	England (2)	Adelaide	1920–21
6	Australia (3)	v	England (3)	Sydney	1924–25
6	Australia (4)	v	England (2)	Melbourne	1928–29

In 1930 and 1934 *Australia regained the Ashes on August 22 both years – a date which happened to be their captain WM Woodfull's birthday. Australia lost the Ashes in 1932–33 on the day that AA Jackson (164 in his first Test 1928–29) died, at the age of 23.*

Four great left-handers: Joe Darling and Neil Harvey of Australia (ABOVE) *and Eddie Paynter and Frank Woolley of England*

5.20 *Highest Percentage of Boundaries in a Century*

ENGLAND

Percentage in Boundaries	6s	5s	4s	Score			
76.51	1	–	27	149*	Botham IT	Headingley	1981
74.58	6	–	13	118	Botham IT	Old Trafford	1981
71.43	1	–	21	126	Hutchings KL	Melbourne	1907–08
70.19	–	1	17	104	Jessop GL	Oval	1902
68.97	–	–	20	116	MacLaren AC	Sydney	1901–02
68.89	–	–	31	180	Dexter ER	Edgbaston	1961
68.38	–	–	20	117	Read WW	Oval	1884
67.22	–	–	20	119	Gunn G	Sydney	1907–08
66.67	–	–	22	132	Hendren EH	Old Trafford	1934
64.23	–	–	22	137	Woolmer RA	Old Trafford	1977

Botham hit one 6 and 19 4s in reaching his century at Headingley in 1981, the highest proportion of boundaries for England in 100.

AUSTRALIA

Percentage in Boundaries	6s	5s	4s	Score			
75.25	–	–	19	101	Darling J	Sydney	1897–98
75.00	–	–	30	160	Darling J	Sydney	1897–98
72.53	–	–	33	182	Morris AR	Headingley	1948
67.80	–	–	20	118	Chappell IM	Oval	1972
67.42	1	2	26	178	Darling J	Adelaide	1897–98
67.23	2	–	17	119	Hilditch AMJ	Headingley	1985
67.13	–	–	24	143	Trott GHS	Lord's	1896
67.05	–	–	29	173*	Bradman DG	Headingley	1948
66.09	–	–	19	115	Chappell GS	Adelaide	1982–83
66.02	–	–	17	103	Gregory SE	Lord's	1896

Both Darling (160) and Morris (182) hit 20 4s in reaching three figures, the highest proportion of boundaries for Australia in reaching 100.

The following batsmen reached centuries with a 6:

England	Barrington KF (132*)	Adelaide	1962–63
	Barrington KF (115)	Melbourne	1965–66
	Botham IT (118)	Old Trafford	1981

Australia	Darling J (178)	Adelaide	1897–98
	Walters KD (103)	Perth	1974–75
	McCosker RB (107)	Trent Bridge	1977

Hon. FS Jackson (Eng) reached his century with a hit off G Giffen onto the pavilion stand at The Oval in 1893, a stroke worth 4 runs.

5.21 *150 Runs in a Match Without a Century*

ENGLAND

188 (95 & 93)	Woolley FE	Lord's	1921
170 (94 & 76)	Hutton L	Adelaide	1946–47
169 (70 & 99)	Dexter ER	Brisbane	1962–63
165 (73 & 92)	Steele DS	Headingley	1975
159 (97 & 62)	Tyldesley JT	Melbourne	1903–04
155 (92 & 63)	Knott APE	Oval	1972
154 (81 & 73)	Richardson PE	Trent Bridge	1956
152 (88 & 64)	Edrich JH	Edgbaston	1968
152 (78 & 74)	Hobbs JB	Trent Bridge	1930
150 (99 & 51)	Gooch GA	Melbourne	1979–80

AUSTRALIA

195 (98 & 97)	Hill C	Adelaide	1901–02
172 (89 & 83)	Border AR	Sydney	1982–83
167 (81 & 86)	Walters KD	Old Trafford	1968
166 (88 & 78)	Lawry WM	Melbourne	1965–66
162 (72 & 90)	Taylor JM	Melbourne	1924–25
154 (86 & 68)	Taylor JM	Melbourne	1924–25
153 (77 & 76*)	Gregory JM	Melbourne	1920–21
153 (65 & 88)	McCabe SJ	Trent Bridge	1934
151 (88 & 63*)	Bardsley W	Lord's	1921
150 (63 & 87)	Ryder J	Adelaide	1928–29

5.22 *250 Runs in a Match*

ENGLAND

364 (364)	Hutton L	Oval	1938
306 (287 & 19)	Foster RE	Sydney	1903–04
303 (176 & 127)	Sutcliffe H	Melbourne	1924–25
296 (119* & 177)	Hammond WR	Adelaide	1928–29

ENGLAND			
260 (147 & 103*)	Compton DCS	Adelaide	1946–47
256 (256)	Barrington KF	Old Trafford	1964
251 (251)	Hammond WR	Sydney	1928–29

AUSTRALIA			
334 (334)	Bradman DG	Headingley	1930
321 (244 & 77)	Bradman DG	Oval	1934
315 (311 & 4*)	Simpson RB	Old Trafford	1964
307 (307)	Cowper RM	Melbourne	1965–66
304 (304)	Bradman DG	Headingley	1934
289 (201* & 88)	Ryder J	Adelaide	1924–25
288 (266 & 22)	Ponsford WH	Oval	1934
283 (13 & 270)	Bradman DG	Melbourne	1936–37
271 (232 & 39)	McCabe SJ	Trent Bridge	1938
266 (136 & 130)	Bardsley W	Oval	1909
255 (254 & 1)	Bradman DG	Lord's	1930

5.23 *Most Runs in a Series* *(500 or more)*

ENGLAND		M	I	NO	Runs	HS	Av	100	50	0s
Hammond WR	1928–29	5	9	1	905	251	113.13	4	–	–
Sutcliffe H	1924–25	5	9	0	734	176	81.56	4	2	1
Gower DI	1985	6	9	0	732	215	81.33	3	1	–
Hobbs JB	1911–12	5	9	1	662	187	82.75	3	1	–
Boycott G	1970–71	5	10	3	657	142*	93.86	2	5	–
Edrich JH	1970–71	6	11	2	648	130	72.00	2	4	–
Barrington KF	1962–63	5	10	2	582	132*	72.75	2	3	–
Hobbs JB	1924–25	5	9	0	573	154	63.67	3	2	1
Compton DCS	1948	5	10	1	562	184	62.44	2	2	1
Edrich JH	1968	5	9	0	554	164	61.56	1	4	–
Hutton L	1950–51	5	10	4	533	156*	88.83	1	4	–
Barrington KF	1964	5	8	1	531	256	75.86	1	2	–
Gatting MW	1985	6	9	3	527	160	87.83	2	3	–
Hobbs JB	1920–21	5	10	0	505	123	50.50	2	1	–

AUSTRALIA		M	I	NO	Runs	HS	Av	100	50	0s
Bradman DG	1930	5	7	0	974	334	139.14	4	–	–
Bradman DG	1936–37	5	9	0	810	270	90.00	3	1	2

AUSTRALIA		M	I	NO	Runs	HS	Av	100	50	0s
Bradman DG	1934	5	8	0	758	304	94.75	2	1	–
Morris AR	1948	5	9	1	696	196	87.00	3	3	–
Bradman DG	1946–47	5	8	1	680	234	97.14	2	3	1
Stackpole KR	1970–71	6	12	0	627	207	52.25	2	2	1
Chappell GS	1974–75	6	11	0	608	144	55.27	2	5	–
Border AR	1985	6	11	2	597	196	66.33	2	1	–
Lawry WM	1965–66	5	7	0	592	166	84.57	3	2	1
Trumper VT	1903–04	5	10	1	574	185*	63.78	2	3	1
Ponsford WH	1934	4	7	1	569	266	94.83	2	1	–
Collins HL	1920–21	5	9	0	557	162	61.89	2	3	–
Taylor JM	1924–25	5	10	0	541	108	54.10	1	4	1
Darling J	1897–98	5	8	0	537	178	67.13	3	–	–
Border AR	1981	6	12	3	533	123*	59.22	2	3	1
Hill C	1901–02	5	10	0	521	99	52.10	–	4	1
McDonald CC	1958–59	5	9	1	519	170	64.88	2	1	0
Brown WA	1938	4	8	1	512	206*	73.14	2	1	0
Bradman DG	1948	5	9	2	508	173*	72.57	2	1	2
Morris AR	1946–47	5	8	1	503	155	71.86	3	1	0

5.24 *Highest Average in a Series in Each Era*

(Qualification: 3 completed innings)

Era 1 1876–99

ENGLAND	M	I	NO	Runs	HS	Av	
Ranjitsinhji KS	2	4	1	235	154*	78.33	1896
Shrewsbury A	3	5	1	284	106	71.00	1893
Hayward TW	5	7	1	413	137	68.83	1899
Jackson Hon. FS	2	3	0	199	103	66.33	1893
Shrewsbury A	3	4	0	243	164	60.75	1886

AUSTRALIA	M	I	NO	Runs	HS	Av	
Scott HJH	3	4	1	220	102	73.33	1884
Bannerman C	2	4	1	209	165*	69.67	1876–77
Darling J	5	8	0	537	178	67.13	1897–98
Murdoch WL	3	4	0	266	211	66.50	1884
Hill C	3	5	0	301	135	60.20	1899

Era 2 1901–12

ENGLAND	M	I	NO	Runs	HS	Av	
Hobbs JB	5	9	1	662	187	82.75	1911–12
Jackson Hon.FS	5	9	2	492	144*	70.28	1905
Foster RE	5	9	1	486	287	60.75	1903–04
Fry CB	4	7	1	348	144	58.00	1905
Rhodes W	5	9	1	463	179	57.88	1911–12

AUSTRALIA	M	I	NO	Runs	HS	Av	
Trumper VT	5	10	1	574	185*	63.78	1903–04
Noble MA	5	10	3	417	133	59.57	1903–04
Ransford VS	5	9	3	353	143*	58.83	1909
Armstrong WW	4	7	4	159	55*	53.00	1901–02
Hill C	5	10	0	521	99	52.10	1901–02

Era 3 1920–38

ENGLAND	M	I	NO	Runs	HS	Av	
Hutton L	3	4	0	473	364	118.25	1938
Hammond WR	5	9	1	974	251	113.13	1928–29
Paynter E	4	6	2	407	216*	101.75	1938
Sutcliffe H	4	7	2	436	161	87.20	1930
Sutcliffe H	5	9	0	734	176	81.56	1924–25

AUSTRALIA	M	I	NO	Runs	HS	Av	
Bradman DG	5	7	0	974	334	139.14	1930
Bradman DG	4	6	2	434	144*	108.50	1938
Ponsford WH	4	7	1	569	266	94.83	1934
Bradman DG	5	8	0	758	304	94.75	1934
Macartney CG	5	6	1	473	151	94.60	1926

Era 4 1946–68

ENGLAND	M	I	NO	Runs	HS	Av	
May PBH	5	7	2	453	101	90.60	1956
Hutton L	5	10	4	533	156*	88.83	1950–51
D'Oliveira BL	2	4	1	263	158	87.67	1968

ENGLAND	M	I	NO	Runs	HS	Av	
Barrington KF	5	8	1	531	256	75.86	1964
Barrington KF	5	10	2	582	132*	72.75	1962–63

AUSTRALIA	M	I	NO	Runs	HS	Av	
Bradman DG	5	8	1	680	234	97.14	1946–47
Simpson RB	3	4	0	355	225	88.75	1965–66
Morris AR	5	9	1	696	196	87.00	1948
Lawry WM	5	7	0	592	166	84.57	1965–66
Barnes SG	4	6	2	329	141	82.25	1948

Era 5 1970–85

ENGLAND	M	I	NO	Runs	HS	Av	
Boycott G	3	5	2	442	191	147.33	1977
Boycott G	5	10	3	657	142*	93.86	1970–71
Gatting MW	6	9	3	527	160	87.83	1985
Gower DI	6	9	0	732	215	81.33	1985
Edrich JH	6	11	2	648	130	72.00	1970–71

AUSTRALIA	M	I	NO	Runs	HS	Av	
McCosker RB	4	7	2	414	127	82.80	1975
Chappell GS	3	6	2	317	114	79.25	1979–80
Chappell IM	4	6	0	429	192	71.50	1975
Hughes KJ	5	8	1	469	137	67.00	1982–83
Border AR	6	11	2	597	196	66.33	1985

5.25 *Scorers of 99, 98, 97*

ENGLAND				AUSTRALIA			
99*	Boycott G	Perth	1979–80	99	Hill C	Melbourne	1901–02
99	Paynter E	Lord's	1938	99	Macartney CG	Lord's	1912
99	Dexter ER	Brisbane	1962–63	†99	Chipperfield AG	Trent Bridge	1934
99	Gooch GA	Melbourne	1979–80	99	Miller KR	Adelaide	1950–51
98*	Gower DI	Sydney	1979–80	99	Cowper RM	Melbourne	1965–66
†98	Jardine DR	Adelaide	1928–29	99	Edwards R	Lord's	1975
†98	Larwood H	Sydney	1932–33				

ENGLAND				AUSTRALIA			
98	Washbrook C	Headingley	1956	99	Hughes KJ	Perth	1979–80
97	Tyldesley JT	Melbourne	1903–04	98*	Chappell GS	Sydney	1979–80
				98	Hill C	Adelaide	1901–02
				98	Hill C	Adelaide	1911–12
				98	Richardson AJ	Sydney	1924–25
				98	Lawry WM	Brisbane	1962–63
				98	Booth BC	Old Trafford	1964
				97	Hill C	Adelaide	1901–02

†Indicates those who never made 100 in their E v A Test career

5.26 *Scorers of 190–199*

ENGLAND				AUSTRALIA			
196	Gooch GA	Oval	1985	196	Morris AR	Oval	1948
194	Sutcliffe H	Sydney	1932–33	196	Border AR	Lord's	1985
191	Boycott G	Headingley	1977	193*	Bardsley W	Lord's	1926
				192	Chappell IM	Oval	1975

5.27 *Scorers of 90–99*

There have been 83 scores of between 90 and 99, 43 for England and 40 for Australia.

The following batsmen have scored two or more 90s:

ENGLAND				AUSTRALIA			
May PBH	3	Cowdrey MC	2	Hill C	5	Lawry WM	2
Hayward TW	2	Dexter ER	2	Bannerman AC	2	Marsh RW	2
Woolley FE	2	Greig AW	2	Trott GHS	2		
Hendren EH	2			Andrews TJE	2		

Hill is the only batsman to score 3 successive nineties: 99 at Melbourne, 98 and 97 at Adelaide, in 1901–02.

Three batsmen have also scored 2 nineties in the same series: Woolley and Andrews in 1921, and Dexter in 1962–63.

DG Bradman was never dismissed in the 90s.

5.28 *Carrying Bat Through Innings*

ENGLAND

Score	Total	Mins			
132*	307	325	Abel R	Sydney	1891–92
156*	272	370	Hutton L	Adelaide	1950–51
99*	215	335	Boycott G	Perth	1979–80

AUSTRALIA

Score	Total	Mins			
67*	176	278	Barrett JE	Lord's	1890
193*	383	398	Bardsley W	Lord's	1926
30*	66	81	Woodfull WM	Brisbane*	1928–29
73*	193	235	Woodfull WM	Adelaide	1932–33
206*	422	369	Brown WA	Lord's	1938
60*	116	267	Lawry WM	Sydney	1970–71

*Exhibition Ground

Australia batted 2 men short at Brisbane in 1928–29 and 1 man short at Adelaide in 1932–33.

The following batsmen opened the innings and were last out:

ENGLAND	Score	Total		
Hutton L	30	52	Oval	1948
Boycott G	191	436	Headingley	1977
AUSTRALIA				
Trumper VT	74	122	Melbourne	1903–04
Brown WA	69	201*	Oval	1938
Morris AR	206	371	Adelaide	1950–51
Inverarity RJ	56	125	Oval	1968
Wessels KC	162	341	Brisbane	1982–83

*Australia batted 2 men short

5.29 *0 and 100 in Same Match*

ENGLAND			
102 & 0	Braund LC	Sydney	1903–04
0 & 100	Tyldesley JT	Headingley	1905
122* & 0	Gunn G	Sydney	1907–08
0 & 123	Woolley FE	Sydney	1924–25
145* & 0	Compton DCS	Old Trafford	1948
0 & 113	Sheppard Rev. DS	Melbourne	1962–63
0 & 150	Randall DW	Sydney	1978–79
0 & 118	Botham IT	Old Trafford	1981
137 & 0	Boycott G	Oval	1981

AUSTRALIA			
0 & 153*	Murdoch WL	Oval	1880
0 & 143	Trott GHS	Lord's	1896
188 & 0	Hill C	Melbourne	1897–98
0 & 103*	Bradman DG	Melbourne	1932–33
100 & 0	Fingleton JHW	Brisbane	1936–37
138 & 0	Bradman DG	Trent Bridge	1948
0 & 141	Barnes SG	Lord's	1948
122 & 0	Harvey RN	Old Trafford	1953
0 & 114	Yallop GN	Old Trafford	1981

5.30 *Fastest Innings*

To 50

Mins	ENGLAND		
28	Brown JT (140)	Melbourne	1894–95
35	Hitch JW (51*)	Oval	1921
43	Jessop GL (104)	Oval	1902

Jessop's 50 came off 38 balls

Mins	AUSTRALIA		
36	Lyons JJ (55)	Lord's	1890
36	Ryder J (79)	Sydney	1928–29
40	Darling J (160)	Sydney	1897–98
40	Trumper VT (62)	Sheffield	1902

To 100

Mins	ENGLAND		
75	Jessop GL (104)	Oval	1902
95	Brown JT (140)	Melbourne	1894–95
104	Botham IT (118)	Old Trafford	1981

Jessop's 100 came off 76 balls and Botham's off 86.

Mins	AUSTRALIA		
91	Darling J (160)	Sydney	1897–98
94	Trumper VT (185*)	Sydney	1903–04
99	Bradman DG (334)	Headingley	1930
100	Bonnor GJ (128)	Sydney	1884–85
105	Bradman DG (254)	Lord's	1930

To 200

Mins	ENGLAND		
306	Paynter E (216*)	Trent Bridge	1938
314	Hammond WR (240)	Lord's	1938

Mins	AUSTRALIA		
214	Bradman DG (334)	Headingley	1930
223	McCabe SJ (232)	Trent Bridge	1938
234	Bradman DG (254)	Lord's	1930
241	Gregory SE (201)	Sydney	1894–95

At Perth in 1982–83 *TM Alderman chased and rugby-tackled a pitch-invader. In the tackle Alderman badly dislocated his shoulder and was unable to take any further part in the match or to play again that season.*

To 300

Mins	AUSTRALIA		
336	Bradman DG (334)	Headingley	1930

England's only triple-century was scored in 662 minutes, by L Hutton at The Oval in 1938.

5.31 *Slowest Innings*

To 50

Mins	ENGLAND		
357	Bailey TE (68)	Brisbane	1958–59
306	Tavaré CJ (78)	Old Trafford	1981
280	Boycott G (77)	Perth	1978–79

Tavaré's 50 came off 219 balls and Boycott's off 218.

Mins	AUSTRALIA		
275	Lawry WM (57)	Melbourne	1962–63

To 100

Mins	ENGLAND		
411	Randall DW (150)	Sydney	1978–79
396	Woolmer RA (149)	Oval	1975
378	Boycott G (107)	Trent Bridge	1977

Randall's 100 came off 353 balls and Woolmer's off 320.

Mins	AUSTRALIA		
373	Border AR (123*)	Old Trafford	1981
369	Hughes KJ (129)	Brisbane	1978–79
362	Wood GM (100)	Melbourne	1978–79

Border's 100 came off 311 balls, Hughes's off 297 and Wood's off 265.

To 200

Mins	ENGLAND		
518	Barrington KF (256)	Old Trafford	1964

Mins	AUSTRALIA		
608	Simpson RB (311)	Old Trafford	1964
570	Barnes SG (234)	Sydney	1946–47
535	Cowper RM (307)	Melbourne	1965–66

To 300

Mins	AUSTRALIA		
753	Simpson RB (311)	Old Trafford	1964

England's only triple-century was scored in 662 minutes, by L. Hutton at The Oval in 1938.

Slow Innings

Runs	Mins	Runs per Hour	ENGLAND		
3*	100	1.80	Murray JT (injured)	Sydney	1962–63
7	125	3.36	Miller G	Melbourne	1978–79
9	126	4.29	Tavaré CJ	Perth	1982–83
9	120	4.50	Newham W	Sydney	1887–88
10*	133	4.51	Evans TG	Adelaide	1946–47
38	262	8.70	Bailey TE	Headingley	1953
68	458	8.91	Bailey TE	Brisbane	1958–59
77	454	10.17	Boycott G	Perth	1978–79
53*	308	10.32	Graveney TW	Adelaide	1958–59
78	423	11.06	Tavaré CJ	Old Trafford	1981
89	466	11.46	Tavaré CJ	Perth	1982–83
150	582	15.46	Randall DW	Sydney	1978–79

Runs	Mins	Runs per Hour	AUSTRALIA		
28*	250	6.72	Burke JW	Brisbane	1958–59
31	264	7.05	Mackay KD	Lord's	1956

Runs	Mins	Runs per Hour	AUSTRALIA		
40	289	8.30	Collins HL	Old Trafford	1921
172	600	17.20	Wood GM	Trent Bridge	1985
234	642	21.87	Barnes SG	Sydney	1946–47

5.32 *Most Runs Before Dismissal* (2 or more innings)

ENGLAND			AUSTRALIA		
315 (216* & 99)	Paynter E	1938	313 (123*, 106* & 84)	Border AR	1981
313 (126* & 187)	Hobbs JB	1911–12	289 (201* & 88)	Ryder J	1924–25
296 (119* & 177)	Hammond WR	1928–29	284 (133* & 151)	Macartney CG	1926
271 (80* & 191)	Boycott G	1977	259 (185* & 74)	Trumper VT	1903–04

5.33 *Duck in Debut Innings*

ENGLAND			AUSTRALIA		
Mackinnon FA	Melbourne	1878–79	Gregory EJ	Melbourne	1876–77
Grace GF	Oval	1880	Hodges JH	Melbourne	1876–77
Barlow RG	Melbourne	1881–82	Spofforth FR	Melbourne	1876–77
Studd CT	Oval	1882	Pope RJ	Melbourne	1884–85
Bligh Hon.IFW	Melbourne	1882–83	Marr AP	Melbourne	1884–85
O'Brien TC	Old Trafford	1884	Robertson WR	Melbourne	1884–85
Gunn W	Sydney	1886–87	Trott GHS	Lord's	1888
MacGregor G	Lord's	1890	Gregory SE	Lord's	1890
Mold AW	Lord's	1893	Burn EJK	Lord's	1890
Lilley AFA	Lord's	1896	Darling J	Sydney	1894–95
Young HI	Headingley	1899	Kelly JJ	Lord's	1896
Warner PF	Sydney	1903–04	Trumper VT	Trent Bridge	1899
Denton D	Headingley	1905	Saunders JV	Sydney	1901–02
Brearley W	Old Trafford	1905	Cotter A	Sydney	1903–04
Carr DW	Oval	1909	Park RL	Melbourne	1920–21
Mead CP	Sydney	1911–12	Nagel LE	Sydney	1932–33
Douglas JWHT	Sydney	1911–12	Ward FA	Brisbane	1936–37
Russell CAG	Sydney	1920–21	Fleetwood-Smith LO'B	Melbourne	1936–37
Tyldesley GE	Trent Bridge	1921			

ENGLAND			AUSTRALIA		
Freeman AP	Sydney	1924–25	Moroney J	Brisbane	1950–51
Larwood H	Oval	1926	Hill JC	Trent Bridge	1953
Ames LEG	Sydney	1932–33	Simpson RB	Melbourne	1958–59
Mitchell TB	Brisbane	1932–33	Connolly AN	Melbourne	1965–66
Worthington TS	Brisbane	1936–37	Gleeson JW	Old Trafford	1968
Price WFF	Headingley	1938	Jenner TJ	Brisbane	1970–71
Ikin JT	Brisbane	1946–47	Thomson AL	Brisbane	1970–71
Bedser AV	Brisbane	1946–47	Massie RAL	Lord's	1972
Dollery HE	Lord's	1948	Dymock G	Melbourne	1974–75
Watkins AJ	Oval	1948	Hurst AG	Brisbane	1978–79
Close DB	Melbourne	1950–51	Carlson PH	Adelaide	1978–79
Tattersall R	Adelaide	1950–51	Laird BM	Perth	1979–80
Smith MJK	Edgbaston	1961	Whitney MR	Old Trafford	1981
Knight BR	Brisbane	1962–63	O'Donnell SP	Headingley	1985
Amiss DL	Old Trafford	1968	Holland RG	Lord's	1985
Fletcher KWR	Headingley	1968			
Gooch GA	Edgbaston	1975			
Roope GRJ	Oval	1975			
Emburey JE	Melbourne	1978–79			
Parker PWG	Oval	1981			
Pringle DR	Perth	1982–83			

5.34 *'Pairs of Spectacles'* (0 in each innings)

ENGLAND			AUSTRALIA		
†Grace GF	Oval	1880	McDonnell PS	Sydney	1882–83
Attewell W	Sydney	1891–92	Garrett TW	Sydney	1882–83
Peel R	Adelaide	1894–95	Evans E	Lord's	1886
Peel R	Sydney	1894–95	McShane PG	Sydney	1887–88
Peel R	Oval	1896	Bannerman AC	Lord's	1888
Arnold EG	Sydney	1903–04	Noble MA	Headingley	1899
Knight AE	Melbourne	1903–04	Gregory SE	Headingley	1899
Strudwick H	Trent Bridge	1921	McLeod CE	Sydney	1901–02
Ikin JT	Sydney	1946–47	Darling J	Sheffield	1902
Bedser AV	Oval	1948	Kelly JJ	Sheffield	1902
Warr JJ	Adelaide	1950–51	Trumble H	Sydney	1903–04
Wardle JH	Lord's	1956	Trumper VT	Melbourne	1907–08

ENGLAND			AUSTRALIA		
Trueman FS	Adelaide	1958–59	Saunders JV	Sydney	1907–08
Bailey TE	Melbourne	1958–59	Grimmett CV	Trent Bridge	1930
†Amiss DL	Old Trafford	1968	Fingleton JHW	Adelaide	1932–33
Amiss DL	Adelaide	1974–75	Richardson VY	Sydney	1932–33
Underwood DL	Adelaide	1974–75	Badcock CL	Lord's	1938
Arnold GG	Adelaide	1974–75	Johnson IW	Melbourne	1946–47
†Gooch GA	Edgbaston	1975	†Moroney J	Brisbane	1950–51
Woolmer RA	Trent Bridge	1981	Iverson JB	Melbourne	1950–51
Botham IT	Lord's	1981	Maddocks LV	Headingley	1956
Hemmings EE	Adelaide	1982–83	Harvey RN	Old Trafford	1956
			Mackay KD	Old Trafford	1956
			Benaud R	Headingley	1961
			McKenzie GD	Old Trafford	1968
			Gleeson JW	Sydney	1970–71
			Edwards R	Headingley	1972
			†Dymock G	Melbourne	1974–75
			Marsh RW	Trent Bridge	1977
			Thomson JR	Headingley	1977
			†Hurst AG	Brisbane	1978–79
			Hurst AG	Sydney	1978–79
			†Whitney MR	Old Trafford	1981
			Holland RG	Edgbaston	1985

†Indicates EvA Test debut

5.35 *Three or More Consecutive Ducks*

ENGLAND			AUSTRALIA		
4	Peel R	1894–95	3	McShane PG	1886–87 to 1887–88
3	Arnold EG	1903–04	3	Trumper VT	1907–08
3	Bedser AV	1948 to 1950–51	3	Massie RAL	1972
3	Warr JJ	1950–51	3	Thomson JR	1977
3	Trueman FS	1958–59			
3	Amiss DL	1974–75			
3	Arnold GG	1974–75			

5.36 *Most Ducks in a Career*

ENGLAND				AUSTRALIA			
0s	**Inns**	**Percentage**		**0s**	**Inns**	**Percentage**	
8	33	24.24	Peel R	11	92	11.96	Gregory SE
8	43	18.60	Underwood DL	8	76	10.53	Hill C
7	21	33.33	Amiss DL	7	35	20.00	McKenzie GD
7	51	13.73	Woolley FE	7	74	9.46	Trumper VT
6	53	11.32	Evans TG	6	41	14.63	Benaud R
6	29	20.69	Snow JA	6	63	9.52	Bradman DG
				6	34	17.65	Grimmett CV
				6	68	8.82	Harvey RN
				6	68	8.82	Marsh RW

5.37 *No Ducks or Long Sequence Without One*

Inns without a 0				
57	Edrich JH	Eng	1964–75	Whole career
46	Boycott G	Eng	1964–79	First 46 innings
42	Macartney CG	Aus	1907–26	Whole career
37	Sutcliffe H	Eng	1926–34	Last 37 innings
36	Barrington KF	Eng	1961–68	First 36 innings

5.38 *Run Out Most Frequently*

Run Out	Inns	Percentage		
5	69	7.25	Rhodes W	Eng
5	76	6.58	Hill C	Aus
4	57	7.02	Edrich JH	Eng
4	49	8.16	Bardsley W	Aus
4	92	4.35	Gregory SE	Aus
4	42	9.52	Trott GHS	Aus

WM Lawry (Aus) was run out 3 times in 6 innings, all in 1964.
PA McAlister (Aus) was run out in each innings at Melbourne in 1907–08, as was J Ryder (Aus) at Sydney in 1920–21.
There were 6 run-outs at Sydney in 1920–21, 5 suffered by Australia and 1 by England.

Shrewsbury, for years England's finest professional batsman

Clem Hill, brilliant young Australian left-hander and later captain

Hutton and Compton, pillars of English post-war batting

Stan McCabe, classic Australian hero

5.39 *Batsmen Retired Hurt or Ill*

ENGLAND

49*	Foster RE	Melbourne	1903–04	Ill.
58*	Sutcliffe H	Trent Bridge	1930	Damaged hand.
33*	Ames LEG	Oval	1934	Lumbago.
122*	Hutton L	Sydney	1946–47	Tonsillitis.

AUSTRALIA

165*	Bannerman C	Melbourne	1876–77	Split finger.
0*	Blackham JM	Lord's	1884	Damaged finger.
13*	Trumper VT	Trent Bridge	1905	Strained back.
5*	Ponsford WH	Sydney	1928–29	Broken hand.
41*	Oldfield WAS	Adelaide	1932–33	Fractured skull.
1*	Barnes SG	Old Trafford	1948	Collapsed after fielding injury.
24*	O'Neill NC	Trent Bridge	1964	Damaged hand.
0*	Jarman BN	Lord's	1968	Hit on finger previously broken.
6*	Lawry WM	Edgbaston	1968	Broken finger.
6*	McKenzie GD	Sydney	1970–71	Broken nose.
4*	Dyson J	Brisbane	1982–83	Bruised shoulder.

In addition to the above, 13 batsmen retired hurt or ill and resumed their innings, 9 for England and 4 for Australia. Among these the batsman who added most runs after resuming was DCS Compton (Eng), who retired when 4* after deflecting a ball onto his head and returned to score 145* at Old Trafford in 1948.

5.40 *Most Ducks*

In a Match

11	England (3)	v	Australia (8)	Old Trafford	1888
11	Australia (4)	v	England (7)	Melbourne	1903–04

In a Series

37	Australia (26)	v	England (11)	1978–79
34	Australia (16)	v	England (18)	1903–04

There were 27 ducks, 9 by England and 18 by Australia, in the 3-match series of 1888.

5.41 *Fewest Double Figures in an Innings*

ENGLAND					AUSTRALIA				
	Total	**HS**				**Total**	**HS**		
1	45	17	Sydney	1886–87	1	42	10	Sydney	1887–88
1	52	30	Oval	1948	1	44	16	Oval	1896
					1	36	18	Edgbaston	1902

No batsman reached double figures in Australia's total of 35–8 (highest score 8) at Old Trafford in 1953.

5.42 *Most Double Figures in an Innings*

ENGLAND					AUSTRALIA				
	Total	**Lowest**				**Total**	**Lowest**		
11	475	11	Melbourne	1894–95	10	267	0	Melbourne	1894–95
11	636	11	Sydney	1928–29	10	452	2	Sydney	1924–25
10	437	4	Sydney	1894–95	10	491	0	Old Trafford	1934
10	282–9	0	Melbourne	1907–08	10	509	0	Trent Bridge	1948
10	356	0	Brisbane	1932–33	10	316	0	Melbourne	1962–63
10	533	5	Headingley	1985	10	481	0	Perth	1974–75
					10	241	1	Oval	1985

There were 36 double-figure scores at Melbourne in 1907–08, 17 by Australia and 19 by England.

5.43 *Most 50s in an Innings*

ENGLAND				AUSTRALIA			
	Total				**Total**		
7	627–9d	Old Trafford	1934	6	581	Sydney	1920–21
6	483	Oval	1893	6	695	Oval	1930
6	558	Melbourne	1965–66				

5.44 *Most 50s in a Match*

14	England (8)	v	Australia (6)	Headingley	1948
14	Australia (8)	v	England (6)	Brisbane	1962–63
13	Australia (6)	v	England (7)	Adelaide	1920–21
13	Australia (7)	v	England (6)	Melbourne	1965–66

5.45 *Most 50s in a Series*

49	Australia (27)	v	England (22)	1920–21
45	Australia (21)	v	England (24)	1970–71
41	Australia (20)	v	England (21)	1924–25
40	Australia (18)	v	England (22)	1928–29

5.46 *100 Before Lunch*

First Day

					Mins
103*	Trumper VT (104)	Aus	Old Trafford	1902	113
112*	Macartney CG (151)	Aus	Headingley	1926	116
105*	Bradman DG (334)	Aus	Headingley	1930	112

The most runs for England before lunch on the first day is 98 by CJ Barnett (126) at Trent Bridge in 1938. He reached three figures off the first ball after lunch.

Other Days

							Mins
3rd	113	(41*–154*)	Ranjitsinhji KS (154*)	Eng	Old Trafford	1896	130
2nd	109	(19*–128*)	Mead CP (182*)	Eng	Oval	1921	147

At Old Trafford in 1934 *GOB Allen's first over of the match, in Australia's first innings, was extended by 4 no-balls and 3 off-side wides.*

5.47 *100 in Other Sessions*

Lunch to Tea

						Day
115	(105*–220*)	Bradman DG (334)	Aus	Headingley	1930	1st
107	(43*–150*)	Bradman DG (244)	Aus	Oval	1934	1st
127	(105*–232)	McCabe SJ (232)	Aus	Trent Bridge	1938	3rd

Tea to Close of Play

113	(15*–128)	Bonnor GJ (128)	Aus	Sydney	1884–85	2nd
112	(7*–119*)	Trumper VT (185*)	Aus	Sydney	1903–04	4th
101	(54*–155*)	Bradman DG (254)	Aus	Lord's	1930	2nd
102	(169*–271*)	Bradman DG (304)	Aus	Headingley	1934	2nd
100	(3*–103*)	Walters KD (103)	Aus	Perth	1974–75	2nd
106	(39*–145*)	Botham IT (149*)	Eng	Headingley	1981	4th

5.48 *Most Consecutive 50s*

ENGLAND		
5 (79, 73, 63, 53, 101)	May PBH	1954–55 to 1956
5 (88, 64, 62, 65, 164)	Edrich JH	1968
AUSTRALIA		
4 (96, 58, 81, 188)	Hill C	1897–98
4 (88, 55, 112, 232)	McCabe SJ	1936–37 to 1938
4 (212, 169, 51, 144*)	Bradman DG	1936–37 to 1938
4 (94, 166, 88, 78)	Lawry WM	1964 to 1965–66

Soon after the start of the second Test of 1924–25 *at Melbourne, it was discovered that inferior-quality balls had been supplied. The captains agreed to use them throughout both first innings of the match, England's bowlers getting through eight balls by the time Australia's total reached 200, and Australia's bowlers later getting through seven.*

5.49 *Long Periods Without Scoring*

Before Breaking Duck

Mins				
97	Evans TG (10*)	Eng	Adelaide	1946–47
74	Murray JT (3*)	Eng	Sydney	1962–63
70	Murdoch WL (17)	Aus	Sydney	1882–83
64	Tavaré CJ (9)	Eng	Perth	1982–83

TG Evans took 61 balls to get off the mark.
JT Murray batted with the handicap of a sprained shoulder.

Without Adding to Score

Mins	On				
90	66*	Tavaré CJ (89)	Eng	Perth	1982–83
67	24*	Scotton WH (34)	Eng	Oval	1886
63	10*	Jardine DR (24)	Eng	Brisbane	1932–33
63	13*	Brearley JM (48)	Eng	Edgbaston	1981
60	after reaching century	Gower DI (114)	Eng	Adelaide	1982–83
58	14*	Collins HL (24)	Aus	Lord's	1926

5.50 *Highest Partnerships for Each Wicket*

ENGLAND					Mins
1st	323	Hobbs JB (178) & Rhodes W (179)	Melbourne	1911–12	268
	283	Hobbs JB (154) & Sutcliffe H (176)	Melbourne	1924–25	289
	234	Boycott G (84) & Barber RW (185)	Sydney	1965–66	242
2nd	382	Hutton L (364) & Leyland M (187)	Oval	1938	381
	351	Gooch GA (196) & Gower DI (157)	Oval	1985	337
	331	Robinson RT (148) & Gower DI (215)	Edgbaston	1985	343
3rd	262	Hammond WR (177) & Jardine DR (98)	Adelaide	1928–29	350
	246	Dexter ER (174) & Barrington KF (256)	Old Trafford	1964	325
	210	Ward A (93) & Brown JT (140)	Melbourne	1894–95	145

ENGLAND					Mins
4th	222	Hammond WR (240) & Paynter E (99)	Lord's	1938	182
	192	Denness MH (188) & Fletcher KWR (146)	Melbourne	1974–75	318
	187	May PBH (101) & Washbrook C (98)	Headingley	1956	287
5th	206	Paynter E (216*) & Compton DCS (102)	Trent Bridge	1938	138
	192	Foster RE (287) & Braund LC (102)	Sydney	1903–04	171
	191	Hendren EH (132) & Leyland M (153)	Old Trafford	1934	180
6th	215	Hutton L (364) & Hardstaff J jr (169*)	Oval	1938	206
	215	Boycott G (107) & Knott APE (135)	Trent Bridge	1977	248
	186	Hammond WR (240) & Ames LEG (83)	Lord's	1938	150
7th	143	Woolley FE (133*) & Vine J (36)	Sydney	1911–12	147
	142	Sharp J (105) & Hutchings KL (59)	Oval	1909	105
	135	Miller G (64) & Taylor RW (97)	Adelaide	1978–79	228
8th	124	Hendren EH (169) & Larwood H (70)	Brisbane†	1928–29	118
	121	Compton DCS (145*) & Bedser AV (37)	Old Trafford	1948	150
	117	Botham IT (149*) & Dilley GR (56)	Headingley	1981	80
9th	151	Scotton WH (90) & Read WW (117)	Oval	1884	130
	128	Woolley FE (123) & Freeman AP (50*)	Sydney	1924–25	82
	115	Foster RE (287) & Relf AE (31)	Sydney	1903–04	84
10th	130	Foster RE (287) & Rhodes W (40*)	Sydney	1903–04	66
	98	Briggs J (121) & Hunter J (39*)	Melbourne	1884–85	75
	81*	Lockwood WH (52*) & Rhodes W (38*)	Edgbaston	1902	67

†Exhibition Ground

AUSTRALIA					Mins
1st	244	Simpson RB (225) & Lawry WM (119)	Adelaide	1965–66	255
	201	Lawry WM (106) & Simpson RB (311)	Old Trafford	1964	281
	180	Bardsley W (130) & Gregory SE (74)	Oval	1909	135
2nd	451	Ponsford WH (266) & Bradman DG (244)	Oval	1934	316
	301	Morris AR (182) & Bradman DG (173*)	Headingley	1948	217
	277	McCosker RB (127) & Chappell IM (192)	Oval	1975	358
3rd	276	Bradman DG (187) & Hassett AL (128)	Brisbane	1946–47	278
	249	Bradman DG (169) & McCabe SJ (112)	Melbourne	1936–37	163
	229	Bradman DG (334) & Kippax AF (77)	Headingley	1930	163

AUSTRALIA					Mins
4th	388	Ponsford WH (181) & Bradman DG (304)	Headingley	1934	341
	243	Bradman DG (232) & Jackson AA (73)	Oval	1930	270
	221	Trott GHS (143) & Gregory SE (103)	Lord's	1896	160
5th	405	Barnes SG (234) & Bradman DG (234)	Sydney	1946–47	393
	219	Simpson RB (311) & Booth BC (98)	Old Trafford	1964	213
	216	Border AR (196) & Ritchie GM (94)	Lord's	1985	270
6th	346	Fingleton JHW (136) & Bradman DG (270)	Melbourne	1936–37	364
	219	Redpath IR (171) & Chappell GS (108)	Perth	1970–71	272
	187	Kelleway C (78) & Armstrong WW (158)	Sydney	1920–21	150
7th	165	Hill C (188) & Trumble H (46)	Melbourne	1897–98	152
	150	Miller KR (145*) & Johnson IW (77)	Sydney	1950–51	160
	134	Ryder J (201*) & Andrews TJE (72)	Adelaide	1924–25	112
8th	243	Hartigan RJ (116) & Hill C (160)	Adelaide	1907–08	245
	173	Pellew CE (116) & Gregory JM (100)	Melbourne	1920–21	125
	154	Bonnor GJ (128) & Jones SP (40)	Sydney	1884–85	105
	154	Tallon D (92) & Lindwall RR (100)	Melbourne	1946–47	88
9th	154	Gregory SE (201) & Blackham JM (74)	Sydney	1894–95	73
	108	Ryder J (201*) & Oldfield WAS (47)	Adelaide	1924–25	118
	104	Marsh RW (91) & Gleeson JW (30)	Old Trafford	1972	82
10th	127	Taylor JM (108) & Mailey AA (46*)	Sydney	1924–25	79
	120	Duff RA (104) & Armstrong WW (45*)	Melbourne	1901–02	148
	88	Murdoch WL (153*) & Moule WH (34)	Oval	1880	90

5.51 *Players Who Have Participated in Most 100 Partnerships*

ENGLAND	Total	1st	2nd	3rd	4th	5th	6th	7th	8th	9th	10th	Highest
Hobbs JB	22	16	4	1	–	–	–	1	–	–	–	323
Sutcliffe H	21	15	4	1	–	–	1	–	–	–	–	283
Boycott G	17	8	2	2	3	–	2	–	–	–	–	234
Edrich JH	17	5	5	4	2	1	–	–	–	–	–	178
Hutton L	15	6	5	3	–	–	1	–	–	–	–	382
Hammond WR	12	–	3	4	3	1	1	–	–	–	–	262
Cowdrey MC	11	2	1	2	3	2	1	–	–	–	–	182
Gower DI	11	–	4	4	3	–	–	–	–	–	–	351

AUSTRALIA	Total	1st	2nd	3rd	4th	5th	6th	7th	8th	9th	10th	Highest
Bradman DG	21	–	8	6	2	4	1	–	–	–	–	451
Chappell GS	14	–	1	5	5	2	1	–	–	–	–	220
Chappell IM	14	–	11	2	–	1	–	–	–	–	–	277
Hill C	12	–	6	1	2	1	–	1	1	–	–	243
Harvey RN	12	–	3	4	4	1	–	–	–	–	–	202
Morris AR	11	4	3	4	–	–	–	–	–	–	–	301
Woodfull WM	11	4	6	–	1	–	–	–	–	–	–	235
Lawry WM	10	5	1	2	1	1	–	–	–	–	–	244

5.52 *Centuries by Brothers in Same Test*

	6s	4s	Mins				
118	–	20	330	Chappell IM	Aus	Oval	1972
113	–	17	243	Chappell GS			

The Chappell brothers added 201 in 243 minutes for the 3rd wicket.

5.53 *Unusual Dismissals*

No batsman on either side has been out handled the ball, hit the ball twice or obstructed the field.

The following dismissals were remarkable:

At The Oval in 1880 GJ Bonnor (Aus) was caught at long-on by GF Grace off a steepling hit. By the time the catch was made the batsmen had turned for their third run.

At The Oval in 1882 SP Jones (Aus) (6) was run out by WG Grace though the batsman had merely left his crease to do some 'gardening'.

At The Oval in 1884 the Hon. A Lyttelton, England's wicketkeeper, came on to bowl lobs and took 4–19 off 12 four-ball overs.

At The Oval in 1905 WW Armstrong (Aus) was caught by AO Jones substituting for England's wicketkeeper AFA Lilley.

At Trent Bridge in 1921 GE Tyldesley (Eng) was struck on the head by a bouncer from JM Gregory which then fell on his wicket.

At Sydney in 1936–37 M Leyland became the first batsman to be given out under the 'new' lbw ruling extended to include a ball pitching on the off side of the wicket.

5.54 *Fewest Innings to 1000 and 2000 Runs*

1000 Runs

Inns			
13	Bradman DG	Aus	1928–29 to 1930
14	Hammond WR	Eng	1928–29 to 1930
15	Sutcliffe H	Eng	1924–25 to 1926
16	Morris AR	Aus	1946–47 to 1948
17	Hutton L	Eng	1938 to 1948
20	Edrich JH	Eng	1964 to 1968
21	Barrington KF	Eng	1961 to 1964
21	Compton DCS	Eng	1938 to 1948
21	Hobbs JB	Eng	1907–08 to 1911–12
21	Stackpole KR	Aus	1965–66 to 1972
21	Woodfull WM	Aus	1926 to 1930

2000 Runs

Inns			
29	Bradman DG	Aus	1928–29 to 1934
31	Sutcliffe H	Eng	1924–25 to 1932–33
34	Hutton L	Eng	1938 to 1953
36	Barrington KF	Eng	1961 to 1968
37	Morris AR	Aus	1946–47 to 1954–55
38	Hammond WR	Eng	1928–29 to 1936–37
40	Hobbs JB	Eng	1907–08 to 1924–25

5.55 *Youngest Players to 1000 and 2000 Runs*

1000 Runs

	Years	Days	Inns			
England	25	229	31	Gower DI	Perth	1982–83
Australia	21	318	13	Bradman DG	Headingley	1930

2000 Runs

	Years	Days	Inns			
England	28	150	48	Gower DI	Oval	1985
Australia	25	328	29	Bradman DG	Headingley	1934

5.56 *Low-Order Batsmen (9, 10, 11) Top-Scoring* (Completed Totals Only)

ENGLAND

Number	Score		Total		
9	52	Absolom CA	113	Melbourne	1878–79
9	55	Bates W	294	Melbourne	1882–83
10	117	Read WW	346	Oval	1884
9	17	Lohmann GA	45	Sydney	1886–87
9	37	Flowers W	151	Sydney	1886–87
10	17	Briggs J	53	Lord's	1888
9	33	Tate MW	146	Sydney	1924–25
10	76	Macaulay GG	294	Headingley	1926
9	63	Laker JC	165	Trent Bridge	1948
9	35	Wardle JH	154	Sydney	1954–55
9	30	Underwood DL	166	Brisbane	1974–75

AUSTRALIA

Number	Score		Total		
10	51*	Garrett TW	181	Sydney	1884–85
11	50	Spofforth FR	163	Melbourne	1884–85
9	10	Garrett TW	42	Sydney	1887–88
9	25*	Blackham JM	82	Sydney	1887–88
9	20*	Ferris JJ	60	Lord's	1888
9	22	Lyons JJ	81	Old Trafford	1888
11	16	McKibbin TR	44	Oval	1896
10	104	Duff RA	353	Melbourne	1901–02
9	160	Hill C	506	Adelaide	1907–08
9	23	Oldfield WAS	125	Oval	1926

AUSTRALIA

Number	Score		Total		
9	62	Lindwall RR	275	Oval	1953
9	36	Hogg RM	116	Brisbane	1978–79

Several of the above, notably Read, Lyons, Duff and Hill, were recognised batsmen going in much lower than their usual position. They have been included for the sake of completeness.

In addition to the above, batsmen at No. 8 have top-scored on 25 further occasions, 12 for England and 13 for Australia.

5.57 *High Averages by Numbers 10 and 11*

ENGLAND	M	I	NO	Runs	HS	Av	
Rhodes W	5	7	6	67	38*	67.00	1902
Freeman AP	2	4	2	80	50*	40.00	1924–25
Underwood DL	4	4	4	69	45*	–	1968
AUSTRALIA	**M**	**I**	**NO**	**Runs**	**HS**	**Av**	
Toshack ERH	4	4	3	51	20*	51.00	1948
Johnson IW	4	6	4	116	41*	58.00	1954–55
Lillee DK	4	4	2	115	73*	57.50	1975

5.58 *Most Sixes in an Innings*

ENGLAND			AUSTRALIA		
6 Botham IT (118)	Old Trafford	1981	5 Loxton SJE (93)	Headingley	1948
3 Chapman APF (121)	Lord's	1930	4 Marsh RW (91)	Old Trafford	1972
3 Wyatt RES (78)	Adelaide	1932–33	3 O'Reilly WJ (37*)	Sydney	1936–37
3 Parks JM (52)	Brisbane	1965–66	3 Lawry WM (106)	Old Trafford	1964
			3 Lillee DK (73*)	Lord's	1975

ENGLAND	AUSTRALIA		
	3 Hughes KJ (117)	Lord's	1980
	3 Hughes KJ (137)	Sydney	1982–83

J Darling (73) at Old Trafford in 1905 made 5 hits clean out of the playing area (4 runs each time) and at the same ground in 1902 made 4 such hits, 2 of them right out of the ground (6 runs) in his innings of 51.
GJ Bonnor (85) at Melbourne in 1882–83 hit 4 fives, the equivalent of 4 sixes under the modern scoring system.

5.59 *Most Runs off an Over*

22 IT Botham (19, with 2 sixes and 1 four) and CJ Tavaré (3) off DK Lillee (Old Trafford 1981). The new ball had just been taken. Botham's score progressed from 35 to 54. He went on to 118.

21 VY Richardson (4 4 4 4 2 3 from the first 6 balls of an 8-ball over from JWHT Douglas, Melbourne 1924–25). Richardson's score progressed from 109 to 130. He was out for 138.

20 DW Hookes (fours off the third, fourth, fifth, sixth and seventh balls of an 8-ball over from AW Greig, Centenary Test, Melbourne, 1976–77). Hookes progressed from 36 to 56, at which score he was dismissed.

5.60 *Odd Incidents While Batting*

At The Oval in 1896 FA Iredale was run out by a long throw from KS Ranjitsinhji while attempting a fifth run for the stroke.

At Sydney in the first Test of 1897–98 CE McLeod, who was partially deaf, was run out by England wicketkeeper W Storer after leaving his crease when bowled by T Richardson, not having heard the umpire's call of no-ball.

At Melbourne in the fourth Test of 1897–98 AC MacLaren (Eng) complained that a fly had hit him in the eye just as H Trumble bowled to him. He was caught at short leg off an indeterminate stroke.

At Sheffield in 1902 the smoke from factory chimneys hampered a number of batsmen during England's first innings.

At Headingley in 1921 the Hon. LH Tennyson damaged his left hand while fielding but scored 63 and 36 batting one-handed for England. He hit 10 fours in his first innings, which lasted 70 minutes.

In the second Test of 1924–25, at Melbourne, VY Richardson (138) was run out by APF Chapman while attempting a fourth run on an overthrow.

At Sydney in 1932–33 H Sutcliffe (Eng) when 43 played a ball from WJ O'Reilly onto his wicket without disturbing the bails, and went on to 194, his highest Test score. The same kind of good fortune favoured L Hutton (Eng) **at Trent Bridge in 1938** when facing EL McCormick in the third over of the match. He went on to score 100.

At Trent Bridge in 1948 opening batsman SG Barnes took a souvenir stump and ran from the field prematurely. It transpired that Australia still needed a further run for victory – which was soon gained, without further loss, by 8 wickets.

At Brisbane in 1950–51 AJW McIntyre was run out while going for a fourth run off a hook shot during England's position of crisis in the second innings.

At The Oval in 1953 Australian captain AL Hassett pulled away from the wicket as FS Trueman bowled after being distracted by a swallow which swooped across the pitch. Trueman released the ball, which missed the stumps.

At Old Trafford in 1956, when Australia were facing defeat against the off-spin of JC Laker (19-90 in the match), their captain, IW Johnson, appealed unsuccessfully for a suspension of play because sawdust from the damp turf was blowing into his eyes while he batted.

At Trent Bridge in 1964 Australia's wicketkeeper ATW Grout declined to run out FJ Titmus after the batsman was impeded by NJN Hawke the bowler.

At The Oval in 1964 England's ER Dexter's bat split clean in two as he played a stroke off NJN Hawke, one half landing near cover point.

At Adelaide in 1965–66 England batsman MC Cowdrey was run out after mistaking a cry from the opposing wicketkeeper as a call from his own batting partner.

At Adelaide in 1978–79 Australian opening batsman WM Darling collapsed after being hit by a ball from fast bowler RGD Willis, and it was thought that his life was saved by fieldsman JE Emburey, who removed Darling's chewing-gum, stopped him from swallowing his tongue, and then administered prompt resuscitation.

At Perth in 1979–80 DK Lillee (Aus) batted for a few minutes on the second day with a metal (aluminium) bat, scoring 3 runs with it before the England captain JM Brearley objected to it and the umpires ordered Lillee to revert to a wooden bat.

SECTION 6
The Bowlers

ABOVE LEFT *S F Barnes: five wickets 12 times*
ABOVE CENTRE *C T B Turner: 101 wickets in only 17 Tests*
ABOVE RIGHT *Hugh Trumble: 141 wickets*

RIGHT *Larwood, England's destroyer in 1932–33*
BELOW *Lillee and Thomson, Australia's 'Terror Twins' of the mid-1970s*

6.1 *Leading Bowlers by Average* (Qualification 10 wickets)

ENGLAND	M	Balls	Mdns	Runs	Wkts	Av	Best	5wi	10wm
Martin F	1	287	21	102	12	8.50	6–50	2	1
Ellison RM	2	455	20	185	17	10.88	6–77	2	1
Lohmann GA	15	3301	326	1002	77	13.01	8–35	5	3
Barnes W	21	2289	271	793	51	15.55	6–28	3	–
Bates W	15	2364	282	821	50	16.42	7–28	4	1
Peel R	20	5216	444	1715	102	16.81	7–31	6	2
Laker JC	15	4010	203	1444	79	18.28	10–53	5	2
Morley F	4	972	124	296	16	18.50	5–56	1	–
Briggs J	31	4941	334	1993	97	20.55	6–45	7	3
Lockwood WH	12	1970	100	884	43	20.56	7–71	5	1
Ulyett G	23	2527	286	992	48	20.67	7–36	1	–
Steel AG	13	1364	108	605	29	20.86	3–27	–	–
Brearley W	3	669	23	355	17	20.88	5–110	1	–
Appleyard R	5	812	32	273	13	21.00	3–13	–	–
Flowers W	8	858	92	296	14	21.14	5–46	1	–
Blythe C	9	2085	99	877	41	21.39	6–44	3	1
Gunn JR	6	997	54	387	18	21.50	5–76	1	–
Barnes SF	20	5749	262	2288	106	21.58	7–60	12	1
Foster FR	8	1894	76	742	34	21.82	6–91	3	–
Young HI	2	556	38	262	12	21.83	4–30	–	–
Miller G	14	2713	113	856	39	21.95	5–44	1	–
Peate E	9	2096	250	682	31	22.00	6–85	2	–
Hearne JT	11	2936	209	1070	48	22.29	6–41	4	1
Barlow RG	17	2456	325	767	34	22.56	7–40	3	–
Attewell W	10	2850	326	626	27	23.19	4–42	–	–
Shaw A	7	1099	155	285	12	23.75	5–38	1	–
Brown FR	6	1184	23	524	22	23.82	5–49	1	–
Rhodes W	41	5796	234	2616	109	24.00	8–68	6	1
Bosanquet BJT	7	970	10	604	25	24.16	8–107	2	–
Dilley GR	5	906	29	418	17	24.59	4–24	–	–

AUSTRALIA	M	Balls	Mdns	Runs	Wkts	Av	Best	5wi	10wm
Horan TP	15	373	45	143	11	13.00	6–40	1	–
Ferris JJ	8	2030	224	684	48	14.25	5–26	4	–
Iverson JB	5	1108	29	320	21	15.24	6–27	1	–
Kendall T	2	563	56	215	14	15.36	7–55	1	–

AUSTRALIA	M	Balls	Mdns	Runs	Wkts	Av	Best	5wi	10wm
Turner CTB	17	5179	457	1670	101	16.53	7–43	11	2
Hogg RM	11	2629	94	952	56	17.00	6–74	5	2
Meckiff I	4	898	24	292	17	17.18	6–38	1	–
Massie RAL	4	1195	58	409	23	17.78	8–53	2	1
Spofforth FR	18	4185	416	1731	94	18.41	7–44	7	4
Boyle HF	12	1743	175	641	32	20.03	6–42	1	–
Trumble H	31	7895	448	2945	141	20.89	8–65	9	3
Lillee DK	29	8516	361	3507	167	21.00	7–89	11	4
Palmer GE	17	4417	452	1678	78	21.51	7–65	6	2
Archer RG	12	2445	126	761	35	21.74	5–53	1	–
Trumble JW	7	600	59	222	10	22.20	3–29	–	–
Miller KR	29	5717	225	1949	87	22.40	7–60	3	1
Lindwall RR	29	6728	216	2559	114	22.45	7–63	6	–
Alderman TM	7	2208	91	977	43	22.72	6–135	4	–
Hurst AG	6	1634	44	577	25	23.08	5–28	1	–
Davidson AK	25	5993	221	1996	84	23.76	6–64	5	–
Midwinter WE	8	949	104	333	14	23.79	5–78	1	–
Thomson JR	21	4957	166	2418	100	24.18	6–46	5	–
Johnston WA	17	5263	224	1818	75	24.24	5–35	3	–
Hordern HV	5	1665	42	780	32	24.38	7–90	4	2
Higgs JD	6	1580	47	471	19	24.79	5–148	1	–
Noble MA	39	6895	353	2860	115	24.87	7–17	9	2
Saunders JV	12	3268	108	1620	64	25.31	5–28	5	–
O'Reilly WJ	19	7864	439	2587	102	25.36	7–54	8	3
Pascoe LS	6	1599	58	736	29	25.38	5–59	1	–
Laver F	15	2361	121	964	37	26.05	8–31	2	–

6.2 *Most Wickets in an Innings*

ENGLAND	O	M	R	W	Ground	Year
Laker JC	51.2	23	53	10	Old Trafford	1956
Laker JC	16.4	4	37	9	Old Trafford	1956
Lohmann GA	25	12	35	8	Sydney	1886–87
Verity H	22.3	8	43	8	Lord's	1934
Willis RGD	15.1	3	43	8	Headingley	1981
Lohmann GA	43.2	18	58	8	Sydney	1891–92
Rhodes W	15	0	68	8	Melbourne	1903–04

ENGLAND	O	M	R	W	Ground	Year
Braund LC	28.5	6	81	8	Melbourne	1903–04
Richardson T	36.1	7	94	8	Sydney	1897–98
Bosanquet BJT	32.4	2	107	8	Trent Bridge	1905
White JC	64.5	21	126	8	Adelaide	1928–29
Rhodes W	11	3	17	7	Edgbaston	1902
Tyson FH	12.3	1	27	7	Melbourne	1954–55
Bates W	26.2	14	28	7	Melbourne	1882–83
Peel R	26.2	17	31	7	Old Trafford	1888
Lohmann GA	30.2	17	36	7	Oval	1886
Ulyett G	39.1	23	36	7	Lord's	1884
Barlow RG	34.2	20	40	7	Sydney	1882–83
Snow JA	17.5	5	40	7	Sydney	1970–71
Barlow RG	52	34	44	7	Old Trafford	1886
Bedser AV	17.2	7	44	7	Trent Bridge	1953
Underwood DL	31.3	19	50	7	Oval	1968
Bedser AV	38.3	16	55	7	Trent Bridge	1953
Rhodes W	15.2	3	56	7	Melbourne	1903–04
Statham JB	28	6	57	7	Melbourne	1958–59
Barnes SF	22.4	6	60	7	Sydney	1907–08
Verity H	36	15	61	7	Lord's	1934
Emmett T	59	31	68	7	Melbourne	1878–79
Lockwood WH	40.3	17	71	7	Oval	1899
Bates W	33	14	74	7	Melbourne	1882–83
Willis RGD	30.1	7	78	7	Lord's	1977
Titmus FJ	37	14	79	7	Sydney	1962–63
Wright DVP	29	4	105	7	Sydney	1946–47
Underwood DL	29	3	113	7	Adelaide	1974–75
Barnes SF	64	17	121	7	Melbourne	1901–02
Richardson T	68	23	168	7	Old Trafford	1896

AUSTRALIA	O	M	R	W	Ground	Year
Mailey AA	47	8	121	9	Melbourne	1920–21
Laver F	18.2	7	31	8	Old Trafford	1909
†Trott AE	27	10	43	8	Adelaide	1894–95
†Massie RAL	27.2	9	53	8	Lord's	1972
Trumble H	31	13	65	8	Oval	1902
†Massie RAL	32.5	7	84	8	Lord's	1972
McDermott CJ	36	3	141	8	Old Trafford	1985
Walker MHN	42.2	7	143	8	Melbourne	1974–75
Noble MA	7.4	2	17	7	Melbourne	1901–02

AUSTRALIA	O	M	R	W	Ground	Year
Hazlitt GR	21.4	8	25	7	Oval	1912
Trumble H	6.5	0	28	7	Melbourne	1903–04
Turner CTB	38	23	43	7	Sydney	1887–88
Spofforth FR	28	15	44	7	Oval	1882
Spofforth FR	41.1	23	44	7	Sydney	1882–83
Spofforth FR	36.3	18	46	7	Oval	1882
O'Reilly WJ	41.4	24	54	7	Trent Bridge	1934
†Kendall T	33.1	12	55	7	Melbourne	1876–77
Macartney CG	25.3	6	58	7	Headingley	1909
†Miller KR	22	4	60	7	Brisbane	1946–47
Spofforth FR	35	16	62	7	Melbourne	1878–79
Lindwall RR	22	3	63	7	Sydney	1946–47
Laver F	31.3	14	64	7	Trent Bridge	1905
Palmer GE	52.2	25	65	7	Melbourne	1882–83
Palmer GE	58	36	68	7	Sydney	1881–82
Gregory JM	20	1	69	7	Melbourne	1920–21
Lawson GF	43.1	14	81	7	Lord's	1981
Jones E	36.1	11	88	7	Lord's	1899
Lillee DK	31.4	4	89	7	Oval	1981
†Hordern HV	42.2	11	90	7	Sydney	1911–12
Hornibrook PM	31.2	9	92	7	Oval	1930
Noble MA	41.1	10	100	7	Sydney	1903–04
Hawke NJN	33.7	6	105	7	Sydney	1965–66
Giffen G	52	14	117	7	Sydney	1884–85
Giffen G	54	17	128	7	Oval	1893
Cotter A	40	4	148	7	Oval	1905
McKenzie GD	60	15	153	7	Old Trafford	1964
O'Reilly WJ	59	9	189	7	Old Trafford	1934

†On debut

6.3 *Most Wickets in a Match*

ENGLAND

Match	Innings	Name	Ground	Year
19–90	9–37 & 10–53	Laker JC	Old Trafford	1956
15–104	7–61 & 8–43	Verity H	Lord's	1934
15–124	7–56 & 8–68	Rhodes W	Melbourne	1903–04
14–99	7–55 & 7–44	Bedser AV	Trent Bridge	1953

ENGLAND

Match	Innings	Name	Ground	Year
14–102	7–28 & 7–74	Bates W	Melbourne	1882–83
13–163	6–42 & 7–121	Barnes SF	Melbourne	1901–02
13–244	7–168 & 6–76	Richardson T	Old Trafford	1896
13–256	5–130 & 8–126	White JC	Adelaide	1928–29
†12–102	6–50 & 6–52	Martin F	Oval	1890
12–104	7–36 & 5–68	Lohmann GA	Oval	1886
12–136	6–49 & 6–87	Briggs J	Adelaide	1891–92
11–68	7–31 & 4–37	Peel R	Old Trafford	1888
11–74	5–29 & 6–45	Briggs J	Lord's	1886
11–76	6–48 & 5–28	Lockwood WH	Old Trafford	1902
11–88	5–58 & 6–30	Trueman FS	Headingley	1961
11–102	6–44 & 5–58	Blythe C	Edgbaston	1909
11–113	5–58 & 6–55	Laker JC	Headingley	1956
11–173	6–39 & 5–134	Richardson T	Lord's	1896
11–176	6–78 & 5–98	Botham IT	Perth	1979–80
11–215	7–113 & 4–102	Underwood DL	Adelaide	1974–75
†11–228	6–130 & 5–98	Tate MW	Sydney	1924–25
10–49	5–29 & 5–20	Woolley FE	Oval	1912
10–57	6–41 & 4–16	Voce W	Brisbane	1936–37
10–58	5–18 & 5–40	Peel R	Sydney	1887–88
10–60	6–41 & 4–19	Hearne JT	Oval	1896
10–82	4–37 & 6–45	Underwood DL	Headingley	1972
10–87	8–35 & 2–52	Lohmann GA	Sydney	1886–87
†10–104	6–77 & 4–27	Ellison RM	Edgbaston	1985
10–105	5–46 & 5–59	Bedser AV	Melbourne	1950–51
10–124	5–96 & 5–28	Larwood H	Sydney	1932–33
10–130	4–45 & 6–85	Tyson FH	Sydney	1954–55
10–142	8–58 & 2–84	Lohmann GA	Sydney	1891–92
10–148	5–34 & 5–114	Briggs J	Oval	1893
†10–156	5–49 & 5–107	Richardson T	Old Trafford	1893
†10–179	5–102 & 5–77	Farnes K	Trent Bridge	1934
10–204	8–94 & 2–110	Richardson T	Sydney	1897–98
10–253	6–125 & 4–128	Botham IT	Oval	1981

†On debut

AUSTRALIA

Match	Innings	Name	Ground	Year
†16–137	8–84 & 8–53	Massie RAL	Lord's	1972
14–90	7–46 & 7–44	Spofforth FR	Oval	1882
13–77	7–17 & 6–60	Noble MA	Melbourne	1901–02
13–110	6–48 & 7–62	Spofforth FR	Melbourne	1878–79
13–236	4–115 & 9–121	Mailey AA	Melbourne	1920–21
12–87	5–44 & 7–43	Turner CTB	Sydney	1887–88
12–89	6–59 & 6–30	Trumble H	Oval	1896
12–173	8–65 & 4–108	Trumble H	Oval	1902
†12–175	5–85 & 7–90	Hordern HV	Sydney	1911–12
†11–82	5–45 & 6–37	Grimmett CV	Sydney	1924–25
11–85	7–58 & 4–27	Macartney CG	Headingley	1909
11–103	5–51 & 6–52	Noble MA	Sheffield	1902
11–117	4–73 & 7–44	Spofforth FR	Sydney	1882–83
11–129	4–75 & 7–54	O'Reilly WJ	Trent Bridge	1934
11–134	6–47 & 5–87	Lawson GF	Brisbane	1982–83
11–138	6–60 & 5–78	Lillee DK	Melbourne	1979–80
11–159	7–89 & 4–70	Lillee DK	Oval	1981
11–165	6–26 & 5–139	Lillee DK	Melbourne	1976–77
11–165	7–68 & 4–97	Palmer GE	Sydney	1881–82
10–63	5–27 & 5–36	Turner CTB	Lord's	1888
10–66	5–30 & 5–36	Hogg RM	Melbourne	1978–79
10–122	5–65 & 5–57	Hogg RM	Perth	1978–79
10–122	5–66 & 5–56	O'Reilly WJ	Headingley	1938
10–126	7–65 & 3–61	Palmer GE	Melbourne	1882–83
10–128	4–75 & 6–53	Trumble H	Old Trafford	1902
10–129	5–63 & 5–66	O'Reilly WJ	Melbourne	1932–33
10–144	4–54 & 6–90	Spofforth FR	Sydney	1884–85
10–152	5–72 & 5–80	Miller KR	Lord's	1956
10–160	4–88 & 6–72	Giffen G	Sydney	1891–92
10–161	5–95 & 5–66	Hordern HV	Sydney	1911–12
10–164	7–88 & 3–76	Jones E	Lord's	1899
10–181	5–58 & 5–123	Lillee DK	Oval	1972
10–201	5–107 & 5–94	Grimmett CV	Trent Bridge	1930
10–239	4–129 & 6–110	Fleetwood-Smith LO'B	Adelaide	1936–37
10–302	5–160 & 5–142	Mailey AA	Adelaide	1920–21

†On debut

6.4 *Five Wickets in an Innings on Most Occasions*

ENGLAND		AUSTRALIA	
12 Barnes SF	5 Trueman FS	11 Grimmett CV	6 Mailey AA
11 Richardson T	4 Bates W	11 Lillee DK	6 Palmer GE
8 Botham IT	4 Hearne JT	11 Turner CTB	5 Davidson AK
7 Bedser AV	4 Snow JA	9 Noble MA	5 Hogg RM
7 Briggs J	4 Underwood DL	9 Trumble H	5 Saunders JV
7 Willis RGD		8 O'Reilly WJ	5 Thomson JR
6 Peel R		7 Giffen G	4 Alderman TM
6 Rhodes W		7 Spofforth FR	4 Benaud R
6 Tate MW		6 Cotter A	4 Ferris JJ
5 Laker JC		6 Lawson GF	4 Hawke NJN
5 Lockwood WH		6 Lindwall RR	4 Hordern HV
5 Lohmann GA		6 McKenzie GD	

6.5 *Five Wickets in an Innings*

ENGLAND (203)		O	M	R	W	Ground	Year
Allen GOB	(1)	6	0	36	5	Brisbane	1936–37
Arnold GG	(1)	29	7	86	5	Sydney	1974–75
Barlow RG	(3)	31	22	19	5	Oval	1882
		34.2	20	40	7	Sydney	1882–83
		52	34	44	7	Old Trafford	1886
Barnes SF	(12)	†35.1	9	65	5	Sydney	1901–02
		16.1	5	42	6	Melbourne	1901–02
		64	17	121	7		
		20	9	49	6	Sheffield	1902
		27.4	4	72	5	Melbourne	1907–08
		22.4	6	60	7	Sydney	1907–08
		35	16	63	6	Headingley	1909
		27	9	56	5	Old Trafford	1909
		23	9	44	5	Melbourne	1911–12
		46.4	7	105	5	Adelaide	1911–12
		29.1	4	74	5	Melbourne	1911–12
		27	15	30	5	Oval	1912

ENGLAND (203)		O	M	R	W	Ground	Year
Barnes W	(3)	38.3	26	31	6	Melbourne	1884–85
		46	29	28	6	Sydney	1886–87
		29	16	32	5	Oval	1888
Bates W	(4)	26.2	14	28	7	Melbourne	1882–83
		33	14	74	7		
		24.1	10	31	5	Adelaide	1884–85
		20	10	24	5	Sydney	1884–85
Bedser AV	(7)	22	5	46	5	Melbourne	1950–51
		20.3	4	59	5		
		38.3	16	55	7	Trent Bridge	1953
		17.2	7	44	7		
		42.4	8	105	5	Lord's	1953
		45	10	115	5	Old Trafford	1953
		28.5	2	95	6	Headingley	1953
Blythe C	(3)	23	6	44	6	Edgbaston	1909
		24	3	58	5		
		20.3	5	63	5	Old Trafford	1909
Bosanquet BJT	(2)	15	1	51	6	Sydney	1903–04
		32.4	2	107	8	Trent Bridge	1905
Botham IT	(8)	†20	5	74	5	Trent Bridge	1977
		11	3	21	5	Headingley	1977
		35	9	78	6	Perth	1979–80
		45.5	14	98	5		
		39.2	11	95	6	Headingley	1981
		14	9	11	5	Edgbaston	1981
		47	13	125	6	Oval	1981
		24	2	109	5	Lord's	1985
Bowes WE	(3)	50	13	142	6	Headingley	1934
		11.3	3	55	5	Oval	1934
		19	3	49	5	Oval	1938
Bradley WM	(1)	†33	13	67	5	Old Trafford	1899
Braund LC	(3)	†28.4	8	61	5	Sydney	1901–02
		26.1	4	95	5	Melbourne	1901–02
		28.5	6	81	8	Melbourne	1903–04
Brearley W	(1)	31.1	8	110	5	Oval	1905

ENGLAND (203)		O	M	R	W	Ground	Year
Briggs J	(7)	34	22	29	5	Lord's	1886
		38.1	17	45	6		
		37	24	25	5	Oval	1888
		21.5	4	49	6	Adelaide	1891–92
		28	7	87	6		
		14.3	5	34	5	Oval	1893
		35	6	114	5		
Brown DJ	(2)	17	1	63	5	Sydney	1965–66
		14	5	42	5	Lord's	1968
Brown FR	(1)	18	4	49	5	Melbourne	1950–51
Carr DW	(1)	†34	2	146	5	Oval	1909
Clark EW	(1)	20	1	98	5	Oval	1934
Cowans NG	(1)	26	6	77	6	Melbourne	1982–83
Crawford JN	(3)	29	1	79	5	Melbourne	1907–08
		23.5	3	48	5	Melbourne	1907–08
		36	10	141	5	Sydney	1907–08
Douglas JWHT	(1)	17.5	6	46	5	Melbourne	1911–12
Edmonds PH	(1)	†20	7	28	5	Headingley	1975
Ellison RM	(2)	†31.5	9	77	6	Edgbaston	1985
		17	3	46	5	Oval	1985
Emburey JE	(1)	43.4	14	82	5	Headingley	1985
Emmett T	(1)	59	31	68	7	Melbourne	1878–79
Farnes K	(3)	†40.2	10	102	5	Trent Bridge	1934
		†25	3	77	5		
		28.5	5	96	6	Melbourne	1936–37
Fender PGH	(2)	32	3	122	5	Melbourne	1920–21
		20	1	90	5	Sydney	1920–21
Fielder A	(1)	30.2	4	82	6	Sydney	1907–08
Flowers W	(1)	46	24	46	5	Sydney	1884–85
Foster FR	(3)	†31.3	5	92	5	Sydney	1911–12
		38	9	91	6	Melbourne	1911–12
		26	9	36	5	Adelaide	1911–12

ENGLAND (203)		O	M	R	W	Ground	Year
Geary G	(2)	18	5	35	5	Sydney	1928–29
		81	36	105	5	Melbourne	1928–29
Gunn JR	(1)	41.4	14	76	5	Adelaide	1901–02
Hammond WR	(1)	15.2	1	57	5	Adelaide	1936–37
Hearne JT	(4)	†36	14	76	5	Lord's	1896
		26.1	10	41	6	Oval	1896
		20.1	7	42	5	Sydney	1897–98
		35.4	13	98	6	Melbourne	1897–98
Hirst GH	(3)	29	5	77	5	Oval	1902
		16.5	4	48	5	Melbourne	1903–04
		23.5	4	58	5	Edgbaston	1909
Hollies WE	(1)	†56	14	131	5	Oval	1948
Illingworth R	(1)	51	22	87	6	Headingley	1968
Jackson Hon.FS	(1)	14.5	2	52	5	Trent Bridge	1905
Jones IJ	(1)	29	3	118	6	Adelaide	1965–66
Laker JC	(5)	29	10	58	5	Headingley	1956
		41.3	21	55	6		
		16.4	4	37	9	Old Trafford	1956
		51.2	23	53	10		
		46	9	107	5	Sydney	1958–59
Larwood H	(3)	14.4	4	32	6	Brisbane*	1928–29
		31	5	96	5	Sydney	1932–33
		18	4	28	5		
Lever P	(1)	11	2	38	6	Melbourne	1974–75
Lock GAR	(1)	21	9	45	5	Oval	1953
Lockwood WH	(5)	†45	11	101	6	Lord's	1893
		40.3	17	71	7	Oval	1899
		20.1	5	48	6	Old Trafford	1902
		17	5	28	5		
		20	6	45	5	Oval	1902

ENGLAND (203)		O	M	R	W	Ground	Year
Lohmann GA	(5)	30.2	17	36	7	Oval	1886
		37	14	68	5		
		25	12	35	8	Sydney	1886–87
		19	13	17	5	Sydney	1887–88
		43.2	18	58	8	Sydney	1891–92
Martin F	(2)	†27	9	50	6	Oval	1890
		†30.2	12	52	6		
Miller G	(1)	27.1	6	44	5	Sydney	1978–79
Morley F	(1)	†32	9	56	5	Oval	1880
Parkin CH	(2)	20	2	60	5	Adelaide	1920–21
		29.4	12	38	5	Old Trafford	1921
Peate E	(2)	45	24	43	5	Sydney	1881–82
		40	14	85	6	Lord's	1884
Peebles IAR	(1)	71	8	204	6	Oval	1930
Peel R	(6)	†40.1	15	51	5	Adelaide	1884–85
		18.3	9	18	5	Sydney	1887–88
		33	14	40	5		
		26.2	17	31	7	Old Trafford	1888
		30	9	67	6	Sydney	1894–95
		12	5	23	6	Oval	1896
Pocock PI	(1)	†33	10	79	6	Old Trafford	1968
Relf AE	(1)	45	14	85	5	Lord's	1909
Rhodes W	(6)	11	3	17	7	Edgbaston	1902
		17.1	3	63	5	Sheffield	1902
		40.2	10	94	5	Sydney	1903–04
		15.2	3	56	7	Melbourne	1903–04
		15	0	68	8		
		25	0	83	5	Old Trafford	1909
Richardson T	(11)	†23.4	5	49	5	Old Trafford	1893
		†44	15	107	5		
		55.3	13	181	5	Sydney	1894–95
		23	6	57	5	Melbourne	1894–95
		21	4	75	5	Adelaide	1894–95

ENGLAND (203)		O	M	R	W	Ground	Year
Richardson T *continued*		45.2	7	104	6	Melbourne	1894–95
		11.3	3	39	6	Lord's	1896
		47	15	134	5		
		68	23	168	7	Old Trafford	1896
		42.3	16	76	6		
		36.1	7	94	8	Sydney	1897–98
Sharpe JW	(1)	51	20	84	6	Melbourne	1891–92
Shaw A	(1)	†34	16	38	5	Melbourne	1876–77
Shuttleworth K	(1)	†17.5	2	47	5	Brisbane	1970–71
Snow JA	(4)	32.3	6	114	6	Brisbane	1970–71
		17.5	5	40	7	Sydney	1970–71
		32	13	57	5	Lord's	1972
		31	8	92	5	Trent Bridge	1972
Statham JB	(3)	16.3	0	60	5	Melbourne	1954–55
		28	6	57	7	Melbourne	1958–59
		21	3	53	5	Old Trafford	1961
Tate MW	(6)	†55.1	11	130	6	Sydney	1924–25
		†33.7	8	98	5		
		33.3	8	99	6	Melbourne	1924–25
		25.5	6	75	5	Melbourne	1924–25
		39.3	6	115	5	Sydney	1924–25
		39	9	124	5	Headingley	1930
Titmus FJ	(2)	37	14	79	7	Sydney	1962–63
		47.2	9	103	5	Sydney	1962–63
Trueman FS	(5)	28	2	90	5	Lord's	1956
		22	5	58	5	Headingley	1961
		15.5	5	30	6		
		20	1	62	5	Melbourne	1962–63
		25	8	48	5	Lord's	1964
Tyson FH	(2)	18.4	1	85	6	Sydney	1954–55
		12.3	1	27	7	Melbourne	1954–55
Ulyett G	(1)	39.1	23	36	7	Lord's	1884

ENGLAND (203)		O	M	R	W	Ground	Year
Underwood DL	(4)	31.3	19	50	7	Oval	1968
		21	6	45	6	Headingley	1972
		29	3	113	7	Adelaide	1974–75
		32.5	13	66	6	Old Trafford	1977
Verity H	(3)	19	9	33	5	Sydney	1932–33
		36	15	61	7	Lord's	1934
		22.3	8	43	8		
Voce W	(1)	20.6	5	41	6	Brisbane	1936–37
Wardle JH	(1)	24.4	6	79	5	Sydney	1954–55
Warren AR	(1)	†19.2	5	57	5	Headingley	1905
White JC	(3)	56.5	20	107	5	Melbourne	1928–29
		60	16	130	5	Adelaide	1928–29
		64.5	21	126	8		
Willis RGD	(7)	21.7	4	61	5	Melbourne	1974–75
		30.1	7	78	7	Lord's	1977
		26	6	88	5	Trent Bridge	1977
		29.3	5	102	5	Oval	1977
		18.5	5	44	5	Perth	1978–79
		15.1	3	43	8	Headingley	1981
		29.4	3	66	5	Brisbane	1982–83
Woolley FE	(2)	9.4	3	29	5	Oval	1912
		7.4	1	20	5		
Wright DVP	(2)	43.6	4	167	5	Brisbane	1946–47
		29	4	105	7	Sydney	1946–47

†On debut *Exhibition Ground

AUSTRALIA (220)		O	M	R	W	Ground	Year
Alderman TM	(4)	†19	3	62	5	Trent Bridge	1981
		35.3	6	135	6	Headingley	1981
		23.1	8	42	5	Edgbaston	1981
		52	19	109	5	Old Trafford	1981
Archer RG	(1)	28.2	7	53	5	Oval	1956

AUSTRALIA (220)		O	M	R	W	Ground	Year
Armstrong WW	(3)	51	14	122	5	Headingley	1905
		15.3	7	27	5	Edgbaston	1909
		24.5	11	35	6	Lord's	1909
Benaud R	(4)	33.4	10	83	5	Sydney	1958–59
		27	6	91	5	Adelaide	1958–59
		32	11	70	6	Old Trafford	1961
		42	12	115	6	Brisbane	1962–63
Blackie DD	(1)	44	13	94	6	Melbourne	1928–29
Boyle HF	(1)	25	9	42	6	Old Trafford	1884
Bright RJ	(1)	34	17	68	5	Edgbaston	1981
Callaway ST	(1)	26.3	13	37	5	Adelaide	1894–95
Connolly AN	(1)	39	13	72	5	Headingley	1968
Cooper WH	(1)	†61	19	120	6	Melbourne	1881–82
Cotter A	(6)	15.2	2	40	6	Melbourne	1903–04
		40	4	148	7	Oval	1905
		21.5	0	101	6	Sydney	1907–08
		33	4	142	5	Melbourne	1907–08
		16	2	38	5	Headingley	1909
		27.4	1	95	6	Oval	1909
Davidson AK	(5)	25.5	7	64	6	Melbourne	1958–59
		24.3	6	42	5	Lord's	1961
		47	23	63	5	Headingley	1961
		23.1	4	75	6	Melbourne	1962–63
		10.6	2	25	5	Sydney	1962–63
Dymock G	(1)	17.2	4	34	6	Perth	1979–80
Ferris JJ	(4)	†61	30	76	5	Sydney	1886–87
		45	16	71	5	Sydney	1886–87
		23	11	26	5	Lord's	1888
		23	8	49	5	Oval	1890
Fleetwood-Smith LO'B	(2)	†25.6	2	124	5	Melbourne	1936–37
		30	1	110	6	Adelaide	1936–37

AUSTRALIA (220)		O	M	R	W	Ground	Year
Garrett TW	(2)	36.1	10	78	6	Sydney	1881–82
		54.2	23	80	5	Melbourne	1881–82
Giffen G	(7)	52	14	117	7	Sydney	1884–85
		28	10	72	6	Sydney	1891–92
		26.4	6	43	5	Lord's	1893
		54	17	128	7	Oval	1893
		78.2	21	155	6	Melbourne	1894–95
		28	11	76	5	Adelaide	1894–95
		15	7	26	5	Sydney	1894–95
Gilmour GJ	(1)	†31.2	10	85	6	Headingley	1975
Gregory JM	(3)	20	1	69	7	Melbourne	1920–21
		19	5	58	6	Trent Bridge	1921
		28.7	2	111	5	Sydney	1924–25
Grimmett CV	(11)	†11.7	2	45	5	Sydney	1924–25
		†19.4	3	37	6		
		39	11	88	5	Headingley	1926
		44.1	9	131	6	Brisbane*	1928–29
		52.1	12	102	5	Adelaide	1928–29
		32	6	107	5	Trent Bridge	1930
		30	4	94	5		
		53	13	167	6	Lord's	1930
		56.2	16	135	5	Headingley	1930
		58.3	24	81	5	Trent Bridge	1934
		26.3	10	64	5	Oval	1934
Hawke NJN	(4)	31.3	11	75	5	Headingley	1964
		25.4	8	47	6	Oval	1964
		33.7	6	105	7	Sydney	1965–66
		21	6	54	5	Adelaide	1965–66
Hazlitt GR	(1)	21.4	8	25	7	Oval	1912
Higgs JD	(1)	59.6	15	148	5	Sydney	1978–79
Hogg RM	(5)	†28	8	74	6	Brisbane	1978–79
		30.5	9	65	5	Perth	1978–79
		17	2	57	5		
		17	7	30	5	Melbourne	1978–79
		17	5	36	5		
Holland RG	(1)	†32	12	68	5	Lord's	1985

AUSTRALIA (220)		O	M	R	W	Ground	Year
Horan TP	(1)	37.1	22	40	6	Sydney	1884–85
Hordern HV	(4)	†27	4	85	5	Sydney	1911–12
		†42.2	11	90	7		
		37	8	95	5	Sydney	1911–12
		25	5	66	5		
Hornibrook PM	(1)	31.2	9	92	7	Oval	1930
Hurst AG	(1)	10.6	2	28	5	Sydney	1978–79
Iverson JB	(1)	19.4	8	27	6	Sydney	1950–51
Johnson IW	(1)	30.1	12	42	6	Sydney	1946–47
Johnston WA	(3)	†25	11	36	5	Trent Bridge	1948
		11	2	35	5	Brisbane	1950–51
		24.5	2	85	5	Melbourne	1954–55
Jones E	(3)	26.2	3	82	6	Sydney	1897–98
		33	6	88	5	Trent Bridge	1899
		36.1	11	88	7	Lord's	1899
Kendall T	(1)	†33.1	12	55	7	Melbourne	1876–77
Laver F	(2)	31.3	14	64	7	Trent Bridge	1905
		18.2	7	31	8	Old Trafford	1909
Lawson GF	(6)	43.1	14	81	7	Lord's	1981
		32	5	108	5	Perth	1982–83
		18.3	4	47	6	Brisbane	1982–83
		35.3	11	87	5		
		24	6	66	5	Adelaide	1982–83
		39.4	10	103	5	Trent Bridge	1985
Lillee DK	(11)	†28.3	0	84	5	Adelaide	1970–71
		30	8	66	6	Old Trafford	1972
		24.2	7	58	5	Oval	1972
		32.2	8	123	5		
		15	8	15	5	Edgbaston	1975
		13.3	2	26	6	Melbourne	1976–77
		34.4	7	139	5		
		33.1	9	60	6	Melbourne	1979–80
		33	6	78	5		
		16.4	2	46	5	Trent Bridge	1981
		31.4	4	89	7	Oval	1981

AUSTRALIA (220)		O	M	R	W	Ground	Year
Lindwall RR	(6)	22	3	63	7	Sydney	1946–47
		27.4	7	70	5	Lord's	1948
		16.1	5	20	6	Oval	1948
		20.4	2	57	5	Trent Bridge	1953
		23	4	66	5	Lord's	1953
		35	10	54	5	Headingley	1953
Lyons JJ	(1)	20.1	7	30	5	Lord's	1890
Macartney CG	(1)	25.3	6	58	7	Headingley	1909
McCool CL	(2)	32.4	4	109	5	Sydney	1946–47
		21.4	5	44	5	Sydney	1946–47
McDermott CJ	(2)	29.2	5	70	6	Lord's	1985
		36	3	141	8	Old Trafford	1985
McDonald EA	(2)	22.4	10	32	5	Trent Bridge	1921
		47	9	143	5	Oval	1921
Mackay KD	(1)	68	21	121	5	Oval	1961
McKenzie GD	(6)	†29	13	37	5	Lord's	1961
		33	3	89	5	Adelaide	1962–63
		24	5	53	5	Trent Bridge	1964
		60	15	153	7	Old Trafford	1964
		35.2	3	134	5	Melbourne	1965–66
		21.7	4	48	6	Adelaide	1965–66
McLeod CE	(2)	48	24	65	5	Adelaide	1897–98
		47	8	125	5	Old Trafford	1905
McLeod RW	(1)	†28.4	12	55	5	Melbourne	1891–92
Mailey AA	(6)	32.1 29.2	3 3	160 142	5 5	Adelaide	1920–21
		47	8	121	9	Melbourne	1920–21
		36.2	5	119	5	Sydney	1920–21
		24	2	92	5	Melbourne	1924–25
		33.5	3	138	6	Oval	1926
Mallett AA	(1)	52	20	114	5	Headingley	1972
Malone MF	(1)	†47	20	63	5	Oval	1977

AUSTRALIA (220)		O	M	R	W	Ground	Year
Massie RAL	(2)	†32.5	7	84	8	Lord's	1972
		†27.2	9	53	8		
Meckiff I	(1)	15.2	3	38	6	Melbourne	1958–59
Midwinter WE	(1)	†54	23	78	5	Melbourne	1876–77
Miller KR	(3)	†22	4	60	7	Brisbane	1946–47
		34.1	9	72	5	Lord's	1956
		36	12	80	5		
Noble MA	(9)	†17	1	49	6	Melbourne	1897–98
		33	7	84	5	Adelaide	1897–98
		7.4	2	17	7	Melbourne	1901–02
		26	5	60	6		
		24	7	54	5	Sydney	1901–02
		33	4	98	6	Melbourne	1901–02
		19	6	51	5	Sheffield	1902
		21	4	52	6		
		41.1	10	100	7	Sydney	1903–04
O'Connor JDA	(1)	†21	6	40	5	Adelaide	1907–08
O'Reilly WJ	(8)	34.3	17	63	5	Melbourne	1932–33
		24	5	66	5		
		41.4	24	54	7	Trent Bridge	1934
		59	9	189	7	Old Trafford	1934
		40.6	13	102	5	Brisbane	1936–37
		23	7	51	5	Melbourne	1936–37
		34.1	17	66	5	Headingley	1938
		21.5	8	56	5		
Palmer GE	(6)	58	36	68	7	Sydney	1881–82
		45.2	23	46	5	Sydney	1881–82
		52.2	25	65	7	Melbourne	1882–83
		66.3	25	103	5	Melbourne	1882–83
		75	26	111	6	Lord's	1884
		73	37	81	5	Adelaide	1884–85
Pascoe LS	(1)	18	5	59	5	Lord's	1980
Philpott PI	(1)	†28.1	3	90	5	Brisbane	1965–66

AUSTRALIA (220)		O	M	R	W	Ground	Year
Saunders JV	(5)	†24.1	8	43	5	Sydney	1901–02
		15.3	4	50	5	Sheffield	1902
		21.4	4	65	5	Adelaide	1907–08
		15.2	8	28	5	Melbourne	1907–08
		35.1	5	82	5	Sydney	1907–08
Sievers MW	(1)	11.2	5	21	5	Melbourne	1936–37
Simpson RB	(1)	15	3	57	5	Sydney	1962–63
Spofforth FR	(7)	25	9	58	6	Melbourne	1878–79
		35	16	62	7		
		36.3	18	46	7	Oval	1882
		28	15	44	7		
		41.1	23	44	7	Sydney	1882–83
		48.1	22	90	6	Sydney	1884–85
		20	8	30	5	Sydney	1884–85
Thomson JR	(5)	†17.5	3	46	6	Brisbane	1974–75
		25	4	93	5	Perth	1974–75
		18	8	38	5	Edgbaston	1975
		31	6	73	5	Brisbane	1982–83
		14.5	2	50	5	Sydney	1982–83
Toshack ERH	(2)	†20.7	2	82	6	Brisbane	1946–47
		20.1	6	40	5	Lord's	1948
Trott AE	(1)	†27	10	43	8	Adelaide	1894–95
Trumble H	(9)	40	10	59	6	Oval	1896
		25	9	30	6		
		39.3	16	60	5	Headingley	1899
		44	18	74	6	Adelaide	1901–02
		25	4	62	5	Melbourne	1901–02
		25	9	53	6	Old Trafford	1902
		31	13	65	8	Oval	1902
		10.5	2	34	5	Melbourne	1903–04
		6.5	0	28	7	Melbourne	1903–04
Turner CTB	(11)	†18	11	15	6	Sydney	1886–87
		53	29	41	5	Sydney	1886–87
		50	27	44	5	Sydney	1887–88
		38	23	43	7		

AUSTRALIA (220)		O	M	R	W	Ground	Year
Turner CTB *continued*		25	9	27	5	Lord's	1888
		24	8	36	5		
		60	24	112	6	Oval	1888
		55	21	86	5	Old Trafford	1888
		33.2	14	51	5	Melbourne	1891–92
		36	16	67	6	Lord's	1893
		20	9	32	5	Melbourne	1894–95
Walker MHN	(2)	42.2	7	143	8	Melbourne	1974–75
		17.3	5	48	5	Edgbaston	1975
Wall TW	(2)	†26	5	66	5	Melbourne	1928–29
		34.1	10	72	5	Adelaide	1932–33
Ward FA	(1)	†46	16	102	6	Brisbane	1936–37
Yardley B	(1)	42.4	15	107	5	Perth	1982–83

†On debut *Exhibition Ground

6.6 *Most Wickets in an Innings on Debut*

ENGLAND				AUSTRALIA			
Martin F	6–50	Oval	1890	Trott AE	8–43	Adelaide	1894–95
Martin F	6–52	Oval	1890	Massie RAL	8–53	Lord's	1972
Ellison RM	6–77	Edgbaston	1985	Massie RAL	8–84	Lord's	1972
Pocock PI	6–79	Old Trafford	1968	Kendall T	7–55	Melbourne	1876–77
Lockwood WH	6–101	Lord's	1893	Miller KR	7–60	Brisbane	1946–47

6.7 *Most Wickets in a Match on Debut*

ENGLAND				AUSTRALIA			
Martin F	12–102	Oval	1890	Massie RAL	16–137	Lord's	1972
Tate MW	11–228	Sydney	1924–25	Hordern HV	12–175	Sydney	1911–12
Ellison RM	10–104	Edgbaston	1985	Grimmett CV	11–82	Sydney	1924–25
Richardson T	10–156	Old Trafford	1893	Miller KR	9–77	Brisbane	1946–47
Farnes K	10–179	Trent Bridge	1934	Toshack ERH	9–99	Brisbane	1946–47

ABOVE LEFT *O'Reilly: 102 wickets in only four series*
ABOVE *'Demon' Spofforth: earliest bowler of influence*

BELOW *Laker and Bedser, successive series record-holders with 46 and 39 wickets*
LEFT *Underwood, taker of 105 wickets in 29 Tests*

6.8 *Most Wickets in a Series*

ENGLAND

6 Tests	Series	M	Balls	Runs	Wkts	Av	Best	5wi	10wm
Botham IT	1981	6	1635	700	34	20.59	6–95	4	1
Botham IT	1985	6	1510	855	31	27.58	5–109	1	–
Snow JA	1970–71	6	1805	708	31	22.84	7–40	2	–
Willis RGD	1981	6	1516	666	29	22.97	8–43	1	–
Botham IT	1978–79	6	1268	567	23	24.65	4–42	–	–
Miller G	1978–79	6	1417	346	23	15.04	5–44	1	–
Willis RGD	1978–79	6	1123	461	20	23.05	5–44	1	–
Emburey JE	1985	6	1492	544	19	28.63	5–82	1	–
Hendrick M	1978–79	5	1160	299	19	15.74	3–19	–	–
Ellison RM	1985	2	455	185	17	10.88	6–77	2	1
Greig AW	1974–75	6	1341	681	17	40.06	4–56	–	–
Underwood DL	1974–75	5	1480	595	17	35.00	7–113	1	1
Willis RGD	1974–75	5	1124	522	17	30.71	5–61	1	–
5 Tests									
Laker JC	1956	5	1703	442	46	9.61	10–53	4	2
Bedser AV	1953	5	1591	682	39	17.49	7–44	5	1
Tate MW	1924–25	5	2528	881	38	23.18	6–99	5	1
Barnes SF	1911–12	5	1782	778	34	22.88	5–44	3	–
Larwood H	1932–33	5	1322	644	33	19.52	5–28	2	1
Foster FR	1911–12	5	1660	692	32	21.63	6–91	3	–
Richardson T	1894–95	5	1747	849	32	26.53	6–104	4	–
Rhodes W	1903–04	5	1032	488	31	15.74	8–68	3	1
Bedser AV	1950–51	5	1560	482	30	16.07	5–46	2	1
Crawford JN	1907–08	5	1426	742	30	24.73	5–48	3	–
Tyson FH	1954–55	5	1208	583	28	20.82	7–27	2	1
Peel R	1894–95	5	1831	721	27	26.70	6–67	1	–
Willis RGD	1977	5	1000	534	27	19.78	7–78	3	–
Voce W	1936–37	5	1297	560	26	21.54	6–41	1	1
Fielder A	1907–08	4	1299	627	25	25.08	6–82	1	–
White JC	1928–29	5	2440	760	25	30.40	8–126	3	1
Barnes SF	1907–08	5	1640	626	24	26.08	7–60	2	–
Snow JA	1972	5	1235	555	24	23.13	5–57	2	–
Verity H	1934	5	1628	576	24	24.00	8–43	2	1
Wright DVP	1946–47	5	1922	990	23	43.04	7–105	2	–

ENGLAND

4 Tests	Series	M	Balls	Runs	Wkts	Av	Best	5wi	10wm
Bates W	1882–83	4	771	286	19	15.05	7–28	2	1
Farnes K	1938	4	1078	581	17	34.18	4–63	–	–
Bates W	1881–82	4	964	334	16	20.88	4–52	–	–
Barlow RG	1882–83	4	976	343	15	22.87	7–40	1	–
Verity H	1938	4	925	354	14	25.29	4–103	–	–
Wright DVP	1938	3	720	426	12	35.50	4–153	–	–
Peate E	1881–82	4	928	256	11	23.27	5–43	1	–
Snow JA	1975	4	815	355	11	32.27	4–66	–	–
Steel AG	1882–83	4	520	195	11	17.73	3–27	–	–
Bowes WE	1938	2	454	188	10	18.80	5–49	1	–
Midwinter WE	1881–82	4	776	272	10	27.20	4–81	–	–

3 Tests	Series	M	Balls	Runs	Wkts	Av	Best	5wi	10wm
Peel R	1888	3	442	181	24	7.54	7–31	1	1
Richardson T	1896	3	876	439	24	18.29	7–168	4	2
Botham IT	1979–80	3	1039	371	19	19.53	6–78	2	1
Briggs J	1886	3	537	132	17	7.76	6–45	2	1
Briggs J	1891–92	3	699	268	17	15.76	6–49	2	1
Briggs J	1893	2	601	293	16	18.31	5–34	2	1
Lohmann GA	1891–92	3	1130	289	16	18.06	8–58	1	1
Hearne JT	1896	3	636	211	15	14.07	6–41	2	1
Lockwood WH	1893	2	465	234	14	16.71	6–101	1	–
Lohmann GA	1886	3	466	191	13	14.69	7–36	2	1
Underwood DL	1979–80	3	962	405	13	31.15	3–71	–	–
Briggs J	1888	3	337	94	12	7.83	5–25	1	–
Lohmann GA	1888	3	379	144	11	13.09	4–33	–	–
Peate E	1884	3	672	280	11	25.45	6–85	1	–
Ulyett G	1884	3	545	194	11	17.64	7–36	1	–

AUSTRALIA

6 Tests	Series	M	Balls	Runs	Wkts	Av	Best	5wi	10wm
Alderman TM	1981	6	1950	893	42	21.26	6–135	4	–
Hogg RM	1978–79	6	1740	527	41	12.85	6–74	5	2
Lillee DK	1981	6	1870	870	39	22.31	7–89	2	1
Thomson JR	1974–75	5	1401	592	33	17.94	6–46	2	–
McDermott CJ	1985	6	1406	901	30	30.03	8–141	2	–
Hurst AG	1978–79	6	1634	577	25	23.08	5–28	1	–
Lillee DK	1974–75	6	1462	596	25	23.84	4–49	–	–

AUSTRALIA

6 Tests	Series	M	Balls	Runs	Wkts	Av	Best	5wi	10wm
Walker MHN	1974–75	6	1751	684	23	29.74	8–143	1	–
Lawson GF	1985	6	1476	830	22	37.73	5–103	1	–
Higgs JD	1978–79	5	1574	468	19	24.63	5–148	1	–
5 Tests									
Mailey AA	1920–21	5	1465	946	36	26.28	9–121	4	2
Giffen G	1894–95	5	2126	820	34	24.12	6–155	3	–
Lawson GF	1982–83	5	1384	687	34	20.21	6–47	4	1
Hordern HV	1911–12	5	1665	780	32	24.38	7–90	4	2
Noble MA	1901–02	5	1380	608	32	19.00	7–17	4	1
Benaud R	1958–59	5	1866	584	31	18.84	5–83	2	–
Lillee DK	1972	5	1499	548	31	17.68	6–66	3	1
Saunders JV	1907–08	5	1603	716	31	23.10	5–28	3	–
Grimmett CV	1930	5	2098	925	29	31.90	6–167	4	1
McKenzie GD	1964	5	1536	654	29	22.55	7–153	2	–
O'Reilly WJ	1934	5	2002	698	28	24.93	7–54	2	1
Trumble H	1901–02	5	1604	561	28	20.04	6–74	2	–
Johnston WA	1948	5	1856	630	27	23.33	5–36	1	–
Lindwall RR	1948	5	1337	530	27	19.63	6–20	2	–
McDonald EA	1921	5	1235	668	27	24.74	5–32	2	–
O'Reilly WJ	1932–33	5	2302	724	27	26.81	5–63	2	1
Jones E	1899	5	1276	657	26	25.27	7–88	2	1
Lindwall RR	1953	5	1444	490	26	18.85	5–54	3	–
Trumble H	1902	3	1036	371	26	14.27	8–65	2	2
Grimmett CV	1934	5	2379	668	25	26.72	5–64	2	–
O'Reilly WJ	1936–37	5	1982	555	25	22.20	5–51	2	–
4 Tests									
Palmer GE	1881–82	4	1362	522	24	21.75	7–68	2	1
O'Reilly WJ	1938	4	1578	610	22	27.73	5–56	2	1
Lillee DK	1975	4	1242	460	21	21.90	5–15	1	–
Palmer GE	1882–83	4	1081	397	21	18.90	7–65	2	1
Garrett TW	1881–82	3	855	367	18	20.39	6–78	2	–
Spofforth FR	1882–83	4	977	408	18	22.67	7–44	1	1
Thomson JR	1975	4	1051	457	16	28.56	5–38	1	–
Fleetwood-Smith LO'B	1938	4	1307	727	14	51.93	4–34	–	–
Walker MHN	1975	4	1225	486	14	34.71	5–48	1	–
McCormick EL	1938	3	684	345	10	34.50	4–101	–	–

AUSTRALIA

3 Tests	Series	M	Balls	Runs	Wkts	Av	Best	5wi	10wm
Lillee DK	1979–80	3	931	388	23	16.87	6–60	2	1
Turner CTB	1888	3	656	261	21	12.43	6–112	4	1
Trumble H	1896	3	851	339	18	18.83	6–30	2	1
Dymock G	1979–80	3	783	260	17	15.29	6–34	1	–
Giffen G	1893	3	859	342	16	21.38	7–128	2	–
Turner CTB	1891–92	3	934	338	16	21.13	5–51	1	–
Giffen G	1891–92	3	783	397	15	26.47	6–72	1	1
Palmer GE	1884	3	692	260	14	18.57	6–111	1	–
Spofforth FR	1886	3	675	260	14	18.57	4–65	–	–
Hazlitt GR	1912	3	681	218	12	18.17	7–25	1	–
Whitty WJ	1912	3	660	252	12	21.00	4–43	–	–
Ferris JJ	1888	3	478	167	11	15.18	5–26	1	–
McKibbin TR	1896	2	348	162	11	14.73	3–35	–	–
Turner CTB	1893	3	875	315	11	28.64	6–67	1	–
McLeod RW	1891–92	3	664	227	10	22.70	5–55	1	–
Pascoe LS	1979–80	2	563	241	10	24.10	4–80	–	–
Spofforth FR	1884	3	769	301	10	30.10	4–42	–	–

6.9 *Hat-Tricks*

ENGLAND (3)

Bates W	McDonnell PS (No. 5)	bowled 3	1882–83	Melbourne
	Giffen G (No. 6)	c and b 0		
	Bonnor GJ (No. 7)	c Read WW 0		
Briggs J	Giffen WF (No. 8)	bowled 3	1891–92	Sydney
	Callaway ST (No. 10)	c Grace WG 0		
	Blackham JM (No. 9)	lbw 0		
Hearne JT	Hill C (No. 3)	bowled 0	1899	Headingley
	Gregory SE (No. 4)	c MacLaren AC 0		
	Noble MA (No. 5)	c Ranjitsinhji KS 0		

K Farnes would have achieved a hat-trick at Lord's in 1938 had DCS Compton at slip held a catch from L O'B Fleetwood-Smith.

AUSTRALIA (3)

Spofforth FR	Royle VPFA (No. 6)	bowled 3	1878–79	Melbourne
	MacKinnon FA (No. 7)	bowled 0		
	Emmett T (No. 8)	c Horan TP 0		
Trumble H	Jones AO (No. 8)	c Darling J 6	1901–02	Melbourne
	Gunn JR (No. 9)	c Jones SP 2		
	Barnes SF (No. 10)	c and b 0		
Trumble H	Bosanquet BJT (No. 7)	c Gehrs DRA 4	1903–04	Melbourne
	Warner PF (No. 5)	c and b 11		
	Lilley AFA (No. 9)	lbw 0		

6.9a *Three Wickets in Four Balls*

ENGLAND			AUSTRALIA		
Voce W	Sydney	1936–37	Spofforth FR	Oval	1882
Botham IT	Headingley	1985	Spofforth FR	Sydney	1884–85
			O'Reilly WJ	Old Trafford	1934
			Lindwall RR	Adelaide	1946–47
			Mackay KD	Edgbaston	1961
			Lillee DK	Old Trafford	1972
			Lillee DK	Oval	1972

6.10 *Most Runs Conceded by a Bowler*

In an Innings

ENGLAND

204	Peebles IAR	Oval	1930
183	†Price JSE	Old Trafford	1964
181	Richardson T	Sydney	1894–95
176	Bedser AV	Melbourne	1946–47
172	Robins RWV	Lord's	1930
172	†Smith TPB	Sydney	1946–47

†On debut

AUSTRALIA			
298	Fleetwood-Smith LO'B	Oval	1938
191	Grimmett CV	Sydney	1928–29
189	O'Reilly WJ	Old Trafford	1934
186	Mailey AA	Melbourne	1924–25
179	Mailey AA	Sydney	1924–25

In a Match

ENGLAND			
282	†Carr DW	Oval	1909
275	Bedser AV	Melbourne	1946–47
256	†Freeman AP	Sydney	1924–25
256	White JC	Adelaide	1928–29
255	Wright DVP	Melbourne	1946–47

AUSTRALIA			
308	Mailey AA	Sydney	1924–25
302	Mailey AA	Adelaide	1920–21
298	Fleetwood-Smith LO'B	Oval	1938
298	Grimmett CV	Brisbane*	1928–29
272	Grimmett CV	Lord's	1930

†On debut *Exhibition Ground

In a Series

ENGLAND		
990	Wright DVP	1946–47
881	Tate MW	1924–25
876	Bedser AV	1946–47
855	Botham IT	1985
849	Richardson T	1894–95

AUSTRALIA		
1024	Grimmett CV	1928–29
999	Mailey AA	1924–25
946	Mailey AA	1920–21
925	Grimmett CV	1930
901	McDermott CJ	1985

6.11 *Most Balls Delivered by a Bowler*

In an Innings

ENGLAND

486	Geary G	Melbourne	1928–29
462	†Cartwright TW	Old Trafford	1964
453	White JC	Melbourne	1928–29
448	†Kilner R	Adelaide	1924–25
441	†Tate MW	Sydney	1924–25

AUSTRALIA

571	Veivers TR	Old Trafford	1964
522	Fleetwood-Smith LO'B	Oval	1938
510	O'Reilly WJ	Oval	1938
478	Higgs JD	Sydney	1978–79
470	Giffen G	Melbourne	1894–95

†On debut

In a Match

ENGLAND

749	White JC	Adelaide	1928–29
712	†Tate MW	Sydney	1924–25
688	†Freeman AP	Sydney	1924–25
683	White JC	Melbourne	1928–29
632	Tate MW	Sydney	1924–25

AUSTRALIA

708	Giffen G	Sydney	1894–95
656	Grimmett CV	Oval	1930
656	†Ward FA	Brisbane	1936–37
654	Trumble H	Adelaide	1901–02
642	Mackay KD	Oval	1961

†On debut

In a Series

ENGLAND		
2528	Tate MW	1924–25
2440	White JC	1928–29
2226	Tate MW	1928–29
1971	Bedser AV	1946–47
1922	Wright DVP	1946–47

AUSTRALIA		
2390	Grimmett CV	1928–29
2379	Grimmett CV	1934
2302	O'Reilly WJ	1932–33
2126	Giffen G	1894–95
2098	Grimmett CV	1930

6.12 *Most Wickets*

All Matches (Minimum 50 wickets)

ENGLAND	M	Balls	Mdns	Runs	Wkts	Av	Best	5wi	10wm
Botham IT	29	7361	254	3556	136	26.15	6–78	8	2
Willis RGD	35	7294	198	3346	128	26.14	8–43	7	–
Rhodes W	41	5796	234	2616	109	24.00	8–68	6	1
Barnes SF	20	5749	262	2288	106	21.58	7–60	12	1
Underwood DL	29	8000	408	2770	105	26.38	7–50	4	2
Bedser AV	21	7065	209	2859	104	27.49	7–44	7	2
Peel R	20	5216	444	1715	102	16.81	7–31	6	2
Briggs J	31	4941	334	1993	97	20.55	6–45	7	3
Richardson T	14	4497	191	2220	88	25.23	8–94	11	4
Snow JA	20	5073	168	2126	83	25.61	7–40	4	–
Tate MW	20	7686	330	2540	83	30.60	6–99	6	1
Laker JC	15	4010	203	1444	79	18.28	10–53	5	2
Trueman FS	19	4361	83	1999	79	25.30	6–30	5	1
Lohmann GA	15	3301	326	1002	77	13.01	8–35	5	3
Statham JB	22	5405	131	2138	69	30.99	7–57	3	–
Larwood H	15	4053	120	1912	64	29.88	6–32	3	1

ENGLAND	M	Balls	Mdns	Runs	Wkts	Av	Best	5wi	10wm
Verity H	18	4930	257	1656	59	28.07	8–43	3	1
Barnes W	21	2289	271	793	51	15.55	6–28	3	–
Bates W	15	2364	282	821	50	16.42	7–28	4	1

AUSTRALIA	M	Balls	Mdns	Runs	Wkts	Av	Best	5wi	10wm
Lillee DK	29	8516	361	3507	167	21.00	7–89	11	4
Trumble H	31	7895	448	2945	141	20.89	8–65	9	3
Noble MA	39	6895	353	2860	115	24.87	7–17	9	2
Lindwall RR	29	6728	216	2559	114	22.45	7–63	6	–
Grimmett CV	22	9164	427	3439	106	32.44	6–37	11	2
Giffen G	31	6391	434	2791	103	27.10	7–117	7	1
O'Reilly WJ	19	7864	439	2587	102	25.36	7–54	8	3
Turner CTB	17	5179	457	1670	101	16.53	7–43	11	2
Thomson JR	21	4957	166	2418	100	24.18	6–46	5	–
McKenzie GD	25	7486	233	3009	96	31.34	7–153	6	–
Spofforth FR	18	4185	416	1731	94	18.41	7–44	7	4
Miller KR	29	5717	225	1949	87	22.40	7–60	3	1
Mailey AA	18	5201	90	2935	86	34.13	9–121	6	2
Davidson AK	25	5993	221	1996	84	23.76	6–64	5	–
Benaud R	27	7284	289	2641	83	31.82	6–70	4	–
Palmer GE	17	4417	452	1678	78	21.51	7–65	6	2
Johnston WA	17	5263	224	1818	75	24.24	5–35	3	–
Armstrong WW	42	6782	364	2288	74	30.92	6–35	3	–
Gregory JM	21	4888	109	2364	70	33.77	7–69	3	–
Lawson GF	14	3497	119	1802	68	26.50	7–81	6	1
Cotter A	16	3464	63	1916	67	28.60	7–148	6	–
Saunders JV	12	3268	108	1620	64	25.31	5–28	5	–
Jones E	18	3580	152	1757	60	29.28	7–88	3	1
Hogg RM	11	2629	94	952	56	17.00	6–74	5	2
Walker MHN	16	4912	200	1858	56	33.18	8–143	2	–
Mallett AA	16	3995	174	1581	50	31.62	5–114	1	–

At Sydney in 1978–79 *England were denied a new ball in their second innings when the Australian captain, GN Yallop, asked the umpires if he could bowl with an old one. Despite protests from the England captain, JM Brearley, the innings continued, contrary to the Laws, with an old ball, after a 6-minute delay.*

6.13 *Most Wickets in Each Era* (Minimum 30 wickets)

A dot before a player's name indicates an incomplete career record.

Era 1 (1876–77 to 1899)

ENGLAND	M	Balls	Mdns	Runs	Wkts	Av	Best	5wi	10wm
Peel R	20	5216	444	1715	102	16.81	7–31	6	2
Briggs J	31	4941	334	1993	97	20.55	6–45	7	3
Richardson T	14	4497	191	2220	88	25.23	8–94	11	4
Lohmann GA	15	3301	326	1002	77	13.01	8–35	5	3
Barnes W	21	2289	271	793	51	15.55	6–28	3	–
Bates W	15	2364	282	821	50	16.42	7–28	4	1
Hearne JT	11	2936	209	1070	48	22.29	6–41	4	1
Ulyett G	23	2527	286	992	48	20.67	7–36	1	–
Barlow RG	17	2456	325	767	34	22.56	7–40	3	–
Peate E	9	2096	250	682	31	22.00	6–85	2	–
AUSTRALIA									
Giffen G	31	6391	434	2791	103	27.10	7–117	7	1
Turner CTB	17	5179	457	1670	101	16.53	7–43	11	2
Spofforth FR	18	4185	416	1731	94	18.41	7–44	7	4
Palmer GE	17	4417	452	1678	78	21.51	7–65	6	2
•Trumble H	19	4057	241	1615	63	25.63	6–30	3	1
•Jones E	14	3058	129	1519	56	27.13	7–88	3	1
Ferris JJ	8	2030	224	684	48	14.25	5–26	4	–
Garrett TW	19	2708	297	970	36	26.94	6–78	2	–
Boyle HF	12	1743	175	641	32	20.03	6–42	1	–
•Noble MA	9	1808	106	791	32	24.72	6–49	2	–

Era 2 (1901–02 to 1912)

ENGLAND	M	Balls	Mdns	Runs	Wkts	Av	Best	5wi	10wm
Barnes SF	20	5749	262	2288	106	21.58	7–60	12	1
•Rhodes W	31	4202	155	1918	84	22.83	8–68	6	1
Braund LC	20	3731	140	1769	46	38.46	8–81	3	–
•Hirst GH	16	2676	87	1219	46	26.50	5–48	3	–
Blythe C	9	2085	99	877	41	21.39	6–44	3	1
Foster FR	8	1894	76	742	34	21.82	6–91	3	–
Crawford JN	5	1426	36	742	30	24.73	5–48	3	–

AUSTRALIA									
•Noble MA	30	5087	247	2069	83	24.93	7–17	7	2
•Trumble H	14	3838	207	1330	78	17.05	8–65	6	2
Cotter A	16	3464	63	1916	67	28.60	7–148	6	–
Saunders JV	12	3268	108	1620	64	25.31	5–28	5	–
•Armstrong WW	32	5403	287	1872	57	32.84	6–35	3	–
•Laver F	11	2201	114	894	33	27.09	8–31	2	–
Hordern HV	5	1665	42	780	32	24.38	7–90	4	2

Era 3 (1920–21 to 1938)

ENGLAND	M	Balls	Mdns	Runs	Wkts	Av	Best	5wi	10wm
Tate MW	20	7686	330	2540	83	30.60	6–99	5	1
Larwood H	15	4053	120	1912	64	29.88	6–32	3	1
Verity H	18	4930	257	1656	59	28.07	8–43	3	1
Allen GOB	13	2783	58	1603	43	37.28	5–36	1	–
•Voce W	9	2098	44	967	41	23.59	6–41	1	1
Farnes K	8	2153	58	1065	38	28.03	6–96	3	1
•Hammond WR	29	3958	136	1612	36	44.78	5–57	1	–
Parkin CH	9	1999	50	1090	32	34.06	5–38	2	–
White JC	7	2974	148	1033	31	33.32	8–126	3	1
Bowes WE	6	1459	41	741	30	24.70	6–142	3	–

AUSTRALIA									
Grimmett CV	22	9164	427	3439	106	32.44	6–37	11	2
O'Reilly WJ	19	7864	439	2587	102	25.36	7–54	8	3
Mailey AA	18	5201	90	2935	86	34.13	9–121	6	2
Gregory JM	21	4888	109	2364	70	33.77	7–69	3	–
Wall TW	14	3881	115	1663	43	38.67	5–66	2	–
Fleetwood-Smith LO'B	7	2359	54	1190	33	36.06	6–110	2	1
McDonald EA	8	1991	42	1060	33	32.12	5–32	2	–

Era 4 (1946–47 to 1968)

ENGLAND	M	Balls	Mdns	Runs	Wkts	Av	Best	5wi	10wm
Bedser AV	21	7065	209	2859	104	27.49	7–44	7	2
Laker JC	15	4010	203	1444	79	18.28	10–53	5	2
Trueman FS	19	4361	83	1999	79	25.30	6–30	5	1
Statham JB	22	5405	131	2138	69	30.99	7–57	3	–
Bailey TE	23	3300	105	1373	42	32.69	4–22	–	–

ENGLAND	M	Balls	Mdns	Runs	Wkts	Av	Best	5wi	10wm
•Titmus FJ	15	4786	198	1434	40	35.85	7–79	2	–
Wright DVP	11	2989	41	1613	36	44.80	7–105	2	–
Tyson FH	8	1724	21	810	32	25.31	7–27	2	1
Lock GAR	13	3442	194	1128	31	36.39	5–45	1	–
AUSTRALIA									
Lindwall RR	29	6728	216	2559	114	22.45	7–63	6	–
•McKenzie GD	22	6602	219	2658	89	29.86	7–153	6	–
Miller KR	29	5717	225	1949	87	22.40	7–60	3	1
Davidson AK	25	5993	221	1996	84	23.76	6–64	5	–
Benaud R	27	7284	289	2641	83	31.82	6–70	4	–
Johnston WA	17	5263	224	1818	75	24.24	5–35	3	–
Johnson IW	22	4592	187	1590	42	37.86	6–42	1	–
Hawke NJN	12	3176	128	1119	37	30.24	7–105	4	–
Archer RG	12	2445	126	761	35	21.74	5–53	1	–

Era 5 (1970–71 to 1985)

ENGLAND	M	Balls	Mdns	Runs	Wkts	Av	Best	5wi	10wm
Botham IT	29	7361	254	3556	136	26.15	6–78	8	2
Willis RGD	35	7294	198	3346	128	26.14	8–43	7	–
•Underwood DL	25	6741	305	2468	85	29.03	7–113	3	2
•Snow JA	15	3855	124	1618	66	24.52	7–40	4	–
Emburey JE	15	4093	193	1388	48	28.92	5–82	1	–
Greig AW	21	3472	114	1663	44	37.80	4–53	–	–
Hendrick M	13	3082	107	1049	42	24.98	4–41	–	–
Old CM	12	2789	90	1232	40	30.80	4–104	–	–
Miller G	14	2713	113	856	39	21.95	5–44	1	–
Arnold GG	8	1992	51	898	30	29.93	5–86	1	–
AUSTRALIA									
Lillee DK	29	8516	361	3507	167	21.00	7–89	11	4
Thomson JR	21	4957	166	2418	100	24.18	6–46	5	–
Lawson GF	14	3497	119	1802	68	26.50	7–81	6	1
Hogg RM	11	2629	94	952	56	17.00	6–74	5	2
Walker MHN	16	4912	200	1858	56	33.18	8–143	2	–
•Mallett AA	15	3629	159	1417	45	31.49	5–114	1	–
Alderman TM	7	2208	91	977	43	22.72	6–135	4	–
McDermott CJ	6	1406	21	901	30	30.03	8–141	2	–

6.14 *Wicket with First Ball*

ENGLAND			
Bradley WM†	(Laver F c Lilley AFA)	Old Trafford	1899
Arnold EG†	(Trumper VT c Foster RE)	Sydney	1903–04
AUSTRALIA			
Coningham A†	(MacLaren AC c Trott GHS)	Melbourne	1894–95
McCormick EL	(Worthington TS c Oldfield WAS)	Brisbane	1936–37

†Debut in all Tests

6.15 *Bowling Through Innings Unchanged*

In Both Innings

ENGLAND			AUSTRALIA		
Peel R	Old Trafford	1888	Spofforth FR	Oval	1882
Hearne JT	Oval	1896	Turner CTB	Sydney	1887–88
Rhodes W	Melbourne	1903–04	Turner CTB	Lord's	1888
			Turner CTB	Sydney	1894–95
			Trumble H	Oval	1902

In One Innings

ENGLAND			AUSTRALIA		
Shaw A	Melbourne	1876–77	Kendall T	Melbourne	1876–77
Morley F	Sydney	1882–83	Palmer GE	Sydney	1881–82
Barlow RG	Sydney	1882–83	Evans E	Sydney	1881–82
Lohmann GA	Oval	1886	Palmer GE	Sydney	1881–82
Briggs J	Oval	1886	Spofforth FR }	Oval	1882
Lohmann GA	Sydney	1887–88	Spofforth FR }	Oval	1882
Peel R	Sydney	1887–88	Spofforth FR	Sydney	1882–83
Peel R }	Old Trafford	1888	Spofforth FR	Old Trafford	1884
Peel R }	Old Trafford	1888	Spofforth FR	Sydney	1884–85
Lohmann GA	Oval	1890	Spofforth FR	Sydney	1884–85
Martin F	Oval	1890	Palmer GE	Sydney	1884–85
Briggs J	Adelaide	1891–92	Turner CTB	Sydney	1886–87
Lohmann GA	Adelaide	1891–92	Ferris JJ	Sydney	1886–87

ENGLAND			AUSTRALIA		
Attewell W	Adelaide	1891–92	Turner CTB }	Sydney	1887–88
Lockwood WH	Oval	1893	Turner CTB }		
Richardson T	Lord's	1896	Turner CTB }	Lord's	1888
Lohmann GA	Lord's	1896	Turner CTB }		
Hearne JT }	Oval	1896	Ferris JJ	Lord's	1888
Hearne JT }			Turner CTB	Melbourne	1894–95
Braund LC	Sydney	1901–02	Giffen G	Adelaide	1894–95
Barnes SF	Melbourne	1901–02	Turner CTB }	Sydney	1894–95
Blythe C	Melbourne	1901–02	Turner CTB }		
Rhodes W	Edgbaston	1902	Giffen G	Sydney	1894–95
Rhodes W }	Melbourne	1903–04	Trumble H	Oval	1896
Rhodes W }			Trumble H	Melbourne	1901–02
Hirst GH	Edgbaston	1909	Noble MA	Melbourne	1901–02
Blythe C	Edgbaston	1909	Noble MA	Sydney	1901–02
Barnes SF	Old Trafford	1909	Saunders JV	Sydney	1901–02
Voce W	Brisbane	1936–37	Noble MA	Melbourne	1901–02
Allen GOB	Brisbane	1936–37	Trumble H	Old Trafford	1902
Hendrick M	Headingley	1977	Trumble H }	Oval	1902
			Trumble H }		
			Cotter A	Melbourne	1903–04
			Gregory JM	Trent Bridge	1921
			Meckiff I	Melbourne	1958–59
			Massie RAL	Lord's	1972
			Alderman TM	Trent Bridge	1981

The following bowlers bowled unchanged through an innings which closed at a low score

ENGLAND			AUSTRALIA		
Bailey TE	Brisbane (Australia total 32–7d)	1950–51	Johnston WA	Brisbane (England total 68–7d)	1950–51
Bedser AV	Brisbane (Australia total 32–7d)	1950–51			
Laker JC	Old Trafford (Australia total 35–8)	1953			

Smoke from nearby bushfires *made batting difficult for England in the fourth Test of 1897–98, at Melbourne.*

6.16 *Pairs Bowling Unchanged in a Completed Innings*

ENGLAND

Bowlers	Aus Total	Ground	Year
Morley F (2–34) Barlow RG (7–40)	83	Sydney	1882–83
Lohmann GA (7–36) Briggs J (3–28)	68	Oval	1886
Lohmann GA (5–17) Peel R (5–18)	42	Sydney	1887–88
Briggs J (6–49) Lohmann GA (3–46)	100	Adelaide	1891–92
Richardson T (6–39) Lohmann GA (3–13)	53	Lord's	1896
Barnes SF (6–42) Blythe C (4–64)	112	Melbourne	1901–02
Hirst GH (4–28) Blythe C (6–44)	74	Edgbaston	1909
Voce W (4–16) Allen GOB (5–36)	58	Brisbane	1936–37

AUSTRALIA

Bowlers	Eng Total	Ground	Year
Palmer GE (7–68) Evans E (3–64)	133	Sydney	1881–82
Spofforth FR (5–30) Palmer GE (4–32)	77	Sydney	1884–85
Turner CTB (6–15) Ferris JJ (4–27)	45	Sydney	1886–87
Turner CTB (5–36) Ferris JJ (5–26)	62	Lord's	1888
Giffen G (5–26) Turner CTB (4–33)	72	Sydney	1894–95
Trumble H (3–38) Noble MA (7–17)	61	Melbourne	1901–02
Noble MA (5–54) Saunders JV (5–43)	99	Sydney	1901–02

For England TE Bailey (4–22) and AV Bedser (3–9) bowled throughout the Australian innings of 32–7d at Brisbane 1950–51.

6.17 *Most Bowlers in an Innings*

ENGLAND

	Ground	Year
11	Oval	1884
8	Adelaide	1897–98
8	Old Trafford	1899
8	Oval	1899
8	Adelaide	1924–25
8	Adelaide	1936–37
8	Headingley	1948
8	Sydney	1962–63
8	Melbourne	1965–66

AUSTRALIA

	Ground	Year
8	Adelaide	1884–85
8	Melbourne	1884–85
8	Melbourne	1884–85
8	Sydney	1894–95
8	Sydney	1903–04
8	Old Trafford	1953
8	Melbourne	1970–71
8	Oval	1975

6.18 *Most Bowlers in a Match* (Both sides)

18 Oval	1884	15 Sydney	1962–63
15 Melbourne	1884–85	15 Melbourne	1965–66
15 Sydney	1894–95	15 Sydney	1970–71
15 Melbourne	1897–98	15 Oval	1975
15 Headingley	1948		

The fewest bowlers used by both sides in a completed match is 6 – Old Trafford 1888.

6.19 *Bowler Dismissing All 11 Batsmen During Match*

ENGLAND			AUSTRALIA
Laker JC	Old Trafford	1956	(no instance)

6.20 *Top of Bowling Averages in Most Series*

ENGLAND	AUSTRALIA
3 Bates W (1881–82, 1882–83, 1884–85)	3 Lindwall RR (1946–47, 1948, 1953)
2 Briggs J (1886, 1891–92)	2 Davidson AK (1961, 1962–63)
2 Laker JC (1956, 1958–59)	2 Grimmett CV (1924–25, 1926)
2 Lockwood WH (1899, 1902)	2 Horan TP (1882–83, 1884–85)
2 Peel R (1888, 1896)	2 Laver F (1905, 1909)
2 Rhodes W (1903–04, 1926)	2 O'Reilly WJ (1934, 1938)
2 Richardson T (1893, 1894–95)	2 Saunders JV (1901–02, 1907–08)
2 Snow JA (1970–71, 1975)	2 Thomson JR (1974–75, 1982–83)
2 Underwood DL (1968, 1972)	2 Trumble H (1899, 1902)
2 Willis RGD (1977, 1982–83)	2 Turner CTB (1888, 1891–92)
2 Yardley NWD (1946–47, 1948)	2 Wall TW (1928–29, 1932–33)

6.21 *Called for Throwing*

The only bowler to be called for throwing in these Tests is E Jones (Aus), who was called once by J Phillips at Melbourne in 1897–98.

6.22 *Economical Career Bowling* (Minimum 1000 balls)

ENGLAND	Runs per 100 Balls	M	Balls	Mdns	Runs	Wkts	Av	Best
Attewell W	21.96	10	2850	326	626	27	23.19	4–42
Shaw A	25.93	7	1099	155	285	12	23.75	5–38
Lohmann GA	30.35	15	3301	326	1002	77	13.01	8–35
Titmus FJ	31.12	19	5765	228	1794	47	38.17	7–79
Kilner R	31.19	7	2164	66	675	24	28.13	4–51
Barlow RG	31.23	17	2456	325	767	34	22.56	7–40
D'Oliveira BL	31.33	13	1644	71	515	14	36.79	2–15
Miller G	31.55	14	2713	113	856	39	21.95	5–44
Peate E	32.54	9	2096	250	682	31	22.00	6–85
Lock GAR	32.77	13	3442	194	1128	31	36.39	5–45
Illingworth R	32.78	18	3337	180	1094	34	32.18	6–87
Peel R	32.88	20	5216	444	1715	102	16.81	7–31
Tate MW	33.05	20	7686	330	2540	83	30.60	6–99
Verity H	33.59	18	4930	257	1656	59	28.07	8–43
Emburey JE	33.91	15	4093	193	1388	48	28.92	5–82
Hendrick M	34.04	13	3082	107	1049	42	24.98	4–41
Underwood DL	34.63	29	8000	408	2770	105	26.38	7–50
Barnes W	34.64	21	2289	271	793	51	15.55	6–28
Bates W	34.73	15	2364	282	821	50	16.42	7–28
White JC	34.73	7	2974	148	1033	31	33.32	8–126
Allen DA	35.79	10	2492	120	892	28	31.86	4–47
Laker JC	36.01	15	4010	203	1444	79	18.28	10–53
Hemmings EE	36.16	3	1131	59	409	9	45.44	3–68
Hearne JT	36.44	11	2936	209	1070	48	22.29	6–41
Geary G	36.64	9	2628	112	963	27	35.67	5–35

AUSTRALIA	Runs per 100 Balls	M	Balls	Mdns	Runs	Wkts	Av	Best
Evans E	26.84	6	1237	166	322	7	47.43	3–64
Richardson AJ	28.75	9	1812	91	521	12	43.42	2–20
Iverson JB	28.88	5	1108	29	320	21	15.24	6–27
Oxenham RK	28.89	3	1208	72	349	7	49.86	4–67
Ironmonger H	29.07	6	2446	155	711	21	33.86	4–26
Higgs JD	29.81	6	1580	47	471	19	24.79	5–148
Mackay KD	30.94	16	2828	126	875	24	36.46	5–121
Archer RG	31.12	12	2445	126	761	35	21.74	5–53

AUSTRALIA	Runs per 100 Balls	M	Balls	Mdns	Runs	Wkts	Av	Best
Turner CTB	32.25	17	5179	457	1670	101	16.53	7–43
Toshack ERH	32.47	9	2467	120	801	28	28.61	6–82
Dymock G	32.82	7	2008	65	659	25	26.36	6–34
O'Reilly WJ	32.90	19	7864	439	2587	102	25.36	7–54
Bright RJ	33.20	10	2009	135	667	18	37.06	5–68
Davidson AK	33.31	25	5993	221	1996	84	23.76	6–64
Ferris JJ	33.69	8	2030	224	684	48	14.25	5–26
McCool CL	33.72	5	1456	27	491	18	27.28	5–44
Miller KR	33.74	29	5717	225	1949	87	22.40	7–60
Massie RAL	34.23	4	1195	58	409	23	17.78	8–53
Johnston WA	34.54	17	5263	224	1818	75	24.24	5–35
Kelleway C	34.58	18	3340	112	1155	37	31.22	4–27
Johnson IW	34.63	22	4592	187	1590	42	37.86	6–42
Gleeson JW	34.77	13	3391	150	1179	29	40.66	4–83
Howell WP	35.15	16	3508	229	1233	35	35.23	4–43
Macartney CG	35.21	26	2579	122	908	33	27.52	7–58
Hawke NJN	35.23	12	3176	128	1119	37	30.24	7–105

6.23 *Expensive Career Bowling* (Minimum 1000 balls)

ENGLAND	Runs per 100 balls	M	Balls	Mdns	Runs	Wkts	Av	Best
Edrich WJ	60.12	21	1477	24	888	16	55.50	3–50
Allen GOB	57.60	13	2783	58	1603	43	37.28	5–36
Wright DVP	54.97	14	3709	61	2039	48	42.48	7–105
Parkin CH	54.53	9	1999	50	1090	32	34.06	5–38
Douglas JWHT	52.93	17	2318	53	1227	35	35.06	5–46
Crawford JN	52.03	5	1426	36	742	30	24.73	5–48
Jones IJ	51.65	4	1032	15	533	15	35.53	6–118
Bowes WE	50.79	6	1459	41	741	30	24.70	6–142
Jackson Hon. FS	50.35	20	1587	77	799	24	33.29	5–52
Arnold EG	50.26	8	1371	47	689	25	27.56	4–28
Hearne JW	49.61	16	2068	31	1026	16	64.13	4–84
Farnes K	49.47	8	2153	58	1065	38	28.03	6–96
Richardson T	49.37	14	4497	191	2220	88	25.23	8–94
Botham IT	48.31	29	7361	254	3556	136	26.15	6–78
Greig AW	47.90	21	3472	114	1663	44	37.80	4–53

ENGLAND	**Runs per 100 balls**	**M**	**Balls**	**Mdns**	**Runs**	**Wkts**	**Av**	**Best**
Gilligan AER	47.75	5	1087	14	519	10	51.90	3–114
Fielder A	47.69	6	1491	42	711	26	27.35	6–82
Braund LC	47.41	20	3731	140	1769	46	38.46	8–81
Larwood H	47.17	15	4053	120	1912	64	29.88	6–32
Tyson FH	46.98	8	1724	21	810	32	25.31	7–27
Dexter ER	46.90	19	1582	29	742	23	32.26	3–16
Brown DJ	46.88	8	1728	48	810	23	35.22	5–42
Voce W	46.04	11	2450	56	1128	41	27.51	6–41
Hirst GH	46.01	21	3445	118	1585	49	32.35	5–48
Willis RGD	45.87	35	7294	198	3346	128	26.14	8–43

AUSTRALIA	**Runs per 100 balls**	**M**	**Balls**	**Mdns**	**Runs**	**Wkts**	**Av**	**Best**
McDermott CJ	64.08	6	1406	21	901	30	30.03	8–141
Mailey AA	56.43	18	5201	90	2935	86	34.13	9–121
Cotter A	55.31	16	3464	63	1916	67	28.60	7–148
Trott GHS	53.92	24	1890	48	1019	29	35.14	4–71
McDonald EA	53.24	8	1991	42	1060	33	32.12	5–32
Lawson GF	51.53	14	3497	119	1802	68	26.50	7–81
Fleetwood-Smith LO'B	50.45	7	2359	54	1190	33	36.06	6–110
Saunders JV	49.57	12	3268	108	1620	64	25.31	5–28
Hopkins AJY	49.11	17	1183	47	581	21	27.67	4–81
Jones E	49.08	18	3580	152	1757	60	29.28	7–88
Thomson JR	48.78	21	4957	166	2418	100	24.18	6–46
McCormick EL	48.75	7	1356	26	661	21	31.48	4–101
Gregory JM	48.36	21	4888	109	2364	70	33.77	7–69
McKibbin TR	48.06	5	1032	41	496	17	29.18	3–35
Hordern HV	46.85	5	1665	42	780	32	24.38	7–90
Pascoe LS	46.03	6	1599	58	736	29	25.38	5–59
Simpson RB	45.84	19	1828	79	838	16	52.38	5–57
Ward FA	45.27	4	1268	30	574	11	52.18	6–102
Holland RG	45.06	4	1032	41	465	6	77.50	5–68
Yardley B	44.44	9	2660	103	1182	29	40.76	5–107
Alderman TM	44.25	7	2208	91	977	43	22.72	6–135
Giffen G	43.67	31	6391	434	2791	103	27.10	7–117
Fairfax AG	43.47	5	1010	38	439	14	31.36	4–101
Thomson AL	43.05	4	1519	33	654	12	54.50	3–79
Wall TW	42.85	14	3881	115	1663	43	38.67	5–66

6.24 *Most Consecutive Innings Conceding 100 or More Runs*

ENGLAND

5 Wright DVP	Brisbane, Sydney, Melbourne (2), Adelaide 1946–47
4 Richardson T	Sydney, Melbourne, Adelaide, Melbourne 1897–98
4 White JC	Melbourne, Adelaide (2), Melbourne 1928–29
3 Botham IT	Oval (2) 1981, Perth 1982–83
3 Freeman AP	Sydney (2), Adelaide 1924–25

The three innings shown above for AP Freeman were the first three of the four in which he bowled. In the fourth innings he conceded 94 runs.

JT Hearne conceded over 90 but under 100 in four consecutive innings in 1897–98.

AV Bedser conceded in his first five innings (1946–47) 159, 153, 99, 176 and 97 runs.

MW Tate conceded in his first four innings (1924–25) 130, 98, 142 and 99 runs.

IAR Peebles bowled in only two innings (1930) and conceded 150 and 204 runs.

T Richardson conceded over 100 runs in an innings on 12 occasions.

AUSTRALIA

5 Grimmett CV	Oval 1926, Brisbane† (2), Sydney, Melbourne 1928–29
5 Mailey AA	Sydney, Adelaide (2), Melbourne (2) 1920–21
3 Cotter A	Sydney (2), Melbourne 1907–08
3 Fleetwood-Smith LO'B	Melbourne, Adelaide (2) 1936–37
3 Gregory JM	Sydney (2), Melbourne 1924–25
3 Grimmett CV	Lord's (2), Headingley 1930
3 Lawson GF	Old Trafford, Edgbaston, Oval 1985
3 McDermott CJ	Old Trafford, Edgbaston, Oval 1985
3 Mailey AA	Sydney (2), Melbourne 1924–25
3 Mailey AA	Adelaide (2), Melbourne 1924–25
3 Ward FA	Brisbane (2), Sydney 1936–37

†Exhibition Ground

The three innings shown above for FA Ward were the first three of the five in which he bowled. In the other two innings he conceded 60 and 142 runs.

CV Grimmett in eight consecutive innings (Oval 1926 to Adelaide 1928–29) conceded over 100 runs on seven occasions and 96 in the other innings. In all he conceded over 100 runs in an innings on 16 occasions.

AA Mailey in seven consecutive innings (Sydney to Melbourne 1924–25) conceded over 100 on six occasions and 92 in the other innings. In all he conceded over 100 runs in an innings on 14 occasions.

6.25 *Most Consecutive Innings Taking Four or More Wickets*

ENGLAND

6 Briggs J	Sydney, Adelaide (2) 1891–92, Oval (2), Old Trafford 1893
5 Bedser AV	Melbourne (2) 1950–51, Trent Bridge (2), Lord's 1953
5 Laker JC	Headingley (2), Old Trafford (2), Oval 1956
5 Richardson T	Melbourne 1894–95, Lord's (2), Old Trafford (2) 1896
4 Botham IT	Sydney 1978–79, Perth (2), Sydney 1979–80
4 Hearne JT	Oval (2) 1896, Sydney (2) 1897–98
4 Peel R	Sydney (2) 1887–88, Lord's (2) 1888

Bedser and Richardson both took 5 or more wickets in each of the innings above.

AUSTRALIA

8 Turner CTB	Sydney (2) 1886–87, Sydney (2) 1887–88, Lord's (2), Oval, Old Trafford 1888
7 Trumble H	Sheffield, Old Trafford (2), Oval (2) 1902, Melbourne (2) 1903–04
5 Benaud R	Sydney (2), Adelaide (2), Melbourne 1958–59
5 Ferris JJ	Sydney (2), Sydney (2) 1886–87, Sydney 1887–88
5 Lawson GF	Perth, Brisbane (2), Adelaide (2) 1982–83
4 Giffen G	Sydney (2), Melbourne, Adelaide 1894–95
4 Hogg RM	Perth (2), Melbourne (2) 1978–79
4 Lillee DK	Oval 1975, Melbourne (2) 1976–77, Perth 1979–80
4 McDonald EA	Trent Bridge, Lord's (2), Headingley 1921
4 Mailey AA	Adelaide (2), Melbourne (2) 1920–21
4 Palmer GE	Sydney (2), Sydney (2) 1881–82
4 Thomson JR	Perth, Melbourne (2), Sydney 1974–75

Hogg took 5 wickets in each of the 4 innings above.

6.26 *Ten Wickets in a Match on Most Occasions*

ENGLAND

4 Richardson T
3 Briggs J
3 Lohmann GA
2 Bedser AV
2 Botham IT
2 Laker JC
2 Peel R
2 Underwood DL

AUSTRALIA

4 Lillee DK
4 Spofforth FR
3 O'Reilly WJ
3 Trumble H
2 Grimmett CV
2 Hogg RM
2 Hordern HV
2 Mailey AA
2 Noble MA
2 Palmer GE
2 Turner CTB

6.27 *Youngest Players to Take Five Wickets in an Innings*

ENGLAND

Age	Name	Analysis	Ground	Year
21 yrs 31 days	Crawford JN	29–1–79–5	Melbourne	1907–08
21 yrs 72 days	Lohmann GA	30.2–17–36–7	Oval	1886
21 yrs 246 days	†Botham IT	20–5–74–5	Trent Bridge	1977
21 yrs 256 days	Cowans NG	26–6–77–6	Melbourne	1982–83
21 yrs 260 days	†Pocock PI	33–10–79–6	Old Trafford	1968

†On debut

Crawford and Lohmann both took 5 wickets in an innings 3 times before reaching the age of 22; Botham did it twice. Pocock never played another Test against Australia.

AUSTRALIA

Age	Name	Analysis	Ground	Year
19 yrs 95 days	Cotter A	15.2–2–40–6	Melbourne	1903–04
19 yrs 253 days	†Ferris JJ	61–30–76–5	Sydney	1886–87
20 yrs 2 days	†McKenzie GD	29–13–37–5	Lord's	1961
20 yrs 75 days	McDermott CJ	29.2–5–70–6	Lord's	1985
21 yrs 196 days	†Lillee DK	28.3–0–84–5	Adelaide	1970–71

†On debut

Ferris took 5 wickets in an innings twice before reaching the age of 20, and once more before his 22nd birthday. Cotter, McKenzie and McDermott each performed the feat twice before reaching the age of 22.

6.28 *Oldest Players to Take Five Wickets in an Innings*

ENGLAND

Age	Name	Analysis	Ground	Year
40 yrs 72 days	Brown FR	18–4–49–5	Melbourne	1950–51
39 yrs 177 days	Peel R	12–5–23–6	Oval	1896
39 yrs 124 days	Barnes SF	27–15–30–5	Oval	1912
37 yrs 355 days	White JC	64.5–21–126–8	Adelaide	1928–29
37 yrs 264 days	Hirst GH	23.5–4–58–5	Edgbaston	1909

Oldest on Debut

37 yrs 145 days	Carr DW	34–2–146–5	Oval	1909

Barnes took 5 wickets in an innings 4 times after reaching the age of 38.

AUSTRALIA

Age	Name	Analysis	Ground	Year
46 yrs 272 days	Blackie DD	44–13–94–6	Melbourne	1928–29
42 yrs 240 days	Grimmett CV	26.3–10–64–5	Oval	1934
40 yrs 223 days	Mailey AA	33.5–3–138–6	Oval	1926
39 yrs 232 days	Laver F	18.2–7–31–8	Old Trafford	1909
38 yrs 255 days	†Holland RG	32–12–68–5	Lord's	1985

†On debut

Grimmett took 5 wickets in an innings twice after reaching the age of 42, and 6 times in all after reaching the age of 38. Mailey achieved the feat twice after passing his 39th birthday.

6.29 *Penetrative Career Bowling* (Qualification 25 wickets)

ENGLAND	Balls per Wicket	M	Balls	Mdns	Runs	Wkts	Av	Best
Bosanquet BJT	38.80	7	970	10	604	25	24.16	8–107
Lohmann GA	42.87	15	3301	326	1002	77	13.01	8–35
Barnes W	44.88	21	2289	271	793	51	15.55	6–28
Lockwood WH	45.81	12	1970	100	884	43	20.56	7–71
Steel AG	47.03	13	1364	108	605	29	20.86	3–27
Bates W	47.28	15	2364	282	821	50	16.42	7–28
Crawford JN	47.53	5	1426	36	742	30	24.73	5–48
Bowes WE	48.63	6	1459	41	741	30	24.70	6–142
Laker JC	50.76	15	4010	203	1444	79	18.28	10–53
Blythe C	50.85	9	2085	99	877	41	21.39	6–44
Briggs J	50.94	31	4941	334	1993	97	20.55	6–45
Richardson T	51.10	14	4497	191	2220	88	25.23	8–94
Peel R	51.14	20	5216	444	1715	102	16.81	7–31
Ulyett G	52.65	23	2527	286	992	48	20.67	7–36
Rhodes W	53.17	41	5796	234	2616	109	24.00	8–68
Tyson FH	53.88	8	1724	21	810	32	25.31	7–27
Botham IT	54.13	29	7361	254	3556	136	26.15	6–78
Barnes SF	54.24	20	5749	262	2288	106	21.58	7–60

ENGLAND	Balls per Wicket	M	Balls	Mdns	Runs	Wkts	Av	Best
Arnold EG	54.84	8	1371	47	689	25	27.56	4–28
Trueman FS	55.20	19	4361	83	1999	79	25.30	6–30
Foster FR	55.71	8	1894	76	742	34	21.82	6–91
Farnes K	56.66	8	2153	58	1065	38	28.03	6–96
Willis RGD	56.98	35	7294	198	3346	128	26.14	8–43
Fielder A	57.35	6	1491	42	711	26	27.35	6–82
Voce W	59.76	11	2450	56	1128	41	27.51	6–41

AUSTRALIA	Balls per Wicket	M	Balls	Mdns	Runs	Wkts	Av	Best
Ferris JJ	42.29	8	2030	224	684	48	14.25	5–26
Spofforth FR	44.52	18	4185	416	1731	94	18.41	7–44
McDermott CJ	46.87	6	1406	21	901	30	30.03	8–141
Hogg RM	46.95	11	2629	94	956	56	17.00	6–74
Thomson JR	49.57	21	4957	166	2418	100	24.18	6–46
Lillee DK	50.99	29	8516	361	3507	167	21.00	7–89
Saunders JV	51.06	12	3268	108	1620	64	25.31	5–28
Turner CTB	51.28	17	5179	457	1670	101	16.53	7–43
Alderman TM	51.35	7	2208	91	977	43	22.72	6–135
Lawson GF	51.43	14	3497	119	1802	68	26.50	7–81
Cotter A	51.70	16	3464	63	1916	67	28.60	7–148
Hordern HV	52.03	5	1665	42	780	32	24.38	7–90
Boyle HF	54.47	12	1743	175	641	32	20.03	6–42
Pascoe LS	55.14	6	1599	58	736	29	25.38	5–59
Trumble H	55.99	31	7895	448	2945	141	20.89	8–65
Palmer GE	56.63	17	4417	452	1678	78	21.51	7–65
Lindwall RR	59.02	29	6728	216	2559	114	22.45	7–63
Jones E	59.67	18	3580	152	1757	60	29.28	7–88
Noble MA	59.96	39	6895	353	2860	115	24.87	7–17
McDonald EA	60.33	8	1991	42	1060	33	32.12	5–32
Mailey AA	60.48	18	5201	90	2935	86	34.13	9–121
Giffen G	62.05	31	6391	434	2791	103	27.10	7–117
Laver F	63.81	15	2361	121	964	37	26.05	8–31
Trott GHS	65.17	24	1890	48	1019	29	35.14	4–71
Hurst AG	65.36	6	1634	44	577	25	23.08	5–28

SECTION 7
The Wicketkeepers

Alan Knott (batting) and Rod Marsh, two of the most successful wicketkeepers in the history of England – Australia Test cricket

7.1 *Total of Dismissals*

ENGLAND	County	M	Ct	St	Total
Knott APE	Kent	34	97	8	105
Lilley AFA	Warks	32	65	19	84
Evans TG	Kent	31	64	12	76
Taylor RW	Derbys	17	54	3	57
Strudwick H	Surrey	17	37	5	42
Ames LEG	Kent	17	33	4	37
Duckworth G	Lancs	10	23	3	26
Downton PR	Middx	7	21	1	22
Parks JM	Sussex	10	17	4	21
Murray JT	Middx	6	18	1	19
MacGregor G	Middx	7	14	3	17
Pilling R	Lancs	8	10	4	14
Smith AC	Warks	4	13	–	13
Smith EJ	Warks	7	12	1	13
Hunter J	Yorks	5	8	3	11
Philipson H	Middx	5	8	3	11
Storer W	Derbys	6	11	–	11
Tylecote EFS	Kent	6	5	5	10
Humphries J	Derbys	3	7	–	7
Sherwin M	Notts	3	5	2	7
Young RA	Sussex	2	6	–	6
Brown G	Hants	3	2	2	4
Gay LH	Som	1	3	1	4
Bairstow DL	Yorks	1	2	1	3
Swetman R	Surrey	2	3	–	3
Wood A	Yorks	1	3	–	3
Hone L	MCC	1	2	–	2
Lyttelton Hon. A	Middx	4	2	–	2
Price WFF	Middx	1	2	–	2
Wood H	Surrey	1	1	1	2
Dolphin A	Yorks	1	1	–	1
Gibb PA	Yorks	1	1	–	1
Selby J	Notts	2	1	–	1
Andrew KV	Northants	1	–	–	–

Only players selected to keep wicket are included. Selby played in 6 Tests in all and MacGregor in 8. AJW McIntyre, though a specialist wicketkeeper, did not keep wicket in his only E v A Test.

The following deputised during a match for a wicketkeeper who was injured or called upon to bowl:

Jupp H (for Selby J)	Melbourne	1876–77	
Read WW (for Lyttelton Hon. A)	Oval	1884	
Grace WG (for Lyttelton Hon. A)	Oval	1884	Ct 1
Brown JT (for Lilley AFA)	Old Trafford	1896	
Jones AO (for Lilley AFA)	Oval	1905	Ct 1 as sub
Spooner RH (for Lilley AFA)	Oval	1905	Ct 1
Woolley FE (for Ames LEG)	Oval	1934	Ct 1
Paynter E (for Ames LEG)	Lord's	1938	Ct 1
Graveney TW (for Evans TG)	Adelaide	1958–59	
Parfitt PH (for Murray JT)	Sydney	1962–63	
Barrington KF (for Parks JM)	Melbourne	1965–66	Ct 1

W Storer (Eng) kept wicket and also bowled slow leg-breaks in four Tests in the 1897–98 series.

AUSTRALIA	State	M	Ct	St	Total
Marsh RW	WA	42	141	7	148
Oldfield WAS	NSW	38	59	31	90
Grout ATW	Qld	22	69	7	76
Blackham JM	Vic	32	35	24	59
Kelly JJ	NSW	33	39	16	55
Carter H	NSW	21	35	17	52
Tallon D	Qld	15	38	4	42
Langley GRA	SA	9	35	2	37
Jarman BN	SA	7	18	–	18
Maclean JA	Qld	4	18	–	18
Jarvis AH	SA	9	8	9	17
Maddocks LV	Vic	5	12	1	13
Phillips WB	SA	6	11	–	11
Wright KJ	WA	2	7	1	8
Barnett BA	Vic	4	3	2	5
Love HSB	NSW	1	3	–	3
Saggers RA	NSW	1	3	–	3
Carkeek W	Vic	3	2	–	2
Murdoch WL	NSW	1	1	1	2
Taber HB	NSW	1	2	–	2
Burton FJ	NSW	1	–	1	1

Only players selected to keep wicket are included. Blackham made one additional catch as replacement wicketkeeper for Murdoch (see over).

The following deputised during a match for a wicketkeeper who was injured or indisposed:

Blackham JM (for Murdoch WL)	Sydney	1881–82	Ct 1
Richardson VY (for Oldfield WAS)	Adelaide	1932–33	
Harvey RN (for Langley GRA)	Oval	1956	
Yallop GN (for Maclean JA)	Sydney	1978–79	Ct 1

7.2 *Summary of Wicketkeeping Dismissals*

	Tests	No of Wkts	Total Ct	Total St	Totals	Percentage per Test
England	257	34	551	86	637	2.48
Australia	257	21	539	123	662	2.58

The above figures do not include dismissals made by players who deputised for regular wicketkeepers.

7.3 *Most Dismissals*

In an Innings

Total	Ct	St	ENGLAND		
5	3	2	Parks JM	Sydney	1965–66
5	5	–	Taylor RW	Brisbane	1978–79
Total	**Ct**	**St**	**AUSTRALIA**		
6	6	–	Marsh RW	Brisbane	1982–83
5	1	4	Oldfield WAS	Melbourne	1924–25
5	5	–	Langley GRA	Lord's	1956
5	5	–	Grout ATW	Lord's	1961
5	5	–	Grout ATW	Sydney	1965–66
5	5	–	Marsh RW	Old Trafford	1972
5	5	–	Marsh RW	Trent Bridge	1972
5	5	–	Maclean JA	Brisbane	1978–79

The fourth day of the Adelaide Test match *of 1901–02 was curtailed because of a fierce duststorm.*

In a Match

Total	Ct	St	ENGLAND		
7	6	1	Evans TG	Lord's	1956
7	7	–	Murray JT	Old Trafford	1961
7	6	1	Taylor RW	Perth	1979–80
7	7	–	Taylor RW	Headingley	1981

Total	Ct	St	AUSTRALIA		
9	8	1	Langley GRA	Lord's	1956
9	9	–	Marsh RW	Brisbane	1982–83
8	8	–	Kelly JJ	Sydney	1901–02
8	8	–	Grout ATW	Lord's	1961
8	8	–	Marsh RW	Adelaide	1982–83

In a Series

Total	Ct	St	ENGLAND		Tests
24	21	3	Knott APE	1970–71	6
23	22	1	Knott APE	1974–75	6
20	18	2	Taylor RW	1978–79	6
20	19	1	Downton PR	1985	6
18	16	2	Strudwick H	1924–25	5
18	17	1	Murray JT	1961	5

Total	Ct	St	AUSTRALIA		
28	28	–	Marsh RW	1982–83	5
23	21	2	Marsh RW	1972	5
23	23	–	Marsh RW	1981	6
21	20	1	Grout ATW	1961	5
20	16	4	Tallon D	1946–47	5
20	17	3	Grout ATW	1958–59	5
19	18	1	Langley GRA	1956	3
19	18	1	Marsh RW	1974–75	6
18	10	8	Oldfield WAS	1924–25	5
18	18	–	Maclean JA	1978–79	4

The most stumpings in a series is 9 by AFA Lilley (Eng) in 5 Tests in 1903–04. WAS Oldfield holds the record in a series for Australia (see above).

Oldfield stumps Hammond off the highly-skilled Australian spinner Grimmett at Trent Bridge in 1934

7.4 *Highest Innings by Wicketkeepers*

ENGLAND				AUSTRALIA			
135	Knott APE	Trent Bridge	1977	110*	Marsh RW	Melbourne	1976–77
120	Ames LEG	Lord's	1934	92*	Marsh RW	Melbourne	1970–71
106*	Knott APE	Adelaide	1974–75	92	Tallon D	Melbourne	1946–47
97	Taylor RW	Adelaide	1978–79	91	Marsh RW	Old Trafford	1972
92	Knott APE	Oval	1972	91	Phillips WB	Headingley	1985

7.5 *Most Dismissals for a Particular Bowler*

ENGLAND

Total	Ct	St	Wicketkeeper	Bowler	Period
23	23	–	Taylor RW	Botham IT	1978–83
17	17	–	Knott APE	Snow JA	1968–75
16	16	–	Knott APE	Greig AW	1972–77
15	14	1	Evans TG	Bedser AV	1946–53

AUSTRALIA

Total	Ct	St	Wicketkeeper	Bowler	Period
40	40	–	Marsh RW	Lillee DK	1970–83
22	7	15	Oldfield WAS	Grimmett CV	1924–34
19	19	–	Marsh RW	Lawson GF	1981–83
18	18	–	Grout ATW	McKenzie GD	1961–66
17	17	–	Marsh RW	Thomson JR	1974–83

7.6 *Highest Batting Averages by Wicketkeepers*

(150 runs or more)

ENGLAND	M	I	NO	Runs	HS	Av	100	50
Brown G	3	5	0	250	84	50.00	–	2
Parks JM	10	13	0	497	89	38.23	–	5
Knott APE	34	57	6	1682	135	32.98	2	11
Ames LEG	17	27	2	675	120	27.00	1	4
Lilley AFA	32	47	7	801	84	20.03	–	4
Storer W	6	11	0	215	51	19.55	–	1
Tylecote EFS	6	9	1	152	66	19.00	–	1
Murray JT	6	10	1	163	40	18.11	–	–
Evans TG	31	53	9	783	50	17.80	–	1
Taylor RW	17	32	5	468	97	17.33	–	1
Duckworth G	10	17	6	163	39*	14.82	–	–

A hailstorm *left the field at Sydney white with ice during the third Test in 1884–85.*

AUSTRALIA	M	I	NO	Runs	HS	Av	100	50
Phillips WB	6	11	1	350	91	35.00	–	2
Barnett BA	4	8	1	195	57	27.86	–	1
Marsh RW	42	68	8	1633	110*	27.22	1	9
Carter H	21	35	4	776	72	25.03	–	4
Oldfield WAS	38	62	14	1116	65*	23.25	–	3
Jarvis AH	9	17	3	283	82	20.21	–	1
Tallon D	15	20	2	340	92	18.89	–	2
Kelly JJ	33	52	17	613	46*	17.51	–	–
Maddocks LV	5	9	0	156	69	17.33	–	1
Blackham JM	32	56	10	719	74	15.63	–	4
Grout ATW	22	26	4	301	74	13.68	–	1

Only batting performances by those originally selected to keep wicket are included.

7.7 Wicketkeepers and Byes

No Byes Conceded in Large Totals

Total		Wicketkeeper		
659–8 dec	by Aus	Evans TG	Sydney	1946–47
551	by Eng	Kelly JJ	Sydney	1897–98
532–9 dec	by Aus	Knott APE	Oval	1975
521	by Eng	Oldfield WAS	Brisbane	1928–29
489	by Aus	Strudwick H	Adelaide	1924–25
456	by Eng	Phillips WB	Trent Bridge	1985

APE Knott (Eng) conceded no byes in 6 consecutive innings, from Trent Bridge 1972 to Brisbane 1974–75, while 1556 runs were scored. In 34 Tests he conceded 125 byes, an average of only 3.68 per match.

Most Byes Conceded in an Innings

Byes	Total	Wicketkeeper		
37	327	Woolley FE (Eng)	Oval	1934
26	476	Smith EJ (Eng)	Adelaide	1911–12
24	353	Jarvis AH (Aus)	Lord's	1886
23	345	Duckworth G (Eng)	Old Trafford	1930

Woolley was deputising for LEG Ames, who had to retire with back trouble.

The most byes conceded by an Australian wicketkeeper *in a match* is 35, by JM Blackham at Lord's in 1893.

SECTION 8
The Allrounders

Jack Gregory (ABOVE) *and Ian Botham, two of the most dynamic allrounders in the annals of Ashes cricket*

8.1 *Leading Allrounders*

Qualification: 30 wickets, and a batting average of 20.00.

The 'Index' is calculated by dividing the batting average by the bowling average.

ENGLAND	M	Runs	Av	Wkts	Av	Index
Bates W	15	656	27.33	50	16.42	1.66
Barnes W	21	725	23.39	51	15.55	1.50
Rhodes W	41	1706	31.02	109	24.00	1.29
Foster FR	8	281	28.10	34	21.82	1.29
Ulyett G	23	901	25.03	48	20.67	1.21
Hammond WR	33	2852	51.85	36	44.78	1.16
Botham IT	29	1422	30.26	136	26.15	1.16
Barlow RG	17	591	22.73	34	22.56	1.01
Greig AW	21	1303	36.19	44	37.80	0.96
Miller G	14	479	20.83	39	21.95	0.95
Woolley FE	32	1664	33.28	43	36.16	0.92
Illingworth R	18	663	26.52	34	32.18	0.82
Bailey TE	23	875	25.74	42	32.69	0.79
Hirst GH	21	744	24.80	49	32.35	0.77
Douglas JWHT	17	696	26.77	35	35.06	0.76
Titmus FJ	19	716	28.64	47	38.17	0.75
Emburey JE	15	334	20.88	48	28.92	0.72
Braund LC	20	830	25.15	46	38.46	0.65
Allen GOB	13	479	23.95	43	37.28	0.64

AUSTRALIA	M	Runs	Av	Wkts	Av	Index
Macartney CG	26	1640	43.16	33	27.52	1.57
Miller KR	29	1511	33.58	87	22.40	1.50
Noble MA	39	1905	30.73	115	24.87	1.24
Armstrong WW	42	2172	35.03	74	30.92	1.13
Gregory JM	21	941	34.85	70	33.77	1.03
Davidson AK	25	750	24.19	84	23.76	1.02
Kelleway C	18	874	31.21	37	31.22	1.00
Lindwall RR	29	795	22.08	114	22.45	0.98
Hordern HV	5	173	21.63	32	24.38	0.89
Giffen G	31	1238	23.36	103	27.10	0.86
Walker MHN	16	407	23.94	56	33.18	0.72
McDonald EA	8	101	20.20	33	32.12	0.63
McLeod CE	17	573	23.88	33	40.15	0.59

8.2 *Career Records*

1000 Runs and 100 Wickets

ENGLAND	M	Runs	Av	Wkts	Av	Double Achieved Year	Match
Botham IT	29	1422	30.26	136	26.15	1982–83	22nd
Rhodes W	41	1706	31.02	109	24.00	1920–21	37th
AUSTRALIA							
Giffen G	31	1238	23.36	103	27.10	1896	30th
Noble MA	39	1905	30.73	115	24.87	1905	29th

1000 Runs and 50 Wickets

ENGLAND	M	Runs	Av	Wkts	Av	Year	Match
Botham IT	29	1422	30.26	136	26.15	1982–83	21st
Rhodes W	41	1706	31.02	109	24.00	1911–12	30th
AUSTRALIA							
Armstrong WW	42	2172	35.03	74	30.92	1911–12	30th
Giffen G	31	1238	23.36	103	27.10	1894–95	26th
Miller KR	29	1511	33.58	87	22.40	1953	19th
Noble MA	39	1905	30.73	115	24.87	1903–04	22nd

500 Runs and 100 Wickets

ENGLAND	M	Runs	Av	Wkts	Av	Year	Match
Botham IT	29	1422	30.26	136	26.15	1982–83	22nd
Rhodes W	41	1706	31.02	109	24.00	1920–21	37th
AUSTRALIA							
Giffen G	31	1238	23.36	103	27.10	1896	30th
Lindwall RR	29	795	22.08	114	22.45	1954–55	23rd
Noble MA	39	1905	30.73	115	24.87	1905	29th
Trumble H	31	838	19.95	141	20.89	1902	26th

500 Runs and 50 Wickets

ENGLAND	M	Runs	Av	Wkts	Av	Double Achieved Year	Match
Barnes W	21	725	23.39	51	15.55	1890	20th
Bates W	15	656	27.33	50	16.42	1886–87	15th
Botham IT	29	1422	30.26	136	26.15	1979–80	11th
Briggs J	31	809	18.81	97	20.55	1894–95	20th
Rhodes W	41	1706	31.02	109	24.00	1907–08	22nd
Tate MW	20	578	19.93	83	30.60	1930	17th
AUSTRALIA							
Armstrong WW	42	2172	35.03	74	30.92	1911–12	30th
Benaud R	27	767	19.67	83	31.82	1961	19th
Davidson AK	25	750	24.19	84	23.76	1961	19th
Giffen G	31	1238	23.36	103	27.10	1893	22nd
Gregory JM	21	940	34.85	70	33.77	1924–25	12th
Lindwall RR	29	795	22.08	114	22.45	1953	16th
Miller KR	29	1511	33.58	87	22.40	1953	19th
Noble MA	39	1905	30.73	115	24.87	1901–02	13th
Trumble H	31	838	19.95	141	20.89	1899	18th

8.3 *Best Match Performances*

A Century and Five Wickets in an Innings

ENGLAND	Bat	Bowl	Ground	Year
Botham IT	149*	6–95	Headingley	1981
AUSTRALIA				
Gregory JM	100	7–69	Melbourne	1920–21

One Hundred Runs and Eight Wickets in a Match

ENGLAND				
Allen GOB	35, 68	3–71, 5–36	Brisbane	1936–37
Larwood H	70, 37	6–32, 2–30	Brisbane†	1928–29

†Exhibition Ground

ABOVE LEFT *Lindwall and Miller, one of the greatest fast-bowling duos, with Miller also a high-ranking allrounder*

ABOVE *Wilfred Rhodes: batted no. 11 and no. 1 for England, and took 109 wickets*

LEFT *Bob Simpson, a prolific runmaker, brilliant slip fielder, and useful legspinner*

George Giffen, Australia's answer to W G Grace. He achieved the double of 1000 runs and 100 wickets in these matches

AUSTRALIA				
Giffen G	161, 41	4–75, 4–164	Sydney	1894–95
Gregory JM	100	7–69, 1–32	Melbourne	1920–21
†Trott AE	38*, 72*	0–9, 8–43	Adelaide	1894–95

†On debut

A Fifty and Five Wickets in an Innings

ENGLAND				
Allen GOB	68	5–36	Brisbane	1936–37
Barnes W	58	6–31	Melbourne	1884–85
Barnes W	62	5–32	Oval	1888
Bates W	55	7–28, 7–74	Melbourne	1882–83
Botham IT	50, 149*	6–95	Headingley	1981
Botham IT	85	5–109	Lord's	1985
†Braund LC	58	5–61	Sydney	1901–02
Fender PGH	59	5–122	Melbourne	1920–21
Flowers W	56	5–46	Sydney	1884–85
†Foster FR	56	5–92	Sydney	1911–12
Foster FR	71	5–36	Adelaide	1911–12
Geary G	66	5–35	Sydney	1928–29
Hirst GH	58*	5–77	Oval	1902
Jackson Hon. FS	82*	5–52	Trent Bridge	1905
Larwood H	70	6–32	Brisbane‡	1928–29
Woolley FE	62	5–29, 5–20	Oval	1912

AUSTRALIA				
Armstrong WW	66	5–122	Headingley	1905
Benaud R	51	6–115	Brisbane	1962–63
Giffen G	53	7–128	Oval	1893
Giffen G	58	5–76	Adelaide	1894–95
Gregory JM	100	7–69	Melbourne	1920–21
Lawson GF	50	5–108	Perth	1982–83
Lindwall RR	50	5–66	Lord's	1953
Lyons JJ	55	5–30	Lord's	1890
†Miller KR	79	7–60	Brisbane	1946–47
Noble MA	56	5–54	Sydney	1901–02
Noble MA	53*	7–100	Sydney	1903–04
Simpson RB	91	5–57	Sydney	1962–63
†Trott AE	72*	8–43	Adelaide	1894–95
Trumble H	56	5–60	Headingley	1899
Trumble H	62*	6–74	Adelaide	1901–02
Trumble H	64*	8–65	Oval	1902

†On debut ‡Exhibition Ground

8.4 *Best Performances in a Series*

200 Runs and 20 Wickets

ENGLAND	Year	M	Runs	Av	Wkts	Av
Botham IT	1981	6	399	36.27	34	20.59
Botham IT	1985	6	250	31.25	31	27.58
Braund LC	1901–02	5	256	36.57	21	35.14
Foster FR	1911–12	5	226	32.29	32	21.63
Miller G	1978–79	6	234	23.40	23	15.04
AUSTRALIA						
Giffen G	1894–95	5	475	52.78	34	24.12
Gregory JM	1920–21	5	442	73.67	23	24.17
Gregory JM	1924–25	5	224	24.89	22	37.09
Miller KR	1956	5	203	22.56	21	22.24
Walker MHN	1974–75	6	221	44.20	23	29.74

300 Runs and 15 Wickets

ENGLAND	Year	M	Runs	Av	Wkts	Av
Barnes W	1884–85	5	369	52.71	19	15.37
Botham IT	1981	6	399	36.27	34	20.59
Greig AW	1974–75	6	446	40.55	17	40.06
AUSTRALIA						
Giffen G	1894–95	5	475	52.78	34	24.12
Gregory JM	1920–21	5	442	73.67	23	24.17
Kelleway C	1920–21	5	330	47.14	15	21.00
Miller KR	1946–47	5	384	76.80	16	20.88
Miller KR	1950–51	5	350	43.75	17	17.71
Noble MA	1903–04	5	417	59.57	16	20.50

In the first two Tests in Australia in 1876–77, *J Selby had to keep wicket for England because the selected wicketkeeper for the tour, E Pooley, was in prison in New Zealand after trying a gambling trick on the locals.*

SECTION 9
The Fieldsmen

Greg Chappell, a technically admirable batsman, also excelled in the field, holding a record 61 catches, most of them at slip

9.1 *Most Catches in Career*

ENGLAND	Tests	Catches	AUSTRALIA	Tests	Catches
Botham IT	29	44	Chappell GS	35	61
Hammond WR	33	43	Trumble H	31	45
Cowdrey MC	43	40	Armstrong WW	42	37
Grace WG	22	39*	Border AR	24	35
Braund LC	20	37	Benaud R	27	32
Greig AW	21	37	Chappell IM	30	31
Rhodes W	41	36	Gregory JM	21	30
Woolley FE	32	36*	Hill C	41	30
MacLaren AC	35	29	Simpson RB	19	30
Shrewsbury A	23	29	Redpath IR	23	29
Graveney TW	22	24	Davidson AK	25	28
Hutton L	27	22	Noble MA	39	26
Lohmann GA	15	22	Harvey RN	37	25
Trueman FS	19	21	Trumper VT	40	25
Brearley JM	19	20	Giffen G	31	24
Gower DI	26	20	Gregory SE	52	24
Barnes W	21	19	Darling J	31	23
Barrington KF	23	19	Walters KD	36	23
Edrich WJ	21	19	Bannerman AC	28	21
Chapman APF	16	18	McCabe SJ	24	21
			Trott GHS	24	21

*Total includes one catch taken while keeping wicket

9.2 *Most Catches*

In an Innings

ENGLAND			AUSTRALIA		
4 Braund LC	Sheffield	1902	4 Chappell GS	Perth	1974–75
4 Braund LC	Sydney	1907–08	4 Harvey RN	Sydney	1962–63
4 Larwood H	Brisbane*	1928–29	4 Loxton SJE	Brisbane	1950–51
4 May PBH	Adelaide	1954–55			
4 Parfitt PH	Trent Bridge	1972	3 Barnes SG	Brisbane	1946–47
4 Rhodes W	Old Trafford	1905	3 Benaud R	Melbourne	1958–59
4 Woolley FE	Sydney	1911–12	3 Benaud R	Oval	1961
			3 Bonnor GJ	Sydney	1882–83

Walter Hammond catches Hassett at Trent Bridge in 1938. A natural fieldsman as well as being a magnificent batsman, Hammond held England's catches record until overtaken by Botham

LEFT *G L Jessop, remembered for his 75-minute century, but also a constant danger to Australian batsmen from his position in the covers*

ENGLAND			AUSTRALIA		
3 Bates W	Melbourne	1884–85	3 Bonnor GJ	Lord's	1884
3 Botham IT	Sydney	1978–79	3 Border AR	Old Trafford	1981
3 Botham IT	Old Trafford	1981	3 Bruce W	Sydney	1894–95
3 Botham IT	Adelaide	1982–83	3 Chappell GS	Lord's	1972
3 Botham IT	Sydney	1982–83	3 Chappell GS	Perth	1974–75
3 Braund LC	Melbourne	1903–04	3 Chappell GS	Headingley	1975
3 Chapman APF	Brisbane†	1928–29	3 Chappell IM	Sydney	1970–71
3 Cowdrey MC	Melbourne	1958–59	3 Chappell IM	Melbourne	1974–75
3 Cowdrey MC	Lord's	1968	3 Chipperfield AG	Trent Bridge	1934
3 Crawford JN	Sydney	1907–08	3 Darling J	Melbourne	1901–02
3 Douglas JWHT	Oval	1912	3 Darling LS	Melbourne	1936–37
3 Edmonds PH	Edgbaston	1985	3 Davidson AK	Melbourne	1958–59
3 Emmett T	Melbourne	1876–77	3 Fairfax AG	Melbourne	1928–29
3 Grace WG	Old Trafford	1888	3 Giffen G	Sydney	1891–92
3 Grace WG	Sydney	1891–92	3 Giffen G	Oval	1893
3 Graveney TW	Sydney	1962–63	3 Gregory JM	Sydney	1920–21
3 Greig AW	Melbourne	1976–77	3 Gregory JM }	Sydney	1920–21
3 Hammond WR	Trent Bridge	1930	3 Gregory JM }		
3 Hammond WR	Trent Bridge	1934	3 Harvey RN	Sydney	1958–59
3 Hammond WR	Oval	1934	3 Hill C	Melbourne	1901–02
3 Hammond WR	Adelaide	1936–37	3 Hole GB	Lord's	1953
3 Hendrick M	Trent Bridge	1977	3 Iredale FA	Old Trafford	1899
3 Hutton L	Lord's	1948	3 Johnson IW	Melbourne	1950–51
3 Illingworth R	Headingley	1972	3 Jones E	Melbourne	1897–98
3 Jardine DR	Melbourne	1928–29	3 Kent MF	Oval	1981
3 Lock GAR	Headingley	1953	3 McCabe SJ	Lord's	1938
3 Lohmann GA	Lord's	1888	3 Murdoch WL	Sydney	1882–83
3 Oakman ASM	Old Trafford	1956	3 Noble MA	Sydney	1907–08
3 Rhodes W	Oval	1909	3 Redpath IR	Perth	1974–75
3 Shrewsbury A	Sydney	1881–82	3 Ryder J	Adelaide	1928–29
3 Shrewsbury A }	Sydney	1887–88	3 Simpson RB	Sydney	1962–63
3 Shrewsbury A }			3 Spofforth FR	Melbourne	1878–79
3 Sims JM	Sydney	1936–37	3 Trott AE	Adelaide	1894–95
3 Smith MJK	Sydney	1965–66	3 Trumble H	Old Trafford	1896
3 Studd GB	Sydney	1882–83	3 Trumble H	Melbourne	1901–02
3 Sutcliffe H	Lord's	1926	3 Worrall J	Adelaide	1894–95
3 Trueman FS	Melbourne	1958–59			

H Strudwick took 3 catches in an innings for England at Melbourne 1903–04 as a substitute fielder (see also section 9.5).

†Exhibition Ground

Most Catches in a Match

ENGLAND			AUSTRALIA		
6 Shrewsbury A	Sydney	1887–88	7 Chappell GS	Perth	1974–75
6 Woolley FE	Sydney	1911–12	6 Gregory JM	Sydney	1920–21
5 Bates W	Melbourne	1884–85	6 Harvey RN	Sydney	1962–63
5 Botham IT	Sydney	1978–79	5 Fairfax AG	Melbourne	1928–29
5 Botham IT	Sydney	1982–83	5 Hole GB	Lord's	1953
5 Braund LC	Sheffield	1902	5 Loxton SJE	Brisbane	1950–51
5 Grace WG	Sydney	1891–92			
5 Hammond WR	Trent Bridge	1934			
5 Oakman ASM	Old Trafford	1956			
5 Rhodes W	Old Trafford	1905			
5 Sutcliffe H	Lord's	1926			

Most Catches in a Series

ENGLAND		AUSTRALIA	
12 Botham IT	1981	15 Gregory JM	1920–21
12 Braund LC	1901–02	14 Chappell GS	1974–75
12 Greig AW	1974–75	12 Border AR	1981
12 Hammond WR	1934	11 Border AR	1985
11 Botham IT	1978–79	11 Chappell IM	1974–75
10 Lock GAR	1956	11 Redpath IR	1974–75
		10 Chappell GS	1979–80
		10 Simpson RB	1964
		10 Trumble H	1901–02

9.3 *Most Caught-and-Bowled*

In an Innings

ENGLAND			AUSTRALIA		
3 Barnes W	Melbourne	1884–85	3 Giffen G	Sydney	1891–92
2 Midwinter WE	Melbourne	1881–82	2 Spofforth FR	Melbourne	1878–79
2 Ulyett G	Lord's	1884	2 Giffen G	Oval	1893
2 Braund LC	Melbourne	1901–02	2 Trott AE	Adelaide	1894–95
2 Braund LC	Melbourne	1903–04	2 Grimmett CV	Headingley	1926
2 Bosanquet BJT	Trent Bridge	1905	2 Blackie DD	Melbourne	1928–29
2 Crawford JN	Sydney	1907–08	2 Johnson IW	Sydney	1954–55
2 Rhodes W	Trent Bridge	1921	2 Benaud R	Melbourne	1958–59
2 Parkin CH	Lord's	1921	2 Philpott PI	Sydney	1965–66
			2 Gleeson JW	Melbourne	1970–71

In a Match

ENGLAND			AUSTRALIA		
4 Barnes W	Melbourne	1884–85	3 Giffen G	Sydney	1891–92

No other players have taken more than 2 'caught-and-bowled' in a match.

In a Career (Career total of all catches in brackets)

ENGLAND	AUSTRALIA
8 Barnes W (19)	15 Trumble H (45)
7 Rhodes W (36)	10 Giffen G (24)
7 Underwood DL (14)	7 Benaud R (32)
6 Woolley FE (36)	5 Spofforth FR (11)
5 Braund LC (37)	5 Johnson IW (14)

Before the Oval Test of 1896 *five England players – R Abel, T Richardson, TW Hayward, W Gunn and GA Lohmann – demanded double the £10 fee offered to professionals. The first three eventually relented, but Gunn and Lohmann never played Test cricket again.*

9.4 *Substitute Catchers*

ENGLAND		AUSTRALIA	
3 Strudwick H	1903–04		
*2 Ealham AGE	1977	2 Andrews TJE	1924–25
†2 Hampshire JH	1970–71	2 Iredale FA	1896
2 Jones AO	1905	2 Loxton SJE	1950–51
2 Shuttleworth K	1970–71		
1 Brockwell W	1896	1 a'Beckett EL	1928–29
1 Chapman APF	1926	†1 Barnett BA	1934
*1 Copley SH	1930	1 Bradman DG	1928–29
*1 Garnett HG	1901–02	1 Brown WA	1936–37
*1 Gould IJ	1982–83	1 Gehrs DRA	1905
‡1 Jarvis AH	1884–85	†1 Gilmour GJ	1975
1 Lever JK	1978–79	1 Gregory SE	1891–92
1 Mead CP	1911–12	1 Hartigan RJ	1909
‡1 Murdoch WL	1884	1 Jenner TJ	1974–75
1 Old CM	1974–75	†1 Kent MF	1981
1 Parfitt PH	1962–63	1 Macartney CG	1911–12
†1 Parks JM	1956	1 McLaren JW	1912
*1 Rees A	1964	1 O'Brien LPJ	1932–33
1 Rhodes W	1899	†1 Oxenham RK	1928–29
*1 Stewart MJ	1961	1 Robinson RH	1936–37
‡1 Turner CTB	1886–87	1 Simpson RB	1958–59
1 Tyldesley JT	1899	*1 Thompson FC	1928–29
1 Vernon GF	1884–85	1 Turner A	1975
1 Willis RGD	1972	†§1 Vine J	1911–12
*1 Wilson JV	1954–55	†1 Waite MG	1938
1 Young RA	1907–08		

*Never played in E v A Tests
†Catch(es) made prior to making debut in E v A Tests
‡Playing for other side in same match
§Member of MCC touring team

At Old Trafford in 1921 *the England captain (Hon. LH Tennyson) mistakenly declared the England first innings contrary to the tour regulations. Australian captain WW Armstrong pointed this out (allegedly at the instigation of his wicketkeeper H Carter) and a delay of some 25 minutes ensued. When the England innings restarted Armstrong bowled his second consecutive over, having bowled the over immediately prior to the abortive declaration.*

9.5 *Famous Missed Catches*

Tate FW

Playing in his first (and only) Test at Old Trafford 1902, FW Tate, a surprise selection anyway, dropped top-scorer J Darling (37 out of 86) in the Australian second innings. Australia went on to win the match by 3 runs when Tate was bowled by JV Saunders for 4.

Carr AW

At Headingley 1926 England dismissed acting Australian captain W Bardsley for 0. England captain Carr dropped CG Macartney fourth ball. Macartney went on to be 112 not out at lunch (the second of 3 batsmen to score a century before lunch in E v A Tests on the first day) and his was the highest pre-lunch score of any of these instances. Macartney was eventually out for 151; Australia totalled 494. England scored 294 and 254–3 and drew the match.

McCosker RB

At Trent Bridge 1977 G Boycott was making his comeback to Test cricket after a self-imposed three-year 'exile'. He had not played against Australia since 1972. After reaching a laborious 20 in over 3 hours he was dropped by RB McCosker at second slip off LS Pascoe. Thus reprieved, he went on to score 107; he scored 80 not out in the second innings and 191 (his 100th first-class century) in the next Test. England won the Trent Bridge Test by 7 wickets and the next Test by an innings and 85 runs.

Tavaré CJ

Perhaps the most famous 'non-dropped catch'. At Melbourne 1982–83, when the last Australian pair AR Border and JR Thomson came together, another 74 runs were needed for victory. Gradually on the fourth day the two inched closer to the target score. On the fifth day, with a possibility of only one ball being delivered to end the match, an estimated 18,000 watched the closing stages of the match free of charge. Border and Thomson took the score to within 4 runs of victory when IT Botham induced an outside edge from Thomson. The ball reached CJ Tavaré at second slip just above head height but he was unable to catch it. Fortunately for England he parried it upwards and G Miller at first slip was able to run round behind Tavaré to complete the catch and England's victory by 3 runs.

SECTION 10
The Umpires

Ian Botham shares a joke with umpire Harold 'Dickie' Bird

Jim Phillips (LEFT) *and Bob Crockett, two fearless and competent Australian umpires*

10.1 *Umpires*

Name	Tests	First Test	Last Test
Alley WE	4	1975	1981
Argall PG	7	1901–02	1907–08
Bailhache RC	12	1974–75	1982–83
Baldwin HG	3	1948	1953
†Bannerman C	12	1886–87	1901–02
Barlow AN	4	1950–51	1950–51
†Barlow RG	1	1899	1899
Bartley TJ	2	1956	1956
Bestwick W	1	1930	1930
Bird HD	10	1975	1985
Borwick EG	15	1932–33	1946–47
†Braund LC	1	1926	1926
Brooks TF	12	1970–71	1978–79
Bryant J	1	1884–85	1884–85
Budd WL	2	1977	1977
Buller JS	10	1956	1968
Burrows RD	1	1926	1926
Butt HR	3	1921	1926
Callaway R	3	1901–02	1901–02
Carlin J	3	1905	1909
Carpenter RP	2	1886	1888
Chester A	1	1896	1896
Chester F	14	1926	1953
Chidgey H	1	1926	1926
Clements C	1	1893	1893
Coady P	1	1878–79	1878–79
Cocks AF	1	1950–51	1950–51
Constant DJ	10	1972	1985
Cooke EJ	1	1948	1948
Cooper GC	1	1950–51	1950–51
Copeland WJ	1	1979–80	1979–80
Cosstick S	1	1876–77	1876–77
*Coulthard G	2	1878–79	1881–82
Crafter AR	3	1978–79	1982–83
†Crapp JF	2	1964	1964
Crockett RM	27	1901–02	1924–25
Cronin PM	1	1979–80	1979–80
Curran WG	1	1911–12	1911–12
Davies D	8	1948	1956
Davies DE	2	1956	1956
Dench CE	1	1909	1909
†Dolphin A	2	1934	1934
Downes G	1	1891–92	1891–92
Draper H	1	1893	1893
Egar CJ	9	1962–63	1965–66
Elder DA	12	1911–12	1928–29

Name	Tests	First Test	Last Test
Elliott CS	10	1961	1972
Elliott EH	6	1882–83	1884–85
Elliott H	2	1953	1953
Elphinston H	3	1950–51	1950–51
Evans DGL	2	1981	1985
†Fagg AE	7	1968	1975
Farrands FH	7	1884	1888
Fisher I	1	1884–85	1884–85
Flynn TP	4	1891–92	1894–95
French RA	5	1978–79	1982–83
Garing C	1	1924–25	1924–25
Greenwood L	1	1882	1882
Hannah W	2	1907–08	1907–08
†Hardstaff J (snr)	6	1930	1934
Hearn W	4	1893	1902
Hele GA	10	1928–29	1932–33
Hide AB	1	1899	1899
†Hill A	1	1890	1890
†Hodges JH	1	1884–85	1884–85
Hoy C	4	1954–55	1958–59
Johnson MW	4	1982–83	1982–83
Jones AC	6	1903–04	1928–29
Laing T	1	1907–08	1907–08
Langridge JG	2	1961	1961
Lee FS	7	1953	1961
†Lillywhite Jas	6	1881–82	1899
McInnes MJ	9	1954–55	1958–59
Mackley A	1	1962–63	1962–63
*McShane PG	1	1884–85	1884–85
Meyer BJ	3	1981	1985
Millward A	1	1921	1921
Moss J	9	1902	1921
Mycroft T	2	1899	1902
Oates TW	2	1930	1930
O'Connell MG	7	1970–71	1979–80
Oslear DO	2	1981	1981
Palmer KE	4	1981	1985
Parris F	1	1909	1909
Parry WR	2	1930	1930
Payne E	1	1884–85	1884–85
Phillips J	24	1884–85	1905
Phillips W	2	1921	1921
Phillipson WE	2	1961	1961
†Price WFF	2	1964	1964
Pullin CK	10	1884	1893
Rawlinson H	1	1886–87	1886–87
Reeves W	1	1926	1926
Reid CA	1	1876–77	1876–77
Rhodes AEG	2	1972	1972
Richards W	6	1899	1909
Richardson CE	2	1902	1902
Robinson E	1	1938	1938
Rowan LP	12	1962–63	1970–71
Rowbotham J	1	1884	1884
Scott JD	10	1936–37	1946–47
Searcy G	1	1894–95	1894–95
Shepherd DR	2	1985	1985
†Sherwin M	1	1899	1899
†Smith EJ	2	1938	1938
Smyth W	3	1962–63	1965–66
Spencer TW	6	1972	1977
Stephenson HH	1	1880	1880
Street AE	4	1912	1926
Street J	1	1890	1890
Swift JS	8	1881–82	1886–87
Terry RB	2	1876–77	1876–77
Thoms RA	2	1880	1882
Titchmarsh VA	3	1899	1905
Tooher JA	1	1891–92	1891–92
Townsend L	1	1958–59	1958–59
Travers J	1	1884–85	1884–85

Name	Tests	First Test	Last Test
Walden FI	4	1934	1938
Watson GA	1	1911–12	1911–12
Webb G	1	1912	1912
Weser DG	2	1978–79	1979–80
West J	1	1886	1886
West JE	1	1905	1905
West WAJ	6	1896	1912
White AA	2	1899	1902
Whitehead AGT	1	1985	1985
Whitehead RV	1	1982–83	1982–83
Whitridge WO	1	1891–92	1891–92
Williams AP	1	1924–25	1924–25
Woolley CN	1	1948	1948
Wright RR	7	1950–51	1958–59
Wykes EF	1	1962–63	1962–63
Yarnold H	1	1968	1968
†Young HI	2	1926	1926
Young W	1	1911–12	1911–12

†Previously played in E v A Tests

*Later played in E v A Tests

In the fifth Test at Melbourne in 1884–85, TW Garrett (playing for Australia in the match) deputised for †JH Hodges after tea on the third day; JC Allen stood in for J Phillips on the third and fourth days.

In the second Test at Sydney in 1886–87, W Gunn (playing for England in the match) deputised for JS Swift on the fourth morning.

In the first Test at Edgbaston in 1975, HD Bird injured his back and †ASM Oakman deputised after tea on the third day; TW Spencer stood in for Bird on the fourth (final) day.

10.2 *Umpired in Most Tests*

Name	Tests
Crockett RM	27
Phillips J	24
Borwick EG	15
Chester F	14
Bailhache RC	12
Bannerman C	12
Brooks TF	12
Elder DA	12
Rowan LP	12
Bird HD	10
Buller JS	10
Constant DJ	10
Elliott CS	10
Hele GA	10
Pullin CK	10
Scott JD	10

SECTION 11
The Grounds

Lord's 1909

11.1 *Test Match Grounds*

Ground	Tests	E won	A won	Drawn
In England				
Edgbaston, Birmingham	7	3	1	3
Headingley, Leeds	19	6	5	8
Lord's, London	28	5	10	13
Old Trafford, Manchester	24	7	4	13
Trent Bridge, Nottingham	15	3	4	8
The Oval, London	29	13	5	11
Bramall Lane, Sheffield	1	0	1	0
Sub-Total	123	37	30	56
In Australia				
Adelaide Oval	23	7	13	3
Exhibition Ground, Brisbane	1	1	0	0
Woolloongabba, Brisbane	12	3	6	3
MCG, Melbourne	47	17	23	7
WACA Ground, Perth	5	1	2	2
SCG, Sydney	46	20	22	4
Sub-Total	134	49	66	19
Total	257	86	96	75

11.1a *Summary of Performances at All Grounds*

Ground	Centuries		5 Wkts/Inns		10 Wkts/Match	
	E	A	E	A	E	A
Edgbaston	7	1	6	6	2	0
Headingley	9	14	16	15	3	2
Lord's	17	22	18	23	3	4
Old Trafford	16	13	19	11	5	1
Trent Bridge	9	12	9	14	2	2
Oval	27	22	30	23	6	5
Sheffield	0	1	2	3	0	1
Sub-Total	85	85	100	95	21	15

Ground	Centuries		5 Wkts/Inns		10 Wkts/Match	
	E	A	E	A	E	A
Adelaide	20	27	14	20	3	2
Brisbane*	1	0	1	1	0	0
Brisbane	2	13	6	12	1	1
Melbourne	37	38	39	44	4	8
Perth	4	6	3	6	1	1
Sydney	30	29	40	42	7	8
Sub-Total	94	113	103	125	16	20
Total	179	198	203	220	37	35

*Exhibition Ground

11.2 *Record Attendances and Gate Receipts for Each Ground Staging 5 or More Tests*

Ground	Record Attendance	(Year)	Record Receipts	(Year)
Edgbaston	83000	(1961)	£318500.00	(1985)
Headingley	158000	(1948)	£321250.00	(1985)
Lord's	137915	(1953)	£668312.00	(1985)
Old Trafford	140000	(1961)	£368968.00	(1985)
Trent Bridge	101886	(1948)	£305000.00	(1985)
Oval	115000	(1953)	£485000.00	(1985)
Adelaide	172346	(1932–33)	$263534.88	(1982–83)
Brisbane	93143	(1932–33)	$315344.55	(1982–83)
Melbourne	350534	(1936–37)	$933152.00	(1982–83)
Perth	84142	(1970–71)	$252052.00	(1982–83)
Sydney	194259	(1946–47)	$680871.73	(1982–83)

A disputed run-out decision *against C Hill (Aus) in the first Test of 1903–04, at Sydney, led to a crowd disturbance, many spectators shouting abuse at umpire RM Crockett and England captain PF Warner, who came close to leading his side from the field. Crockett was afforded police protection at the end of play.*

11.3 *Highest Scores at Each Ground by Era*

ENGLAND	Era 1		Era 2		Era 3		Era 4		Era 5	
Edgbaston	–		376–9d	(1902)	–		409	(1968)	595–5d	(1985)
Headingley	220	(1899)	301	(1905)	391	(1930)	496	(1948)	533	(1985)
Lord's	379	(1884)	310–7d	(1912)	494	(1938)	372	(1953)	436–7d	(1975)
Old Trafford	372	(1899)	446	(1905)	627–9d	(1934)	611	(1964)	482–9d	(1985)
Trent Bridge	193	(1899)	426–5d	(1905)	658–8d	(1938)	441	(1948)	456	(1985)
Oval	576	(1899)	430	(1905)	903–7d	(1938)	494	(1968)	538	(1975)
Sheffield	–		195	(1902)	–		–		–	
Adelaide	499	(1891–92)	501	(1911–12)	447	(1920–21)	460	(1946–47)	470	(1970–71)
Brisbane*	–		–		521	(1928–29)	–		–	
Brisbane	–		–		358	(1936–37)	389	(1962–63)	464	(1970–71)
Melbourne	475	(1894–95)	589	(1911–12)	548	(1924–25)	558	(1965–66)	529	(1974–75)
Perth	–		–		–		–		411	(1982–83)
Sydney	551	(1897–98)	577	(1903–04)	636	(1928–29)	488	(1965–66)	346	(1978–79)

AUSTRALIA	Era 1		Era 2		Era 3		Era 4		Era 5	
Edgbaston	–		151	(1909)	–		516–9d	(1961)	359	(1975)
Headingley	224	(1899)	224–7	(1905)	584	(1934)	458	(1948)	401–9d	(1981)
Lord's	421	(1899)	350	(1909)	729–6d	(1930)	460–7d	(1948)	425	(1985)
Old Trafford	412	(1896)	299	(1902)	491	(1934)	656–8d	(1964)	402	(1981)
Trent Bridge	252	(1899)	221	(1905)	427–6d	(1938)	509	(1948)	539	(1985)
Oval	551	(1884)	363	(1905)	701	(1934)	494	(1961)	532–9d	(1975)

Sheffield	–		289	(1902)	–		–		–	
Adelaide	573	(1897–98)	506	(1907–08)	582	(1920–21)	516	(1965–66)	438	(1982–83)
Brisbane*	–		–		122	(1928–29)	–		–	
Brisbane	–		–		340	(1932–33)	645	(1946–47)	433	(1970–71)
Melbourne	520	(1897–98)	397	(1907–08)	604	(1936–37)	543–8d	(1965–66)	493–9d	(1970–71)
Perth	–		–		–		–		481	(1974–75)
Sydney	586	(1894–95)	485	(1903–04)	581	(1920–21)	659–8d	(1946–47)	405	(1974–75)

*Exhibition Ground

11.4 *Lowest Scores at Each Ground by Era*

ENGLAND	Era 1		Era 2		Era 3		Era 4		Era 5	
Edgbaston	–		121	(1909)	–		195	(1961)	101	(1975)
Headingley	220*	(1899)	87*	(1909)	123	(1938)	167	(1953)	174	(1981)
Lord's	53	(1888)	121	(1909)	187	(1921)	171	(1956)	116	(1972)
Old Trafford	95	(1884)	119	(1909)	‡123–0d	(1934)	165	(1968)	231	(1981)
Trent Bridge	193	(1899)	196	(1905)	112	(1921)	144	(1953)	125	(1981)
Oval	77	(1882)	175	(1912)	145*	(1934)	52	(1948)	191	(1975)
Sheffield	–		145	(1902)	–		–		–	
Adelaide	124	(1894–95)	183	(1907–08)	243	(1936–37)	228*	(1950–51)	169	(1978–79)
Brisbane†	–		–		521	(1928–29)	–		–	
Brisbane	–		–		256	(1936–37)	§122	(1950–51)	166	(1974–75)
Melbourne	75	(1894–95)	61 61	(1901–02) (1903–04)	139	(1932–33)	87	(1958–59)	95	(1976–77)

ENGLAND	Era 1		Era 2		Era 3		Era 4		Era 5	
Perth	–		–		–		–		208 208	(1974–75) (1978–79)
Sydney	45	(1886–87)	99	(1901–02)	146	(1924–25)	104	(1962–63)	123	(1979–80)

*One batsman short
†Exhibition Ground
‡England were not bowled out at Old Trafford during Era 3, so the lowest declared score is shown
§At Brisbane 1950–51 England declared their first innings at 68–7

AUSTRALIA	Era 1		Era 2		Era 3		Era 4		Era 5	
Edgbaston	–		36	(1902)	–		222*	(1968)	121	(1981)
Headingley	172	(1899)	188	(1909)	242	(1938)	120	(1961)	103	(1977)
Lord's	53	(1896)	181	(1905)	118	(1934)	78*	(1968)	268	(1975)
Old Trafford	70	(1888)	147	(1909)	175	(1921)	84	(1956)	130	(1981)
Trent Bridge	252	(1899)	188*	(1905)	144	(1930)	123	(1953)	179	(1981)
Oval	44	(1896)	65	(1912)	123**	(1938)	125	(1968)	129	(1985)
Sheffield	–		194	(1902)	–		–		–	
Adelaide	100	(1891–92)	133	(1911–12)	193*	(1932–33)	111	(1954–55)	160	(1978–79)
Brisbane†	–		–		66**	(1928–29)	–		–	
Brisbane	–		–		58*	(1936–37)	§186	(1958–59)	116	(1978–79)
Melbourne	104	(1876–77)	111	(1903–04)	191	(1932–33)	111	(1954–55)	138	(1976–77)
Perth	–		–		–		–		161	(1978–79)
Sydney	42	(1887–88)	131	(1903–04)	80*	(1936–37)	174	(1965–66)	111	(1978–79)

†Exhibition Ground **Two batsmen short *One batsman short
§At Brisbane 1950–51 Australia declared their second innings at 32–7

11.5 *Record Individual Scores for Each Ground by Era*

ENGLAND

Ground	**Era 1**		**Era 2**		**Era 3**		**Era 4**		**Era 5**	
Edgbaston	–		138	Tyldesley JT (1902)	–		180	Dexter ER (1961)	215	Gower DI (1985)
Headingley	55	Lilley AFA (1899)	144	Jackson Hon. FS (1905)	113	Hammond WR (1930)	143	Washbrook C (1948)	191	Boycott G (1977)
Lord's	164	Shrewsbury A (1886)	107	Hobbs JB (1912)	240	Hammond WR (1938)	145	Hutton L (1953)	175	Edrich JH (1975)
Old Trafford	154*	Ranjitsinhji KS (1896)	128	Jackson Hon. FS (1902)	153	Leyland M (1934)	256	Barrington KF (1964)	160	Gatting MW (1985)
Trent Bridge	93*	Ranjitsinhji KS (1899)	140	MacLaren AC (1905)	216*	Paynter E (1938)	184	Compton DCS (1948)	166	Gower DI (1985)
Oval	170	Grace WG (1886)	144	Fry CB (1905)	364	Hutton L (1938)	164	Edrich JH (1968)	196	Gooch GA (1985)
Sheffield	–		63	MacLaren AC (1902)	–				–	
Adelaide	134	Barnes W (1884–85)	187	Hobbs JB (1911–12)	177	Hammond WR (1928–29)	156*	Hutton L (1950–51)	119*	Boycott G (1970–71)
	134	Stoddart AE (1891–92)								

ENGLAND

Ground	Era 1		Era 2		Era 3		Era 4		Era 5	
Brisbane†	–		–		169	Hendren EH (1928–29)	–		–	
Brisbane	–		–		126	Leyland M (1936–37)	99	Dexter ER (1962–63)	110	Greig AW (1974–75)
Melbourne	173	Stoddart AE (1894–95)	179	Rhodes W (1911–12)	200	Hammond WR (1928–29)	156*	Simpson RT (1950–51)	188	Denness MH (1974–75)
Perth	–		–		–		–		131	Luckhurst BW (1970–71)
Sydney	175	Ranjitsinhji KS (1897–98)	287	Foster RE (1903–04)	251	Hammond WR (1928–29)	185	Barber RW (1965–66)	150	Randall DW (1978–79)

AUSTRALIA

Ground	Era 1		Era 2		Era 3		Era 4		Era 5	
Edgbaston	–		43 43	Gregory SE Ransford VS (1909)	–		114	Harvey RN (1961)	83	Wessels KC (1985)
Headingley	76	Worrall J (1899)	66	Armstrong WW (1905)	334	Bradman DG (1930)	182	Morris AR (1948)	119	Hilditch AMJ (1985)
Lord's	143	Trott GHS (1896)	143*	Ransford VS (1909)	254	Bradman DG (1930)	141	Barnes SG (1948)	196	Border AR (1985)
Old Trafford	108	Iredale FA (1896)	104	Trumper VT (1902)	137	McCabe SJ (1934)	311	Simpson RB (1964)	146*	Border AR (1985)
Trent Bridge	80	Hill C (1899)	54	Hill C (1905)	232	McCabe SJ (1938)	138	Bradman DG (1948)	172	Wood GM (1985)

Oval	211	Murdoch WL (1884)	146	Duff RA (1905)	266	Ponsford WH (1934)	196	Morris AR (1948)	192	Chappell IM (1975)
Sheffield	–		119	Hill C (1902)	–		–		–	
Adelaide	178	Darling J (1897–98)	160	Hill C (1907–08)	212	Bradman DG (1936–37)	225	Simpson RB (1965–66)	136	Stackpole KR (1970–71)
Brisbane†	–		–		33	Ryder J (1928–29)	–		–	
Brisbane	–		–		100	Fingleton JHW (1936–37)	187	Bradman DG (1946–47)	207	Stackpole KR (1970–71)
Melbourne	188	Hill C (1897–98)	133*	Armstrong WW (1907–08)	270	Bradman DG (1936–37)	307	Cowper RM (1965–66)	114	Chappell GS (1979–80)
Perth	–		–		–		–		171	Redpath IR (1970–71)
							234	Barnes SG		
Sydney	201	Gregory SE (1894–95)	185*	Trumper VT (1903–04)	187*	McCabe SJ (1932–33)	234	Bradman DG (1946–47)	144	Chappell GS (1974–75)

†Exhibition Ground

11.6 *Runs and Averages per Wicket by Grounds*

	ENGLAND			AUSTRALIA		
Ground	**Runs Scored**	**Wkts Lost**	**Av**	**Runs Scored**	**Wkts Lost**	**Av**
Edgbaston	3026	91	33.25	2328	101	23.05
Headingley	8877	292	30.40	9080	311	29.20
Lord's	12383	422	29.34	11939	398	30.00
Old Trafford	10098	315	32.06	9635	375	25.69
Trent Bridge	6578	217	30.31	6613	216	30.62
Oval	14371	443	32.44	12688	470	27.00
Sheffield	340	20	17.00	483	20	24.15
Sub-Total	55673	1800	30.93	52766	1891	27.90
Adelaide	13141	414	31.74	13824	392	35.27
Brisbane*	863	18	47.94	188	17	11.06
Brisbane	5465	204	26.79	6085	174	34.97
Melbourne	22169	798	27.78	23495	804	29.22
Perth	2914	96	30.35	2473	75	32.97
Sydney	21756	806	26.99	21964	793	27.70
Sub-Total	66308	2336	28.39	68029	2255	30.17
Total	121981	4136	29.49	120795	4146	29.14

*Exhibition Ground

11.7 *Records for Each Ground*

Edgbaston (Birmingham)

First Test 1902 Played 7 England won 3 Australia won 1 Drawn 3

Highest Match Aggregates	1112–23 wickets	(1961)	Drawn
	1072–25 wickets	(1985)	England inns & 118 runs
	841–23 wickets	(1968)	Drawn
Lowest Match Aggregates	451–30 wickets	(1909)	England 10 wickets
	458–21 wickets	(1902)	Drawn
	633–30 wickets	(1975)	Australia inns & 85 runs

	ENGLAND	AUSTRALIA
Highest Totals	595–5d (1985)	516–9d (1961)
	409 (1968)	359 (1975)
	401–4 (1961)	335 (1985)
Lowest Totals	101 (1975)	36 (1902)
	121 (1909)	74 (1909)
	173 (1975)	121 (1981)
Highest Individual Innings	215 Gower DI (1985)	114 Harvey RN (1961)
	180 Dexter ER (1961)	83 Wessels KC (1985)
	148 Robinson RT (1985)	82 O'Neill NC (1961)
	138 Tyldesley JT (1902)	76 Simpson RB (1961)
	112 Subba Row R (1961)	71 Chappell IM (1968)
Best Innings Bowling Analyses	7–17 Rhodes W (1902)	5–15 Lillee DK (1975)
	6–44 Blythe C (1909)	5–27 Armstrong WW (1909)
	6–77 Ellison RM (1985)	5–38 Thomson JR (1975)
	5–11 Botham IT (1981)	5–42 Alderman TM (1981)
	5–58 Blythe C (1909)	5–48 Walker MHN (1975)
	5–58 Hirst GH (1909)	
Best Match Bowling Analyses	11–102 Blythe C (1909)	8–107 Alderman TM (1981)
	10–104 Ellison RM (1985)	7–60 Lillee DK (1975)
	9–86 Hirst GH (1909)	7–88 Bright RJ (1981)
	8–26 Rhodes W (1902)	7–95 Walker MHN (1975)
	6–63 Emburey JE (1981)	5–54 Armstrong WW (1909)
Highest Run Aggregates	238 Gower DI (79.33)	141 Chappell IM (70.50)
	191 Edrich JH (47.75)	114 Harvey RN (114.00)
	190 Dexter ER (95.00)	93 Wessels KC (46.50)
	171 Subba Row R (85.50)	89 Border AR (22.25)
	162 Tyldesley JT (81.00)	82 Cowper RM (82.00)
		82 O'Neill NC (82.00)
Highest Wicket Aggregates	12 Hirst GH (9.25)	11 Lillee DK (15.64)
	11 Blythe C (9.27)	8 Alderman TM (13.38)
	10 Ellison RM (10.40)	7 Bright RJ (12.57)
	10 Botham IT (23.50)	7 Walker MHN (13.57)
	8 Rhodes W (4.25)	6 Armstrong WW (19.67)
		6 Thomson JR (26.67)

	ENGLAND	AUSTRALIA
Most Appearances	3 Gooch GA 2 (19 players)	2 (12 players)

ENGLAND		**Record Wicket Partnerships**	
1st	105*	Hobbs JB (62*) Fry CB (35*)	1902
2nd	331	Robinson RT (148) Gower DI (215)	1985
3rd	100	Gower DI (215) Gatting MW (100*)	1985
4th	161	Dexter ER (180) Barrington KF (48*)	1961
5th	38	Fletcher KWR (51) Knott APE (38)	1975
6th	91	Tyldesley JT (138) Hirst GH (48)	1902
7th	51	Graveney TW (96) Illingworth R (27)	1968
8th	34	Tyldesley JT (138) Braund LC (14)	1902
9th	50	Emburey JE (37*) Taylor RW (8)	1981
10th	81*	Lockwood WH (52*) Rhodes W (38*)	1902

AUSTRALIA		**Record Wicket Partnerships**	
1st	80	McCosker RB (80) Turner A (37)	1975
2nd	111	Cowper RM (57) Chappell IM (71)	1968
3rd	146	Harvey RN (114) O'Neill NC (82)	1961
4th	58	Border AR (40) Yallop GN (30)	1981
5th	51	Hughes KJ (47) Yallop GN (30)	1981
6th	79	Edwards R (56) Marsh RW (61)	1975
7th	88	Simpson RB (76) Mackay KD (64)	1961
8th	58	Lawson GF (53) McDermott CJ (35)	1985
9th	59	Lawson GF (53) Thomson JR (28*)	1985
10th	26	O'Connor JDA (13) Whitty WJ (9*)	1909

Headingley (Leeds)

First Test 1899 Played 19 England won 6 Australia won 5 Drawn 8

Highest Match Aggregates	1723–31 wickets	(1948)	Australia 7 wickets
	1311–35 wickets	(1985)	England 5 wickets
	1159–34 wickets	(1968)	Drawn
Lowest Match Aggregates	566–31 wickets	(1972)	England 9 wickets
	608–30 wickets	(1956)	England inns & 42 runs
	635–29 wickets	(1899)	Drawn

	ENGLAND		AUSTRALIA	
Highest Totals	533	(1985)	584	(1934)
	496	(1948)	566	(1930)
	436	(1977)	494	(1926)
Lowest Totals	87†	(1909)	103	(1977)
†One batsman absent ill	123	(1938)	111	(1981)
	167	(1953)	120	(1961)
Highest Individual Innings	191	Boycott G (1977)	334	Bradman DG (1930)
	175	Robinson RT (1985)	304	Bradman DG (1934)
	149*	Botham IT (1981)	182	Morris AR (1948)
	144	Jackson Hon. FS (1905)	181	Ponsford WH (1934)
	143	Washbrook C (1948)	173*	Bradman DG (1948)
Best Innings Bowling Analyses	8–43	Willis RGD (1981)	7–58	Macartney CG (1909)
	6–30	Trueman FS (1961)	6–85	Gilmour GJ (1975)
	6–45	Underwood DL (1972)	6–135	Alderman TM (1981)
	6–55	Laker JC (1956)	5–38	Cotter A (1909)
	6–63	Barnes SF (1909)	5–54	Lindwall RR (1953)
Best Match Bowling Analyses	11–88	Trueman FS (1961)	11–85	Macartney CG (1909)
	11–113	Laker JC (1956)	10–122	O'Reilly WJ (1938)
	10–82	Underwood DL (1972)	9–157	Gilmour GJ (1975)
	8–95	Hendrick M (1977)	9–194	Alderman TM (1981)
	8–115	Willis RGD (1981)	8–158	Lindwall RR (1953)
Highest Run Aggregates	308	Edrich JH (38.50)	963	Bradman DG (192.60)
	306	Washbrook C (102.00)	427	Harvey RN (61.00)
	291	Boycott G (58.20)	318	Macartney CG (63.60)
	281	Hammond WR (46.83)	269	Armstrong WW (53.50)
	279	Edrich WJ (46.50)	269	Chappell IM (44.83)
Highest Wicket Aggregates	19	Botham IT (19.47)	20	Grimmett CV (22.20)
	18	Underwood DL (14.06)	15	O'Reilly WJ (17.07)
	17	Trueman FS (14.94)	15	Lindwall RR (25.87)
	15	Laker JC (24.60)	13	Macartney CG (11.46)
	11	Willis RGD (16.55)	13	Lillee DK (22.31)
	11	Illingworth R (18.00)	13	McKenzie GD (22.54)
	11	Lock GAR (25.64)		

Most Appearances	4 Edrich JH, Hobbs JB, Knott APE, Underwood DL	4 Bradman DG, Harvey RN, Marsh RW, Walters KD

ENGLAND		**Record Wicket Partnerships**	
1st	168	Hutton L (81) Washbrook C (143)	1948
2nd	112	Edrich JH (62) Steele DS (73)	1975
3rd	153	Edrich WJ (111) Bedser AV (79)	1948
4th	187	May PBH (101) Washbrook C (98)	1956
5th	80	Robinson RT (175) Botham IT (60)	1985
6th	123	Boycott G (191) Knott APE (57)	1977
7th	93	Hayward TW (40*) Lilley AFA (55)	1899
8th	117	Botham IT (149*) Dilley GR (56)	1981
9th	108	Geary G (35*) Macaulay GG (76)	1926
10th	61	Brown DJ (14) Underwood DL (45*)	1968

AUSTRALIA		**Record Wicket Partnerships**	
1st	71	Bardsley W (25) Andrews TJE (92)	1921
2nd	301	Morris AR (182) Bradman DG (173*)	1948
3rd	229	Bradman DG (334) Kippax AF (77)	1930
4th	388	Ponsford WH (181) Bradman DG (304)	1934
5th	112	Hughes KJ (89) Yallop GN (58)	1981
6th	58	Trumper VT (32) Kelly JJ (33)	1899
7th	80	Phillips WB (91) O'Donnell SP (24)	1985
8th	105	Burge PJP (160) Hawke NJN (37)	1964
9th	89	Burge PJP (160) Grout ATW (37)	1964
10th	55	Lindwall RR (77) Toshack ERH (12*)	1948

Lord's (London)

First Test 1884 Played 28 England won 5 Australia won 10 Drawn 13

Highest Match Aggregates	1601–29 wickets	(1930)	Australia 7 wickets
	1368–37 wickets	(1953)	Drawn
	1362–34 wickets	(1938)	Drawn
Lowest Match Aggregates	102–2 wickets	(1902)	Drawn
	291–40 wickets	(1888)	Australia 61 runs
	556–20 wickets	(1968)	Drawn

	ENGLAND		AUSTRALIA	
Highest Totals	494	(1938)	729–6d	(1930)
	475–3d	(1926)	460–7d	(1948)
	440	(1934)	425	(1985)
Lowest Totals	53	(1888)	53	(1896)
†One batsman retired hurt	62	(1888)	60	(1888)
	116	(1972)	78†	(1968)
Highest Individual Innings	240	Hammond WR (1938)	254	Bradman DG (1930)
	175	Edrich JH (1975)	206*	Brown WA (1938)
	173	Duleepsinhji KS (1930)	196	Border AR (1985)
	164	Shrewsbury A (1886)	193*	Bardsley W (1926)
	148	Steel AG (1884)	155	Woodfull WM (1930)
Best Innings Bowling Analyses	8–43	Verity H (1934)	8–53	Massie RAL (1972)
	7–36	Ulyett G (1884)	8–84	Massie RAL (1972)
	7–61	Verity H (1934)	7–81	Lawson GF (1981)
	7–78	Willis RGD (1977)	7–88	Jones E (1899)
	6–39	Richardson T (1896)	6–35	Armstrong WW (1909)
Best Match Bowling Analyses	15–104	Verity H (1934)	16–137	Massie RAL (1972)
	11–74	Briggs J (1886)	10–63	Turner CTB (1888)
	11–173	Richardson T (1896)	10–152	Miller KR (1956)
	9–118	Willis RGD (1977)	10–164	Jones E (1899)
	8–50	Peel R (1888)	8–45	Ferris JJ (1888)
Highest Run Aggregates	395	Shrewsbury A (65.93)	551	Bradman DG (78.71)
	364	Woolley FE (60.67)	411	Bardsley W (102.75)
	334	Jackson Hon. FS (47.71)	411	Chappell GS (68.50)
	333	Boycott G (55.50)	390	Border AR (195.00)
	327	Edrich JH (54.50)	379	Brown WA (75.80)
Highest Wicket Aggregates	21	Verity H (11.24)	19	Turner CTB (14.63)
	19	Trueman FS (21.16)	17	Lillee DK (34.35)
	15	Briggs J (7.27)	16	Massie RAL (8.56)
	14	Peel R (12.36)	15	Lindwall RR (14.87)
	13	Willis RGD (15.62)	14	Lawson GF (22.07)
	13	Bedser AV (30.31)		
Most Appearances	5	Grace WG, Jackson Hon. FS, Lilley AFA	8	Gregory SE
			5	Blackham JM, Marsh RW
	4	(17 players)	4	(15 players)

ENGLAND		Record Wicket Partnerships	
1st	182	Hobbs JB (119) Sutcliffe H (82)	1926
2nd	168	Hutton L (145) Graveney TW (78)	1953
3rd	140	Woolley FE (87) Hendren EH (127*)	1926
4th	222	Hammond WR (240) Paynter E (99)	1938
5th	163	Watson W (109) Bailey TE (71)	1953
6th	186	Hammond WR (240) Ames LEG (83)	1938
7th	131	Gatting MW (75*) Botham IT (85)	1985
8th	76	Steel AG (148) Lyttelton Hon. A (31)	1884
9th	53	Relf AE (17) Lilley AFA (47)	1909
10th	39	Trueman FS (25) Statham JB (11*)	1961

AUSTRALIA		Record Wicket Partnerships	
1st	162	Woodfull WM (155) Ponsford WH (81)	1930
2nd	231	Woodfull WM (155) Bradman DG (254)	1930
3rd	192	Bradman DG (254) Kippax AF (83)	1930
4th	221	Trott GHS (143) Gregory SE (103)	1896
5th	216	Border AR (196) Ritchie GM (94)	1985
6th	142	Gregory SE (57) Graham H (107)	1893
7th	117	Mackay KD (31) Benaud R (97)	1956
8th	85	Brown WA (206*) O'Reilly WJ (42)	1938
9th	66	Edwards R (99) Lillee DK (73*)	1975
10th	69	Scott HJH (75) Boyle HF (26*) Lillee DK (73*) Mallett AA (14)	1884 1975

Old Trafford (Manchester)

First Test 1884 Played 24 England won 7 Australia won 4 Drawn 13

Highest Match Aggregates	1307–20 wickets	(1934)	Drawn
	1271–18 wickets	(1964)	Drawn
	1190–40 wickets	(1961)	Australia 54 runs
Lowest Match Aggregates	217–10 wickets	(1912)	Drawn
	323–30 wickets	(1888)	England inns & 21 runs
	457–29 wickets	(1884)	Drawn

Two England players *have severely injured themselves on boundary fences in Australia. At Brisbane 1954–55 DCS Compton fractured a bone in his left hand while fielding, while at Sydney 1970–71, JA Snow dislocated and fractured a finger in his right hand while attempting a catch.*

	ENGLAND	AUSTRALIA
Highest Totals	627–9d (1934)	656–8d (1964)
	611 (1964)	491 (1934)
	482–9d (1985)	432 (1961)
Lowest Totals	95 (1884)	70 (1888)
	119 (1909)	81 (1888)
	120 (1902)	84 (1956)
Highest Individual Innings	256 Barrington KF (1964)	311 Simpson RB (1964)
	174 Dexter ER (1964)	146* Border AR (1985)
	160 Gatting MW (1985)	137 McCabe SJ (1934)
	154* Ranjitsinhji KS (1896)	123* Border AR (1981)
	153 Leyland M (1934)	122 Harvey RN (1953)
Best Innings Bowling Analyses	10–53 Laker JC (1956)	8–31 Laver F (1909)
	9–37 Laker JC (1956)	8–141 McDermott CJ (1985)
	7–31 Peel R (1888)	7–153 McKenzie GD (1964)
	7–44 Barlow RG (1886)	7–189 O'Reilly WJ (1934)
	7–168 Richardson T (1896)	6–42 Boyle HF (1884)
Best Match Bowling Analyses	19–90 Laker JC (1956)	10–128 Trumble H (1902)
	13–244 Richardson T (1896)	9–56 Laver F (1909)
	11–68 Peel R (1888)	9–197 Alderman TM (1981)
	11–76 Lockwood WH (1902)	8–106 Lillee DK (1972)
	10–156 Richardson T (1893)	8–141 McDermott CJ (1985)
Highest Run Aggregates	339 Barrington KF (113.00)	379 Lawry WM (75.80)
	325 Jackson Hon.FS (54.17)	370 Simpson RB (123.33)
	292 Ranjitsinhji KS (73.00)	302 Walters KD (50.33)
	266 Dexter ER (88.67)	288 Border AR (144.00)
	226 Sutcliffe H (75.33)	276 Trumper VT (34.50)
Highest Wicket Aggregates	23 Richardson T (17.39)	21 Trumble H (21.38)
	22 Laker JC (6.50)	14 Lillee DK (21.29)
	17 Rhodes W (16.12)	14 McKenzie GD (26.00)
	13 Snow JA (21.23)	12 Spofforth FR (14.08)
	12 Briggs J (24.58)	12 Giffen G (28.00)

Most Appearances	5 Grace WG, Lilley AFA, MacLaren AC 4 Boycott G, Briggs J, Jackson Hon. FS, Rhodes W	6 Gregory SE 4 Armstrong WW, Bardsley W, Blackham JM, Darling J, Giffen G, Kelly JJ, Macartney CG, Noble MA, Trumble H, Trumper VT

ENGLAND		Record Wicket Partnerships	
1st	174	Richardson PE (104) Cowdrey MC (80)	1956
2nd	124	Washbrook C (85*) Edrich WJ (53)	1948
3rd	246	Dexter ER (174) Barrington KF (256)	1964
4th	160	Woolmer RA (137) Greig AW (76)	1977
5th	191	Hendren EH (132) Leyland M (153)	1934
6th	149	Tavaré CJ (78) Botham IT (118)	1981
7th	113	Hayward TW (130) Lilley AFA (58)	1899
8th	121	Compton DCS (145*) Bedser AV (37)	1948
9th	95	Allen GOB (61) Verity H (60*)	1934
10th	56	Allott PJW (52*) Willis RGD (11)	1981

AUSTRALIA		Record Wicket Partnerships	
1st	201	Lawry WM (106) Simpson RB (311)	1964
2nd	196	Brown WA (72) McCabe SJ (137)	1934
3rd	144	Lawry WM (81) Walters KD (81)	1968
4th	173	Harvey RN (122) Hole GB (66)	1953
5th	219	Simpson RB (311) Booth BC (98)	1964
6th	127*	Border AR (146*) Phillips WB (39*)	1985
7th	64	Bruce W (68) Trumble H (35)	1893
8th	87	Fairfax AG (49) Grimmett CV (50)	1930
9th	104	Marsh RW (91) Gleeson JW (30)	1972
10th	98	Davidson AK (77*) McKenzie GD (32)	1961

Trent Bridge (Nottingham)

First Test 1899 Played 15 England won 3 Australia won 4 Drawn 8

Highest Match Aggregates	1496–24 wickets	(1938)	Drawn
	1213–32 wickets	(1948)	Australia 8 wickets
	1191–22 wickets	(1985)	Drawn

Lowest Match Aggregates	32–0 wickets	(1926)	Drawn
	521–30 wickets	(1921)	Australia 10 wickets
	617–29 wickets	(1964)	Drawn

	ENGLAND	AUSTRALIA
Highest Totals	658–8d (1938)	539 (1985)
	456 (1985)	509 (1948)
	441 (1948)	427–6 (1938)
Lowest Totals	112 (1921)	123 (1953)
†One batsman absent hurt	125 (1981)	144 (1930)
	141 (1934)	148† (1956)
Highest Individual Innings	216* Paynter E (1938)	232 McCabe SJ (1938)
	184 Compton DCS (1948)	172 Wood GM (1985)
	166 Gower DI (1985)	170* Edwards R (1972)
	140 MacLaren AC (1905)	146 Ritchie GM (1985)
	135 Knott APE (1977)	144* Bradman DG (1938)
Best Innings Bowling Analyses	8–107 Bosanquet BJT (1905)	7–54 O'Reilly WJ (1934)
	7–44 Bedser AV (1953)	7–64 Laver F (1905)
	7–55 Bedser AV (1953)	6–58 Gregory JM (1921)
	5–52 Jackson Hon. FS (1905)	5–32 McDonald EA (1921)
	5–74 Botham IT (1977)	5–36 Johnston WA (1948)
Best Match Bowling Analyses	14–99 Bedser AV (1953)	11–129 O'Reilly WJ (1934)
	10–179 Farnes K (1934)	10–201 Grimmett CV (1930)
	8–136 Bosanquet BJT (1905)	9–130 Alderman TM (1981)
	8–186 Snow JA (1972)	9–183 Johnston WA (1948)
	7–62 Dilley GR (1981)	8–74 McDonald EA (1921)
Highest Run Aggregates	305 Compton DCS (76.25)	526 Bradman DG (75.14)
	280 Hutton L (70.00)	477 McCabe SJ (79.50)
	266 Boycott G (66.50)	293 Brown WA (58.60)
	237 Gower DI (59.25)	281 Hassett AL (56.20)
	216 Paynter E (–)	194 Hill C (48.50)

When the Oval Test of 1921 *was heading for an inevitable draw, Australian captain WW Armstrong demonstrated his boredom by going off to the outfield and reading a newspaper while his bowlers directed themselves.*

Highest Wicket Aggregates	19 Bedser AV (13.58)	18 Grimmett CV (17.83)
	14 Farnes K (25.93)	14 Lillee DK (14.07)
	11 Rhodes W (22.36)	14 O'Reilly WJ (20.93)
	11 Botham IT (28.09)	13 Miller KR (22.31)
	10 Willis RGD (22.10)	9 Alderman TM (14.44)
	10 Laker JC (22.50)	9 Johnston WA (24.33)
Most Appearances	4 Hendren EH	4 Bradman DG
	3 Botham IT, Boycott G, Compton DCS, Evans TG, Hammond WR, Hutton L, Rhodes W, Sutcliffe H, Woolley FE	3 Brown WA, Hassett AL, Lindwall RR, McCabe SJ, Marsh RW, Miller KR, Oldfield WAS, Woodfull WM

ENGLAND		Record Wicket Partnerships	
1st	219	Barnett CJ (126) Hutton L (100)	1938
2nd	117	Luckhurst BW (96) Parfitt PH (46)	1972
3rd	187	Gower DI (166) Gatting MW (74)	1985
4th	93	Compton DCS (184) Hardstaff J jnr (43)	1948
5th	206	Paynter E (216*) Compton DCS (102)	1938
6th	215	Boycott G (107) Knott APE (135)	1977
7th	101	Hendren EH (79) Geary G (53)	1934
8th	47	Sharpe PJ (35*) Allen DA (21)	1964
9th	89	Laker JC (63) Bedser AV (22)	1948
10th	28	Robins RWV (50*) Duckworth G (4)	1930

AUSTRALIA		Record Wicket Partnerships	
1st	89	Fingleton JHW (40) Brown WA (133)	1938
2nd	170	Brown WA (133) Bradman DG (144*)	1938
3rd	146	Edwards R (170*) Chappell GS (72)	1972
4th	112	Brown WA (73) McCabe SJ (88)	1934
5th	120	Bradman DG (138) Hassett AL (137)	1948
6th	161	Wood GM (172) Ritchie GM (146)	1985
7th	69	McCabe SJ (232) Barnett BA (22)	1938
8th	107	Hassett AL (137) Lindwall RR (42)	1948
9th	48	O'Donnell SP (46) Lawson GF (18)	1985
10th	77	McCabe SJ (232) Fleetwood-Smith LO'B (5*)	1938

The Oval (London)

First Test 1880 Played 29 England won 13 Australia won 5 Drawn 11

Highest Match Aggregates	1494–37 wickets	(1934)	Australia 562 runs
	1351–30 wickets	(1930)	Australia inns & 39 runs
	1301–31 wickets	(1975)	Drawn
Lowest Match Aggregates	363–40 wickets	(1882)	Australia 7 runs
	389–38 wickets	(1890)	England 2 wickets
	392–40 wickets	(1896)	England 66 runs

	ENGLAND	AUSTRALIA
Highest Totals	903–7d (1938)	701 (1934)
	576 (1899)	695 (1930)
	538 (1975)	551 (1884)
Lowest Totals	52 (1948)	44 (1896)
	77 (1882)	63 (1882)
	84 (1896)	65 (1912)
Highest Individual Innings	364 Hutton L (1938)	266 Ponsford WH (1934)
	196 Gooch GA (1985)	244 Bradman DG (1934)
	187 Leyland M (1938)	232 Bradman DG (1930)
	182* Mead CP (1921)	211 Murdoch WL (1884)
	170 Grace WG (1886)	196 Morris AR (1948)
Best Innings Bowling Analyses	7–36 Lohmann GA (1886)	8–65 Trumble H (1902)
	7–50 Underwood DL (1968)	7–25 Hazlitt GR (1912)
	7–71 Lockwood WH (1899)	7–44 Spofforth FR (1882)
	6–23 Peel R (1896)	7–46 Spofforth FR (1882)
	6–41 Hearne JT (1896)	7–89 Lillee DK (1981)
Best Match Bowling Analyses	12–102 Martin F (1890)	14–90 Spofforth FR (1882)
	12–104 Lohmann GA (1886)	12–89 Trumble H (1896)
	10–49 Woolley FE (1912)	12–173 Trumble H (1902)
	10–60 Hearne JT (1896)	11–159 Lillee DK (1981)
	10–148 Briggs J (1893)	10–181 Lillee DK (1972)

Highest Run Aggregates	557 Hutton L (111.40) 518 Sutcliffe H (86.33) 504 Grace WG (45.82) 426 Jackson Hon. FS (53.25) 402 Knott APE (50.25)	553 Bradman DG (138.25) 414 Murdoch WL (69.00) 412 Ponsford WH (82.40) 359 Chappell IM (71.80) 341 Bardsley W (48.71)
Highest Wicket Aggregates	21 Briggs J (11.33) 21 Lockwood WH (17.48) 19 Lohmann GA (10.63) 18 Underwood DL (29.22) 16 Bowes WE (18.31) 16 Botham IT (22.56)	27 Lillee DK (17.59) 27 Trumble H (17.67) 20 Spofforth FR (12.50) 18 Grimmett CV (31.89) 15 Lindwall RR (16.73) 15 Cotter A (22.47)
Most Appearances	8 Grace WG 6 Barnes W, Rhodes W 5 Jackson Hon. FS, Knott APE, Lilley AFA, MacLaren AC, Read WW, Woolley FE	7 Blackham JM, Gregory SE 5 Bannerman AC, Giffen G, Trumble H

ENGLAND		**Record Wicket Partnerships**	
1st	185	Jackson Hon. FS (118) Hayward TW (137)	1899
2nd	382	Hutton L (364) Leyland M (187)	1938
3rd	135	Hutton L (364) Hammond WR (59)	1938
4th	156	May PBH (83*) Compton DCS (94)	1956
5th	172	Subba Row R (137) Barrington KF (83)	1961
6th	215	Hutton L (364) Hardstaff J jnr (169*)	1938
7th	142	Sharp J (105) Hutchings KL (59)	1909
8th	90	Read WW (94) Briggs J (53)	1886
9th	151	Scotton WH (90) Read WW (117)	1884
10th	58	Lohmann GA (62*) Wood H (8)	1888

AUSTRALIA		**Record Wicket Partnerships**	
1st	180	Gregory SE (74) Bardsley W (130)	1909
2nd	451	Ponsford WH (266) Bradman DG (244)	1934
3rd	207	Murdoch WL (211) Scott HJH (102)	1884
4th	243	Bradman DG (232) Jackson AA (73)	1930
5th	185	Burge PJP (181) Booth BC (71)	1961
6th	86	Wellham DM (103) Marsh RW (52)	1981
7th	107	Collins HL (61) Gregory JM (73)	1926
8th	83	Gregory SE (117) McLeod CE (31*)	1899
9th	100	Walker MHN (78*) Malone MF (46)	1977
10th	88	Murdoch WL (153*) Moule WH (34)	1880

Sheffield (Bramall Lane)

Only Test 1902 England won 0 Australia won 1 Drawn 0

Match Aggregate	823–40 wickets (1902)	Australia 143 runs
	ENGLAND	**AUSTRALIA**
Highest Total	195 (1902)	289 (1902)
Lowest Total	145 (1902)	194 (1902)
Highest Individual Innings	63 MacLaren AC (1902) 55 Jessop GL (1902) 38 Abel R (1902)	119 Hill C (1902) 62 Trumper VT (1902) 47 Noble MA (1902)
Best Innings Bowling Analyses	6–49 Barnes SF (1902) 5–63 Rhodes W (1902) 3–60 Jackson Hon. FS (1902)	6–52 Noble MA (1902) 5–50 Saunders JV (1902) 5–51 Noble MA (1902)
Best Match Bowling Analyses	7–99 Barnes SF (1902) 6–96 Rhodes W (1902) 4–71 Jackson Hon. FS (1902)	11–103 Noble MA (1902) 5–118 Saunders JV (1902) 4–70 Trumble H (1902)
Highest Run Aggregates	94 MacLaren AC (47.00) 67 Jessop GL (33.50) 46 Abel R (23.00)	137 Hill C (68.50) 67 Hopkins AJY (67.00) 63 Trumper VT (31.50)
Highest Wicket Aggregates	7 Barnes SF (14.14) 6 Rhodes W (16.00) 4 Jackson Hon. FS (17.75)	11 Noble MA (9.36) 5 Saunders JV (23.60) 4 Trumble H (17.50)

ENGLAND		**Best Three Partnerships**	
5th	64	MacLaren AC (63) Jackson Hon. FS (14)	1902
1st	61	MacLaren AC (31) Abel R (38)	1902
2nd	61	Jessop GL (55) Tyldesley JT (14)	1902

AUSTRALIA		**Best Three Partnerships**	
4th	107	Hill C (119) Gregory SE (29)	1902
2nd	60	Trumper VT (62) Hill C (119)	1902
9th	57	Armstrong WW (25) Trumble H (32)	1902

Sydney 1894–95 (ABOVE) *and The Oval 1985*

Adelaide

First Test 1884–85 Played 23 England won 7 Australia won 13 Drawn 3

Highest Match Aggregates	1753–40 wickets	(1920–21)	Australia 119 runs
	1502–29 wickets	(1946–47)	Drawn
	1467–40 wickets	(1924–25)	Australia 11 runs
Lowest Match Aggregates	768–30 wickets	(1891–92)	England inns & 230 runs
	853–40 wickets	(1978–79)	England 205 runs
	870–31 wickets	(1884–85)	England 8 wickets

	ENGLAND		AUSTRALIA	
Highest Totals	501	(1911–12)	582	(1920–21)
	499	(1891–92)	573	(1897–98)
	470	(1970–71)	516	(1965–66)
Lowest Totals	124	(1894–95)	100	(1891–92)
	143	(1894–95)	111	(1954–55)
	169	(1978–79)	133	(1911–12)
Highest Individual Innings	187	Hobbs JB (1911–12)	225	Simpson RB (1965–66)
	177	Hammond WR (1928–29)	212	Bradman DG (1936–37)
	156*	Hutton L (1950–51)	206	Morris AR (1950–51)
	147	Compton DCS (1946–47)	201*	Ryder J (1924–25)
	135*	Russell CAG (1920–21)	178	Darling J (1897–98)
Best Innings Bowling Analyses	8–126	White JC (1928–29)	8–43	Trott AE (1894–95)
	7–113	Underwood DL (1974–75)	6–48	McKenzie GD (1965–66)
	6–49	Briggs J (1891–92)	6–74	Trumble H (1901–02)
	6–87	Briggs J (1891–92)	6–110	Fleetwood-Smith LO'B (1936–37)
	6–118	Jones IJ (1965–66)	5–37	Callaway ST (1894–95)
Best Match Bowling Analyses	13–256	White JC (1928–29)	10–239	Fleetwood-Smith LO'B (1936–37)
	12–136	Briggs J (1891–92)	10–302	Mailey AA (1920–21)
	11–215	Underwood DL (1974–75)	9–122	Lawson GF (1982–83)
	8–119	Peel R (1884–85)	9–173	Benaud R (1958–59)
	8–121	Allen GOB (1932–33)	9–198	Trumble H (1901–02)

	England	Australia
Highest Run Aggregates	601 Hobbs JB (66.78) 482 Hammond WR (60.25) 456 Hutton L (91.20) 357 Barrington KF (119.00) 333 Compton DCS (83.25)	643 Hill C (71.44) 509 Morris AR (101.80) 486 Ryder J (97.20) 466 Bradman DG (66.57) 344 Harvey RN (49.14)
Highest Wicket Aggregates	16 Briggs J (22.19) 14 Barnes SF (24.29) 13 White JC (19.69) 13 Underwood DL (26.54) 12 Peel R (21.50) 12 Richardson T (27.33) 12 Statham JB (28.25)	16 Mailey AA (35.06) 15 Trumble H (26.40) 13 Lillee DK (18.62) 13 McKenzie GD (19.54) 12 Lindwall RR (27.83) 12 Noble MA (29.50)
Most Appearances	5 Cowdrey MC, Hobbs JB 4 Briggs J, Evans TG, Hammond WR, Rhodes W, Willis RGD	5 Armstrong WW, Gregory SE, Hill C, Oldfield WAS 4 Bradman DG, Harvey RN, Noble MA, Trumper VT

ENGLAND		Record Wicket Partnerships	
1st	149	MacLaren AC (67) Hayward TW (90)	1901–02
2nd	169	Edrich JH (130) Fletcher KWR (80)	1970–71
3rd	262	Hammond WR (177) Jardine DR (98)	1928–29
4th	118	Gower DI (114) Botham IT (58)	1982–83
5th	156	Leyland M (83) Ames LEG (78)	1932–33
6th	124	Russell CAG (135*) Douglas JWHT (60)	1920–21
7th	135	Miller G (64) Taylor RW (97)	1978–79
8th	96	Paynter E (77) Verity H (45)	1932–33
9th	85*	Compton DCS (103*) Evans TG (10*)	1946–47
10th	74	MacGregor G (31) Attewell W (43*)	1891–92

AUSTRALIA		Record Wicket Partnerships	
1st	244	Simpson RB (225) Lawry WM (119)	1965–66
2nd	202	Stackpole KR (136) Chappell IM (104)	1970–71
3rd	189	Morris AR (122) Hassett AL (78)	1946–47
4th	194	Kelleway C (147) Armstrong WW (121)	1920–21
		Harvey RN (154) O'Neill NC (100)	1962–63
5th	150	Miller KR (141*) Johnson IW (52)	1946–47
6th	126	Kelleway C (147) Pellew CE (104)	1920–21
7th	134	Ryder J (201*) Andrews TJE (72)	1924–25
8th	243	Hartigan RJ (116) Hill C (160)	1907–08
9th	108	Ryder J (201*) Oldfield WAS (47)	1924–25
10th	81	Trott AE (38*) Callaway ST (41)	1894–95

Brisbane (Exhibition Ground)

Only Test 1928–29 England won 1 Australia won 0 Drawn 0

Match Aggregate	1051–35 wickets (1928–29)	England 675 runs

	ENGLAND	AUSTRALIA
Highest Total	521 (1928–29)	122† (1928–29) †One batsman absent hurt
Lowest Total	342–8d (1928–29)	66§ (1928–29) §Two batsmen absent hurt
Highest Individual Innings	169 Hendren EH (1928–29) 73 Mead CP (1928–29) 70 Larwood H (1928–29)	33 Ryder J (1928–29) 30* Woodfull WM (1928–29) 30 Hendry HSTL (1928–29)
Best Innings Bowling Analyses	6–32 Larwood H (1928–29) 4–7 White JC (1928–29) 3–50 Tate MW (1928–29)	6–131 Grimmett CV (1928–29) 3–142 Gregory JM (1928–29) 3–167 Grimmett CV (1928–29)
Best Match Bowling Analyses	8–52 Larwood H (1928–29) 5–76 Tate MW (1928–29) 4–7 White JC (1928–29)	9–298 Grimmett CV (1928–29) 4–164 Ironmonger H (1928–29) 3–142 Gregory JM (1928–29)
Highest Run Aggregates	214 Hendren EH (107.00) 107 Larwood H (53.50) 100 Jardine DR (100.00)	36 Hendry HSTL (18.00) 34 Ryder J (17.00) 31 Kippax AF (15.50)
Highest Wicket Aggregates	8 Larwood H (6.50) 5 Tate MW (15.20) 4 White JC (1.75)	9 Grimmett CV (33.11) 4 Ironmonger H (41.00) 3 Gregory JM (47.33)

ENGLAND		Best Three Partnerships	
8th	124	Hendren EH (169) Larwood H (70)	1928–29
1st	85	Hobbs JB (49) Sutcliffe H (38)	1928–29
6th	74	Hendren EH (169) Chapman APF (50)	1928–29

AUSTRALIA		Best Three Partnerships	
5th	31	Hendry HSTL (30) Ryder J (33)	1928–29
6th	30	Ryder J (33) Bradman DG (18)	1928–29
2nd	27	Woodfull WM (30*) Kippax AF (15)	1928–29

Brisbane (Woolloongabba)

First Test 1932–33 Played 12 England won 3 Australia won 6 Drawn 3

Highest Match Aggregates	1433–30 wickets	(1962–63)	Drawn
	1150–31 wickets	(1970–71)	Drawn
	1059–33 wickets	(1982–83)	Australia 7 wickets
Lowest Match Aggregates	450–34 wickets	(1950–51)	Australia 60 runs
	665–32 wickets	(1958–59)	Australia 8 wickets
	906–39 wickets	(1936–37)	England 322 runs

	ENGLAND		AUSTRALIA	
Highest Totals	464	(1970–71)	645	(1946–47)
	389	(1962–63)	601–8d	(1954–55)
	358	(1936–37)	443–6d	(1965–66)
Lowest Totals	122	(1950–51)	58†	(1936–37)
	134	(1958–59)	116	(1978–79)
	141	(1946–47)	175	(1932–33)

†One batsman absent ill

In 1950–51 England declared their first innings at 68–7; Australia declared their second innings at 32–7

	ENGLAND	AUSTRALIA
Highest Individual Innings	126 Leyland M (1936–37)	207 Stackpole KR (1970–71)
	110 Greig AW (1974–75)	187 Bradman DG (1946–47)
	99 Dexter ER (1962–63)	166 Lawry WM (1965–66)
	88 Bailey TE (1954–55)	162 Harvey RN (1954–55)
	88 Edrich WJ (1954–55)	162 Wessels KC (1982–83)
Best Innings Bowling Analyses	6–41 Voce W (1936–37)	7–60 Miller KR (1946–47)
	6–114 Snow JA (1970–71)	6–46 Thomson JR (1974–75)
	5–36 Allen GOB (1936–37)	6–47 Lawson GF (1982–83)
	5–47 Shuttleworth K (1970–71)	6–74 Hogg RM (1978–79)
	5–66 Willis RGD (1982–83)	6–82 Toshack ERH (1946–47)
Best Match Bowling Analyses	10–57 Voce W (1936–37)	11–134 Lawson GF (1982–83)
	8–107 Allen GOB (1936–37)	9–77 Miller KR (1946–47)
	8–162 Snow JA (1970–71)	9–99 Toshack ERH (1946–47)
	7–50 Bailey TE (1950–51)	9–105 Thomson JR (1974–75)
	7–54 Bedser AV (1950–51)	8–240 Ward FA (1936–37)

	England	Australia
Highest Run Aggregates	257 Leyland M (64.25) 214 Bailey TE (42.80) 202 Edrich JH (40.40) 192 Barrington KF (48.00) 190 Randall DW (63.33) 190 Boycott G (38.00)	381 Harvey RN (54.43) 357 Lawry WM (71.40) 339 Walters KD (84.75) 325 Bradman DG (65.00) 215 Stackpole KR (107.50)
Highest Wicket Aggregates	19 Willis RGD (16.00) 13 Allen GOB (18.00) 13 Bailey TE (18.92) 10 Voce W (14.90) 10 Bedser AV (34.40)	17 Benaud R (21.71) 14 Miller KR (12.57) 14 Thomson JR (15.79) 11 Lawson GF (12.18) 10 Johnston WA (17.10) 10 O'Reilly WJ (34.60)
Most Appearances	4 Cowdrey MC 3 Bailey TE, Bedser AV, Boycott G, Compton DCS, Edrich JH, Hammond WR, Hutton L, Statham JB, Willis RGD	4 Harvey RN 3 Benaud R, Bradman DG, Burge PJP, Johnson IW, Lawry WM, Lindwall RR, Marsh RW, Miller KR, Morris AR, Redpath IR, Walters KD

ENGLAND — Record Wicket Partnerships

Wkt	Runs	Partnership	Season
1st	114	Jardine DR (46) Sutcliffe H (86)	1932–33
		Pullar G (56) Sheppard Rev. DS (53)	1962–63
2nd	90	Fowler G (83) Gower DI (34)	1982–83
3rd	124	Edrich WJ (88) May PBH (44)	1954–55
4th	99	Barnett CJ (69) Leyland M (126)	1936–37
5th	82	Cowdrey MC (40) Bailey TE (88)	1954–55
6th	95	Gower DI (44) Botham IT (49)	1978–79
7th	64	Parfitt PH (80) Titmus FJ (21)	1962–63
8th	78	D'Oliveira BL (57) Snow JA (34)	1970–71
9th	92	Paynter E (83) Verity H (23*)	1932–33
10th	45	Hutton L (62*) Wright DVP (2)	1950–51

AUSTRALIA — Record Wicket Partnerships

Wkt	Runs	Partnership	Season
1st	136	Lawry WM (98) Simpson RB (71)	1962–63
2nd	151	Stackpole KR (207) Chappell IM (59)	1970–71
3rd	276	Bradman DG (187) Hassett AL (128)	1946–47
4th	170	Yallop GN (102) Hughes KJ (129)	1978–79
5th	187	Lawry WM (166) Walters KD (155)	1965–66

AUSTRALIA

6th	131	McCool CL (95) Johnson IW (47)	1946–47
7th	103	Booth BC (112) Mackay KD (86*)	1962–63
8th	91	Mackay KD (86*) Benaud R (51)	1962–63
9th	29*	Lindwall RR (64*) Johnson IW (24*)	1954–55
10th	52	Walker MHN (41*) Thomson JR (23)	1974–75

Melbourne

First Test 1876–77 Played 47 England won 17 Australia won 23 Drawn 7

Highest Match Aggregates	1619–40 wickets	(1924–25)	Australia 81 runs
	1562–37 wickets	(1946–47)	Drawn
	1554–35 wickets	(1928–29)	Australia 5 wickets
Lowest Match Aggregates	542–39 wickets	(1903–04)	Australia 218 runs
	548–30 wickets	(1878–79)	Australia 10 wickets
	561–30 wickets	(1882–83)	England inns & 27 runs

	ENGLAND		**AUSTRALIA**	
Highest Totals	589	(1911–12)	604	(1936–37)
	558	(1965–66)	600	(1924–25)
	548	(1924–25)	564	(1936–37)
Lowest Totals	61	(1901–02)	104	(1876–77)
	61	(1903–04)	111	(1903–04)
	75	(1894–95)	111	(1954–55)
Highest Individual Innings	200	Hammond WR (1928–29)	307	Cowper RM (1965–66)
	188	Denness MH (1974–75)	270	Bradman DG (1936–37)
	179	Rhodes W (1911–12)	188	Hill C (1897–98)
	178	Hobbs JB (1911–12)	169	Bradman DG (1936–37)
	176	Sutcliffe H (1924–25)	167	Harvey RN (1958–59)
Best Innings Bowling Analyses	8–68	Rhodes W (1903–04)	9–121	Mailey AA (1920–21)
	8–81	Braund LC (1903–04)	8–143	Walker MHN (1974–75)
	7–27	Tyson FH (1954–55)	7–17	Noble MA (1901–02)
	7–28	Bates W (1882–83)	7–28	Trumble H (1903–04)
	7–56	Rhodes W (1903–04)	7–55	Kendall T (1876–77)

Best Match Bowling Analyses	15–124 Rhodes W (1903–04)	13–77 Noble MA (1901–02)
	14–102 Bates W (1882–83)	13–110 Spofforth FR (1878–79)
	13–163 Barnes SF (1901–02)	13–236 Mailey AA (1920–21)
	10–105 Bedser AV (1950–51)	11–138 Lillee DK (1979–80)
	9–81 Barnes W (1884–85)	11–165 Lillee DK (1976–77)
Highest Run Aggregates	1178 Hobbs JB (69.29)	1034 Bradman DG (114.89)
	724 Sutcliffe H (103.43)	634 Armstrong WW (57.64)
	661 Cowdrey MC (50.85)	620 Hill C (32.63)
	505 Hammond WR (42.08)	481 Lawry WM (68.71)
	487 Ulyett G (40.58)	444 Walters KD (44.40)
Highest Wicket Aggregates	35 Barnes SF (18.06)	46 Trumble H (14.04)
	27 Peel R (21.04)	39 Noble MA (13.36)
	22 Bates W (12.59)	27 Lillee DK (16.48)
	22 Bedser AV (20.91)	26 Giffen G (30.27)
	21 Rhodes W (20.67)	24 O'Reilly WJ (13.79)
		24 Spofforth FR (24.92)
		24 Mailey AA (27.29)
Most Appearances	10 Hobbs JB	10 Hill C
	9 Cowdrey MC	9 Armstrong WW
	8 Rhodes W	8 Blackham JM, Giffen G, Gregory SE, Horan TP, Noble MA, Oldfield WAS, Trumper VT
	7 Briggs J, Ulyett G	7 Bannerman AC, Garrett TW, Trumble H
	6 Bates W, Braund LC, Hammond WR, Hayward TW, Hendren EH, MacLaren AC, Willis RGD, Woolley FE	

ENGLAND		**Record Wicket Partnerships**	
1st	323	Hobbs JB (178) Rhodes W (179)	1911–12
2nd	147	Washbrook C (62) Edrich WJ (89)	1946–47
3rd	210	Ward A (93) Brown JT (140)	1894–95
4th	192	Denness MH (188) Fletcher KWR (146)	1974–75
5th	162	MacLaren AC (164) Peel R (73)	1894–95
6th	140	Hendren EH (95) Leyland M (137)	1928–29
7th	133	Whysall WW (76) Kilner R (74)	1924–25
8th	93	Parks JM (71) Titmus FJ (56*)	1965–66
9th	89	Botham IT (119*) Lever JK (12)	1979–80
10th	98	Briggs J (121) Hunter J (39*)	1884–85

AUSTRALIA		Record Wicket Partnerships	
1st	126	Trumper VT (63) Noble MA (64)	1907–08
2nd	180	Redpath IR (72) Chappell IM (111)	1970–71
3rd	249	Bradman DG (169) McCabe SJ (112)	1936–37
4th	172	Cowper RM (307) Walters KD (60)	1965–66
5th	198	Burge PJP (120) Walters KD (115)	1965–66
6th	346	Fingleton JHW (136) Bradman DG (270)	1936–37
7th	165	Hill C (188) Trumble H (46)	1897–98
8th	173	Pellew CE (116) Gregory JM (100)	1920–21
9th	100	Hartkopf AEV (80) Oldfield WAS (39*)	1924–25
10th	120	Duff RA (104) Armstrong WW (45*)	1901–02

Perth

First Test 1970–71 Played 5 England won 1 Australia won 2 Drawn 2

Highest Match Aggregates	1266–31 wickets	(1982–83)	Drawn
	1224–29 wickets	(1970–71)	Drawn
	1024–40 wickets	(1979–80)	Australia 138 runs
Lowest Match Aggregates	868–40 wickets	(1978–79)	England 166 runs
	1005–31 wickets	(1974–75)	Australia 9 wickets
	1024–40 wickets	(1979–80)	Australia 138 runs

	ENGLAND		AUSTRALIA	
Highest Totals	411	(1982–83)	481	(1974–75)
	397	(1970–71)	440	(1970–71)
	358	(1982–83)	424–9d	(1982–83)
Lowest Totals	208	(1974–75)	161	(1978–79)
	208	(1978–79)	190	(1978–79)
	215	(1979–80)	244	(1979–80)
Highest Individual Innings	131	Luckhurst BW (1970–71)	171	Redpath IR (1970–71)
	115*	Edrich JH (1970–71)	117	Chappell GS (1982–83)
	115	Randall DW (1982–83)	115	Border AR (1979–80)
	102	Gower DI (1978–79)	115	Edwards R (1974–75)
	99*	Boycott G (1979–80)	108	Chappell GS (1970–71)

	England		Australia	
Best Innings Bowling Analyses	6–78	Botham IT (1979–80)	6–34	Dymock G (1979–80)
	5–44	Willis RGD (1978–79)	5–57	Hogg RM (1978–79)
	5–98	Botham IT (1979–80)	5–65	Hogg RM (1978–79)
	4–28	Lever JK (1978–79)	5–93	Thomson JR (1974–75)
	4–70	Miller G (1982–83)	5–107	Yardley B (1982–83)
Best Match Bowling Analyses	11–176	Botham IT (1979–80)	10–122	Hogg RM (1978–79)
	6–80	Willis RGD (1978–79)	9–86	Dymock G (1979–80)
	6–160	Snow JA (1970–71)	8–208	Yardley B (1982–83)
	5–48	Lever JK (1978–79)	7–138	Thomson JR (1974–75)
	5–118	Willis RGD (1982–83)	6–147	Lillee DK (1979–80)
Highest Run Aggregates	319	Boycott G (63.80)	371	Chappell GS (74.20)
	254	Gower DI (42.33)	250	Redpath IR (125.00)
	239	Randall DW (39.83)	193	Hughes KJ (38.60)
	200	Luckhurst BW (50.00)	159	Border AR (53.00)
	162	Edrich JH (162.00)	131	Marsh RW (26.20)
Highest Wicket Aggregates	14	Willis RGD (28.29)	14	Lillee DK (31.36)
	13	Botham IT (31.77)	12	Yardley B (26.50)
	8	Miller G (24.50)	11	Dymock G (19.18)
	6	Snow JA (26.67)	10	Hogg RM (12.20)
	5	Lever JK (9.60)	10	Thomson JR (23.80)
Most Appearances	4	Willis RGD	4	Chappell GS, Marsh RW
	3	Botham IT, Boycott G, Gower DI, Miller G, Randall DW, Taylor RW	3	Hughes KJ, Lillee DK
			2	(9 players)

ENGLAND		Record Wicket Partnerships	
1st	171	Boycott G (70) Luckhurst BW (131)	1970–71
2nd	95	Tavaré CJ (89) Gower DI (72)	1982–83
3rd	80	Tavaré CJ (89) Lamb AJ (46)	1982–83
4th	158	Boycott G (77) Gower DI (102)	1978–79
5th	100	Tavaré CJ (89) Randall DW (78)	1982–83
6th	77	Randall DW (115) Taylor RW (31)	1982–83
7th	78*	Edrich JH (115*) Knott APE (30*)	1970–71
8th	66	Titmus FJ (61) Old CM (43)	1974–75
9th	49	Taylor RW (29*) Willis RGD (26)	1982–83
10th	66	Pringle DR (47*) Cowans NG (36)	1982–83

AUSTRALIA		Record Wicket Partnerships	
1st	91	Wiener JM (58) Laird BM (33)	1979–80
2nd	37	Redpath IR (41) Chappell IM (25)	1974–75
3rd	68	Border AR (115) Chappell GS (43)	1979–80
4th	141	Chappell GS (117) Hughes KJ (62)	1982–83
5th	170	Edwards R (115) Walters KD (103)	1974–75
6th	219	Redpath IR (171) Chappell GS (108)	1970–71
7th	67	Redpath IR (171) Marsh RW (44)	1970–71
8th	78	Border AR (115) Lillee DK (19)	1979–80
9th	57	Toohey PM (81*) Dymock G (11)	1978–79
10th	19	Walker MHN (19) Thomson JR (11*)	1974–75

Sydney

First Test 1881–82 Played 46 England won 20 Australia won 22 Drawn 4

Highest Match Aggregates	1541–35 wickets	(1903–04)	England 5 wickets
	1514–40 wickets	(1894–95)	England 10 runs
	1364–40 wickets	(1911–12)	Australia 146 runs
Lowest Match Aggregates	374–40 wickets	(1887–88)	England 126 runs
	421–28 wickets	(1894–95)	Australia inns & 147 runs
	445–40 wickets	(1886–87)	England 13 runs

	ENGLAND		AUSTRALIA	
Highest Totals	636	(1928–29)	659–8d	(1946–47)
	577	(1903–04)	586	(1894–95)
	551	(1897–98)	581	(1920–21)
Lowest Totals	45	(1886–87)	42	(1887–88)
†One batsman absent hurt	65†	(1894–95)	80†	(1936–37)
	72†	(1894–95)	82	(1887–88)
Highest Individual Innings	287	Foster RE (1903–04)	234	Barnes SG (1946–47)
	251	Hammond WR (1928–29)	234	Bradman DG (1946–47)
	231*	Hammond WR (1936–37)	201	Gregory SE (1894–95)
	194	Sutcliffe H (1932–33)	187*	McCabe SJ (1932–33)
	185	Barber RW (1965–66)	185*	Trumper VT (1903–04)

Best Innings Bowling Analyses	8–35 Lohmann GA (1886–87)	7–43 Turner CTB (1887–88)
	8–58 Lohmann GA (1891–92)	7–44 Spofforth FR (1882–83)
	8–94 Richardson T (1897–98)	7–63 Lindwall RR (1946–47)
	7–40 Barlow RG (1882–83)	7–68 Palmer GE (1881–82)
	7–40 Snow JA (1970–71)	7–90 Hordern HV (1911–12)
Best Match Bowling Analyses	11–228 Tate MW (1924–25)	12–87 Turner CTB (1887–88)
	10–58 Peel R (1887–88)	12–175 Hordern HV (1911–12)
	10–87 Lohmann GA (1886–87)	11–82 Grimmett CV (1924–25)
	10–124 Larwood H (1932–33)	11–117 Spofforth FR (1882–83)
	10–130 Tyson FH (1954–55)	11–165 Palmer GE (1881–82)
Highest Run Aggregates	808 Hammond WR (161.60)	690 Gregory SE (40.59)
	654 Hobbs JB (43.60)	677 Trumper VT (45.13)
	510 Woolley FE (46.36)	620 Hill C (31.00)
	494 Gunn G (70.57)	540 Armstrong WW (38.57)
	462 MacLaren AC (46.20)	510 Bradman DG (72.86)
Highest Wicket Aggregates	35 Lohmann GA (9.46)	45 Turner CTB (13.38)
	28 Barnes SF (26.96)	33 Giffen G (17.97)
	25 Peel R (21.28)	32 Spofforth FR (15.06)
	24 Tate MW (23.46)	30 Palmer GE (16.33)
	23 Bates W (19.87)	27 Noble MA (27.59)
	23 Richardson T (29.65)	
Most Appearances	10 Briggs J	10 Gregory SE, Hill C
	8 Bates W, Hobbs JB, Rhodes W	9 Blackham JM
	7 Cowdrey MC, Shrewsbury A, Willis RGD	8 Armstrong WW, Bannerman AC, Garrett TW, Trumper VT
	6 Barlow RG, Braund LC, Hayward TW, MacLaren AC, Peel R, Read JM, Scotton WH, Woolley FE	7 Giffen G, McDonnell PS, Noble MA, Oldfield WAS
		6 Harvey RN, Horan TP, Jones SP, Kelly JJ, Turner CTB

In the 1905 series *the opposing captains, Hon. FS Jackson (Eng) and J Darling (Aus), had been born on the same day. Jackson won the toss in all 5 Tests, topped the batting aggregates and averages and the bowling averages for both sides, and led England to a 2–0 series victory.*

ENGLAND		Record Wicket Partnerships	
1st	234	Boycott G (84) Barber RW (185)	1965–66
2nd	188	Sutcliffe H (194) Hammond WR (112)	1932–33
3rd	129	Hammond WR (231*) Leyland M (42)	1936–37
4th	182	May PBH (92) Cowdrey MC (100*)	1958–59
5th	192	Foster RE (287) Braund LC (102)	1903–04
6th	124	Hirst GH (62) Ranjitsinhji KS (175)	1897–98
7th	143	Woolley FE (133*) Vine J (36)	1911–12
8th	86	Hearne JW (43) Douglas JWHT (32)	1911–12
9th	128	Woolley FE (123) Freeman AP (50*)	1924–25
10th	130	Foster RE (287) Rhodes W (40*)	1903–04

AUSTRALIA		Record Wicket Partnerships	
1st	126	Barnes SG (71) Morris AR (57)	1946–47
2nd	220	Redpath IR (105) Chappell GS (144)	1974–75
3rd	193	Darling J (160) Worrall J (62)	1897–98
4th	199	Bannerman AC (70) McDonnell PS (147)	1881–82
5th	405	Barnes SG (234) Bradman DG (234)	1946–47
6th	187	Kelleway C (78) Armstrong WW (158)	1920–21
7th	150	Miller KR (145*) Johnson IW (77)	1950–51
8th	154	Bonnor GJ (128) Jones SP (40)	1884–85
9th	154	Gregory SE (201) Blackham JM (74)	1894–95
10th	127	Taylor JM (108) Mailey AA (46*)	1924–25

At Melbourne in 1976–77 *a special Test was played to celebrate the centenary of Test cricket. By a remarkable coincidence the result in this 'Centenary Test' was the same as in the first-ever Test match: Australia beat England by 45 runs. England celebrated its own centenary of Test cricket with a special match at Lord's in 1980. Unlike the Melbourne match, this was spoiled by the weather (match drawn) and was further marred by a fracas in front of the pavilion when some MCC members jostled the two umpires after a protracted delay caused by overnight rain.*

On the fourth afternoon of the Brisbane Test of 1946–47 *a torrential thunderstorm, with hail and 79 mph winds, left the ground completely flooded. The pitch-covers and stumps floated away. Against all likelihood play began on time next morning.*

SECTION 12
Laws and Conditions of Play

The LAWS of the NOBLE GAME of CRICKET
as revised by the Club at St. Mary le bone

THE BALL must weigh not less than Five Ounces and a Half, nor more than Five Ounces and Three Quarters. At the beginning of each Innings either party may call for a New Ball.

THE BAT

Must not exceed Four Inches and One Quarter, in the widest part.

THE STUMPS

Must be Twenty-four Inches out of the ground, the BAILS Seven Inches in length.

THE BOWLING CREASE

Must be in a line with the Stumps, three Feet in length, with a Return Crease.

THE POPPING CREASE

Must be Three Feet Ten Inches from the Wicket, and parallel to it.

THE WICKETS

Must be opposite to each other, at the distance of Twenty-two yards.

THE PARTY WHICH GOES FROM HOME

Shall have the choice of the Innings, and the pitching of the Wickets, which shall be pitched within Thirty Yards of a center fixed by the Adversaries.

When the Parties meet at a Third Place, the Bowlers shall toss up for the pitching of the Wickets, and the choice for going in.

It shall not be lawful for either party during a Match, without the consent of the other, to alter the Ground, by rolling, watering, covering, mowing, or beating. This rule is not meant to prevent the Striker from beating the ground with his Bat near where he stands during the Innings, or to prevent the Bowler from filling up holes, watering his ground, or using sawdust, &c. when the ground is wet.

THE BOWLER

Shall deliver the Ball with one foot behind the Bowling Crease, and within the Return Crease, and shall bowl four Balls before he changes Wickets, which he shall do but once in the same Innings.

He may order the Striker at his Wicket, to stand on which side of it he pleases.

THE STRIKER IS OUT

If the Ball is bowled off, or the Stump bowled out of the ground.

Or, if the Ball, from a stroke over or under the Bat, or upon his hand, (but not wrists) is held before it touches the ground, although it be hugged to the body of the Catcher.

Or, if in striking, or at any other time while the Ball is in play, both his feet are over the Popping Crease and his Wicket put down, except his Bat is grounded within it.

Or, if in striking at the ball he hits down his Wicket.

Or, if under pretence of running a Notch, or otherwise, either of the Strikers prevent a Ball from being caught, the Striker of the Ball is out.

Or, if the Ball is struck up, and he wilfully strikes it again.

Or, if in running a Notch, the Wicket is struck down by a throw, or with the Ball in Hand, before his Foot Hand or Bat is grounded over the Popping Crease. But if the Bail is off, the Stump must be struck out of the ground.

Or, if the Striker touches or takes up the Ball while in play, unless at the request of the other Party.

If with his foot or leg he stops the Ball, which the Bowler in the opinion of the Umpire at the Bowler's Wicket shall have pitched in a straight line to the Wicket, and would have hit it.

If the Players have crossed each other, he that runs for the Wicket which is put down, is out; if they are not crossed, he that has left the Wicket which is put down, is out.

When a Ball is caught, no Notch to be reckoned.

When a Striker is run out, the Notch they were running for is not to be reckoned.

If lost Ball is call'd, the Striker shall be allowed four, but if more than four are run before lost Ball is call'd, then the Striker to have all they have run.

When the Ball has been in the Bowler's or Wicket-keeper's hands, it is considered as no longer in play, and the Strikers need not keep within their ground, till the Umpire has called Play, but if the player goes out of his ground with an intent to run before the ball is delivered, the Bowler may put him out.

If the Striker is hurt, he may retire from his Wicket, and have his Innings at any time in that Innings.

If a Striker is hurt, some other Person may be allowed to stand out for him, but not go in.

If any Person stops the Ball with his Hat, the Ball is to be considered as dead, and the opposite Party to add Five Notches to their Score; if any are run, they are to have five in all.

If the Ball is struck up, the Striker may guard his Wicket either with his Bat or his Body.

In single Wicket Matches, if the Striker moves out of his ground to strike at the Ball, he shall be allowed no Notch for such stroke.

THE WICKET KEEPERS

Shall stand at a reasonable distance behind the Wicket, and shall not move till the Ball is out of the Bowler's hand, and shall not by any noise incommode the Striker; and if his hands, knees, foot, or head, be over, or before the Wicket, though the Ball hit it, it shall not be out.

THE UMPIRES

Are the sole judges of fair and unfair play, and all disputes shall be determined by them; each at his own Wicket; but in case of a Catch, which the Umpire at the Wicket cannot see sufficiently to decide upon, he may apply to the other Umpire, whose opinion is conclusive.

They shall allow Two Minutes for each man to come in, and Fifteen Minutes between each Innings; when the Umpire shall call *Play*, the party refusing to Play shall lose the Match.

They are not to order a player out, unless appealed to by the Adversaries.

But if the Bowler's foot is not behind the Bowling Crease, and within the return Crease, when he delivers the Ball, they must, unasked, call *No Ball*.

If the Striker runs a short Notch, the Umpire must call *No Notch*.

The Umpire of the Bowler's Wicket, shall be first applied to decide on all Catches.

The Umpires are not to be changed during the Match, but by the consent of both Parties.

BETS.

If the Notches of one Player are laid against another, the Bets depend on the First Inning, unless otherwise specified.

If the Bets are made upon both Innings, and one Party beats the other in one inning, the Notches in the First Inning shall determine the Bet.

But if the other Party goes in a second time, then the Bet must be determined by the number on the Score.

Published by John Wallis, 13, Warwick-Square, London.

Hours of Play and Intervals

The various hours of play over the years in these matches are too varied to mention. By 1982–83 in Australia and 1985 in England the hours had become standardised as follows: play begins at 11.00, luncheon interval 1.00 to 1.40, tea interval 3.40 to 4.00, close of play at 6.00. In Australia 1982–83 there was for the first time a minimum number of overs – 90 – which had to be bowled in a day's play. (This minimum number, however, was subject to reduction for time lost to weather interference and wickets lost and was also re-calculated in the event of an innings ending during the day's play.) In England in 1985 the minimum number of overs to be bowled was also 90, with deductions being made for weather interference. Once again the minimum number of overs to be bowled was also re-calculated if an innings ended. This re-calculation was based on one over being bowled for each full four minutes of playing time remaining.

Since 1975, in England it has been possible for some of the time lost through weather interference to be made up on any day (except the final day). If, through weather or other interference, more than an hour's play has been lost on any day, an additional hour has been available on that day only (and not on the final day). Originally it was intended that the extra hour could take effect only if play was possible at the original close-of-play time, but since mid-1981 (after crowd protests at Lord's and Headingley) the Test and County Cricket Board have ruled that play may re-start at any time in the extra hour. The extra hour did not (in 1985) affect the minimum number of overs to be bowled in the day.

Luncheon Interval

The luncheon interval has been a regular feature of these Tests since 1876–77. The pre-lunch session of play has varied from 1½ to 2½ hours, with the standard time (see above) now being 2 hours.

Tea Interval

Prior to 1905 **in England** there was no tea interval in Tests, although in 1899 and 1902 there was a short on-field break while tea was taken out to the players. Since the 1905 series the tea interval has been a regular feature, now being taken two hours after the end of the luncheon interval. The tea interval customarily lasts 20 minutes. **In Australia** the tea interval has been a regular feature since 1881–82.

Balls per Over

The over has consisted of 4, 5, 6 or 8 balls as follows:

In England	In Australia
4 balls 1880 to 1888	4 balls 1876–77 to 1887–88
5 balls 1890 to 1899	6 balls 1891–92 to 1920–21
6 balls 1902 to 1985	8 balls 1924–25
	6 balls 1928–29 to 1932–33
	8 balls 1936–37 to 1978–79
	6 balls 1979–80 to 1982–83

For the first time in E v A Tests, in 1985 wides and no-balls not scored from were debited against the bowlers' analyses.

Follow-On

The follow-on has been available in E v A Tests as under:

In England		In Australia	
1880 to 1893	Compulsory after deficit of 80 runs	1876–77 to 1891–92	Compulsory after deficit of 80 runs
1896 to 1899	Compulsory after deficit of 120 runs	1894–95 to 1897–98	Compulsory after deficit of 120 runs
1902 to 1961	Optional after deficit of 150 runs	1901–02	Optional after deficit of 150 runs
1964 to 1985	Optional after deficit of 200 runs	1903–04 to 1950–51	Optional after deficit of 200 runs
		1954–55 to 1965–66	Optional after deficit of 150 runs
		1970–71 to 1982–83	Optional after deficit of 200 runs

Duration of Matches – Matches Played to a Finish

In England all Tests prior to 1912 were limited to three days. Apart from 'timeless' Tests (see below), all Tests between 1912 and 1926 were still limited to three days, between 1930 and 1938 four days, and from 1948 to 1985 five days, apart from occasions where the final Test of a series was extended to maximise the possibility of a result (also see below).
In Australia the Tests of 1876–77 were limited to four days; the 1878–79 Test was limited to three. The 1881–82 series had provision for the usual four days to be extended if necessary (although the first Test was originally scheduled

to last only three days and the final Test was limited to a maximum of four days). Between 1882–83 and 1936–37 all Tests were played to a finish (although the final Test in 1891–92 was limited to a maximum of six days but was completed anyway in four). From 1946–47 to 1958–59 Tests were limited to a maximum of six days, and from 1965–66 to 1982–83 they were limited to a maximum of five days.

'Timeless' Tests in England (all played at The Oval)

1912 Match lasted four days
1926 Match lasted four days
1930 Match lasted six days (no play on fifth day)
1934 Match lasted four days
1938 Match lasted four days

Provision for extra day's play in final Test in England

Other than 'timeless' Tests above, it was possible under tour regulations for the 1948 final Test to be 'timeless' if the difference in matches was no greater than one. This was not applicable as Australia led 3–0 before the fifth Test. In 1953 although there was provision for the final Test to be played if necessary over six days (this was announced after the fourth Test), England won on the fourth day. In 1968 it was agreed that the fifth Test should last six days if the teams were level (not applicable), while in 1972 and 1975 the final Test would be extended to six days if only one match separated the two teams. In both of these years the full six days were taken, Australia winning the 1972 match, while the 1975 Test was drawn. From 1956 to 1964 and from 1977 to 1985 there was no provision for an extra day to be played under any circumstances.

Provisions for final Test in Australia

Prior to 1946–47 no such provisions were necessary as all Tests were played to a finish after 1881–82. In 1946–47 and 1950–51 tour regulations allowed for the final Tests to be played to a finish if the difference in matches won was not greater than one (in the event inapplicable both seasons). In 1954–55 the final Test could have been extended to seven days if the difference in matches won was not greater than one (inapplicable), and in 1958–59 the final Test could have been extended to seven days, or eight in the event of weather interference, in the event of the series being level (again inapplicable). Since 1962–63 there have been no special provisions for the final Test, all matches having been scheduled for a maximum of five days.

Covering of Pitches

In England prior to 1926 there were no regulations regarding the covering of the pitch. Since then the position has been as follows:

1926	The practice applicable at each ground shall be followed so far as covering the pitch prior to the commencement of a Test is concerned.
1930	As for 1926, except the pitch shall not be completely covered after play has begun.
1934 to 1956	The pitch shall be completely protected against rain if necessary before the start of the match. After the first ball is bowled the covers shall not protect more than 3ft 6ins in front of the popping creases at each end.
1961	The whole pitch may be covered until the first ball is bowled. The whole pitch may be covered (a) the night before the match and, if necessary, until the first ball is bowled; and, whenever necessary and possible, at any time prior to that during the preparation of the pitch; and (b) on each night of the match and, if necessary, throughout Sunday. In addition, in the event of rain during the specified hours of play, the pitch shall be completely covered from the time it is decided that no further play is possible on that day.
1964	As for 1961 in effect, but also the bowling ends will be covered to a distance of 4ft in front of the popping creases if, during the hours of play, the match is suspended temporarily owing to weather or light conditions.
1968 to 1977	As for 1964 in effect, but in the event of rain during the specified hours of play, the umpires shall order the pitch to be completely covered as soon as play has been abandoned for the day.
1981 to 1985	The pitch shall be covered as soon as practicable after play is suspended for whatever reason.

In Australia from 1920–21 to 1950–51 the whole of the pitch could be protected prior to the start of a Test, but after the start only the pitch-ends could be covered. From 1946–47 to 1982–83 it was obligatory to protect the whole of the pitch against rain at all times.

Minimum Overs in Last Hour

This regulation was first used in these matches in Australia in 1970–71, when a minimum of 15 8-ball overs had to be bowled after the last hour had been signalled on the final day. This continued to be the case in 1974–75 and 1978–79. In 1979–80 (following the re-introduction of the 6-ball over) and 1982–83 a minimum of 20 overs had to be bowled in the last hour.

In England, since 1972 a minimum of 20 overs have had to be bowled in the last hour of play on the final day.

New Ball

A new ball has been available to the fielding side in E v A Tests as follows:

In England		In Australia	
1880 to 1899	No provision	1876–77 to 1894–95	No provision
1902 to 1905	Practice acknowledged of taking new ball if old one damaged or if bowler had lifted seam to obtain better grip	1897–98 to 1946–47	After 200 runs
		1950–51	After 50 overs
		1954–55 to 1962–63	After 200 runs
		1965–66 to 1978–79	After 65 overs
1909 to 1938	After 200 runs	1979–80 to 1982–83	After 85 overs
1948	After 55 overs		
1953	After 65 overs		
1956	After 200 runs or 75 overs		
1961 to 1964	After 200 runs or 85 overs		
1968 to 1985	After 85 overs		

Boundary Hits

In England prior to 1912 it was the usual practice to award 4 runs to a hit over the boundary and 6 for a hit out of the ground, although this was not universal. Since 1912 all hits full over the boundary in England have counted as 6 runs. In Australia prior to 1907–08 5 runs were awarded for a hit full over the boundary (the players would then change ends) and 6 were awarded for a hit out of the ground. Since 1907–08 all hits full over the boundary in Australia have counted as 6 runs.

Controversy surrounded the Melbourne Test of 1954–55 *after it was found that the pitch was damp on the third morning, following the rest day. It is believed that it was illegally watered. England won on the fifth day by 128 runs.*

The 200th Test between England and Australia, *at Lord's in 1968, was ruined by bad weather, a hailstorm turning the ground into a white lake during the luncheon interval on the opening day. Ultimately only half of the scheduled 30 hours of play was possible.*